This Hallowed Ground: Guides to Civil War Battlefields

SERIES EDITORS

Brooks D. Simpson
Arizona State University

Mark Grimsley
The Ohio State University

Steven E. Woodworth
Texas Christian University

MANASSAS

A BATTLEFIELD GUIDE

ETHAN S. RAFUSE

Cartography by Erin Greb

·

University of Nebraska Press

Lincoln and London

Library of Congress Cataloging-in-Publication Data
Rafuse, Ethan Sepp, 1968–
Manassas: a battlefield guide / Ethan S. Rafuse; cartography by Erin Greb.
pages   cm.
–(This hallowed ground: guides to Civil War battlefields)
Includes bibliographical references.
ISBN 978-0-8032-3643-1 (pbk.: alk. paper)—
ISBN 978-0-8032-5427-5 (epub)—
ISBN 978-0-8032-5428-2 (mobi)—
ISBN 978-0-8032-5426-8 (pdf)
1. Manassas National Battlefield Park (Va.)—Guidebooks.
2. Bull Run, 1st Battle of, Va., 1861. 3. Bull Run, 2nd Battle of, Va., 1862.
I. Greb, Erin, cartographer. II. Title.
E472.183.R34 2014
973.7′31–dc23   2013025744

Set in SwiftEF by Laura Wellington.

Contents

Uniform of the 14th New York
at Bull Run. BLCW 1:167.

Acknowledgments

It is with great pleasure that I express appreciation to the people who helped me put together my second contribution to this distinguished series. As before, the list begins with series editors Mark Grimsley, Brooks Simpson, and Steve Woodworth, who invited me to contribute this volume to the This Hallowed Ground series and offered welcome guidance and encouragement throughout the process. Brooks especially merits appreciation for, among many other things, taking a good chunk of time away from his schedule to accompany me on a field check of significant portions of the guide. I also appreciate all that the folks working for or with the University of Nebraska Press, especially Heather Lundine, Bridget Barry, Sabrina Ehmke Sergeant, Sara Springsteen, Alison Rold, Weston Poor, Rosemary Vestal, Kathryn Owens, Acacia Gentrup, Tish Fobben, and Judith Hoover, did to shepherd this work from raw manuscript to finished book, and the superb work Erin Greb did on the maps that accompany the text.

I also want to thank the distinguished students of the Manassas Campaigns who generously shared their expertise and provided badly needed feedback on earlier drafts of the guide. John J. Hennessy let me know when I was on the right track in the sections on Second Manassas and helped me get back on it when not, while Harry Smeltzer did the same with the sections on First Manassas. Ray Brown, the chief of interpretation and cultural resources management at Manassas National Battlefield Park, could not have been more helpful or supportive of my efforts and provided especially appreciated information and insights on changes that were being made in the park in preparation for the 150th anniversaries of the two battles.

I have been fortunate to have had several opportunities to lead tours and staff rides of the Manassas battlefields. The first of these came during the summer of 1998, when I received training in the art of leading folks around battlefields in general, and Manassas in particular, from Edmund Raus, Chris Bryce, Terri Bard, and James Burgess. Since then I have had the good fortune to take folks around Manassas on a number of occasions and am thankful to those who collaborated with me on those programs, especially the incomparable Ed Bearss, J. Michael Miller, Carol Reardon, Jeffry Wert, and Gary Ecelbarger. I also thank my colleagues at the Department of Military History at the U.S. Army Command and General Staff College for their friendship and collegiality, particularly those members of the department who have collaborated with me on staff rides of various Civil War and Revolutionary War battlefields over the past few years.

As before—indeed, as always—my deepest appreciation is to my wife, Rachel, and daughter, Corinne, for their love and support while I worked on this project. I also am thankful for the support I have received in the course of my efforts from my parents, Robert and Diane Rafuse, and brothers, Jonathan and Stephen Rafuse. Since the last two have yet to have a book dedicated to them, they get this one.

All illustrations reproduced in this book first appeared in the four volumes of *Battles and Leaders of the Civil War*, edited by Robert Underwood Johnson and Clarence Clough Buel (New York: Century, 1887–88). The volume and page number from which each illustration was taken are indicated at the end of each caption.

Off to war. BLCW 1:278.

To Jon and Steve

Introduction

In July 1861 a Union army commanded by Brig. Gen. Irvin McDowell marched out of its camps around Washington hoping to achieve a decisive victory over the army the Confederate States of America had assembled near Manassas Junction, Virginia. Both sides eagerly anticipated the first major clash of arms, were confident that they would achieve victory, and were hopeful that the outcome of the battle would be decisive enough to bring the Civil War to a quick end. The Confederacy was able at the end of the day on July 21 to claim a decisive victory in the hard-fought First Battle of Manassas (Bull Run), which ended with the Union army in full retreat back to Washington and the people of the South exulting in the triumph achieved by their soldiers and their commanders, above all *Pierre G. T. Beauregard, Joseph E. Johnston*, and *Thomas J. "Stonewall" Jackson.*

But the war did not end. Thirteen months later, the two armies found themselves conducting yet another great campaign in northern Virginia that, on August 28–30, 1862, would culminate in a battle at Manassas. Once again, when the fighting was over it was the Confederacy that could claim a decisive victory, with Gen. *Robert E. Lee's* Army of Northern Virginia having spectacularly defeated a Union army commanded by Maj. Gen. John Pope. Indeed rarely, if ever, has an American army operated with the boldness and brilliance the Army of Northern Virginia demonstrated during the Second Manassas Campaign.

This guide is designed to provide visitors to the sites associated with the First and Second Manassas Campaigns with a better understanding of what happened in 1861 and 1862 and why events followed the course they did. It is written for those who have a day to devote to their visit to Manassas and provides detailed excursions for those who have more time to devote to their study of these great campaigns. Visitors need not do any previsit preparation but can simply pick up this book and immediately head out to the field for the main tour, which can be completed in about eight hours. For those with even more time, a number of excursions can add up to an additional day to your visit.

On the way to Manassas. BLCW 1:163.

How to Use This Guide

The main tour is divided into fourteen main stops that will enable you to study the first and second battles of Manassas (also known as Bull Run) in chronological order. That is, the tour follows the battles as they progressed on July 21, 1861, and August 28–30, 1862. Most stops require about twenty to twenty-five minutes to complete. A few, such as Henry Hill and Deep Cut, take a bit longer. The main tour can be completed in approximately eight hours, though if you find yourself short on time, directions are provided on how to combine some of the stops in ways that make both geographical and chronological sense. Few of the stops require a great deal of walking from your vehicle or the Visitor Center, though many offer optional walks and side trips that can enhance your understanding of the terrain and events.

Most of the stops on these tours are divided into two or more substops. Substops seldom ask you to do much additional walking or driving around, though in many cases you are given the option of exploring the battlefield a bit more extensively on foot in a way that may enhance your visiting experience. The substops are simply designed to develop the action at each point in a clear, organized fashion, and there are as many substops as are required to do the job. In the guidebook, each stop and most substops have a section of text married to a map. This enables you to visualize the troop dispositions and movements at each stop without having to flip through the guide looking for maps.

The stops and substops follow a standard format: **Directions, Orientation, What Happened, Analysis,** and **Vignette.**

The **Directions** tell you how to get from one stop to the next. They not only give you driving instructions, but they also ask you, once you have reached a given stop, to walk to a precise spot on the battlefield. When driving, keep an eye on your odometer; distances are given to the nearest tenth of a mile. The directions often suggest points of interest en route from one stop to another. We have found that it works best to give the directions to a given stop first and then to mention the points of interest. These are always introduced by the italicized words *en route*.

Once you've reached a stop, the **Orientation** section describes the terrain around you so that you can quickly pick out the key landmarks and get your bearings.

What Happened is the heart of each stop. It explains the action succinctly but without becoming simplistic, and whenever possible it explains how the terrain affected the fighting.

Some stops have a section called **Analysis,** which explains why a particular decision was made, why a given attack met with success or failure, and so on. The purpose is to give you additional insight into the battle.

Some stops have a section called **Vignette**, designed to give you an additional emotional understanding of the battle by offering a short eyewitness account or by telling a particularly vivid anecdote.

Although the basic tour can be completed in about eight hours, you can also take **Excursions** to places of special interest. These excursion tours follow the same format as the basic tour. The main tour and excursions are structured to give you flexibility in how you approach your study. If you wish to focus on just First Manassas, it is suggested you first do the First Manassas Campaign Excursion, then do the six stops on the main tour devoted to First Manassas, incorporating the *Jackson's* Line Excursion into your stop on Henry Hill. The lengthy Second Manassas Campaign excursion consists of eight stops and involves a considerable amount of driving between stops, so it will take over six hours in itself to complete. To do a complete Second Manassas tour will take two full days, consisting of the Second Manassas Campaign Excursion and first three stops on the Second Manassas battlefield tour, then the last five stops on the tour and Chantilly Excursion on the second.

A few conventions are used in the guidebook to help keep confusion to a minimum. We have tried not to burden the text with a proliferation of names and unit designations. Names of Confederate leaders and units are in italics. The full name and rank of each individual is usually given only the first time he is mentioned at a particular stop.

Directions are particularly important in a guidebook, but they can be confusing. We have tried to make them as foolproof as possible here. At each stop, you are asked to face in a specific direction. To make this as precise as possible, we may ask you to look to your left front, far left, left rear, and so on, according to the system shown below:

straight ahead

left front	*right front*
left	*right*
left rear	*right rear*

behind/directly to the rear

The maps can also help you get your bearings. The monuments are excellent tools for understanding the battlefield as well, and the guidebook uses some monuments and markers to help you orient yourself.

Although this guidebook is intended primarily for use on the battlefield, it also contains information helpful for further study of the battle. Introductory sections at the beginning of each section of the book describe the events that preceded and shaped the battle and help to establish context. The stops for each phase of the main tour are preceded by overviews that outline the main developments of that phase of the battle. Appendixes at the end of the book give the organization of each army (Orders of Battle) and a discussion of tactics and weaponry. Suggestions for further reading are provided as well. Finally, although users might benefit from perusing the guide before visiting the battlefield, such preparation is not essential. You can simply pick up the guide, drive out to the battlefield, and begin your tour immediately.

Ethan S. Rafuse

Mark Grimsley,
Brooks D. Simpson,
& Steven E. Woodworth
SERIES EDITORS

First Manassas

The contest for the Henry Hill. BLCW 1:190.

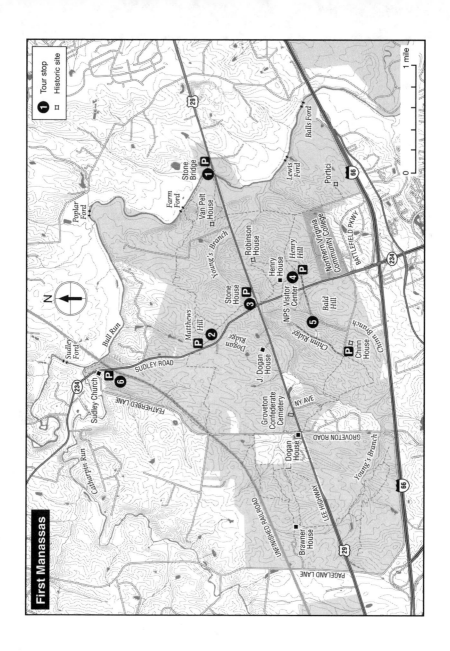

First Manassas

Tour stop
Historic site

N

0   1 mile

The Road to First Manassas

"You are green it is true; but they are green also; you are all green alike." That was the response, Brig. Gen. Irvin McDowell later complained, whenever he told the Lincoln administration that his Army of Northeastern Virginia was not ready to undertake active military operations in July 1861. It was not just President Abraham Lincoln and the members of his administration, however, who expected and demanded that a major battle take place in Virginia that summer. In the aftermath of the April 1861 battle at Fort Sumter a *rage militarie* had seized both the North and the South. Professional military officers like McDowell were acutely conscious of the complexities raising and training armies from scratch entailed and counseled caution. Ultimately, though, they were compelled to yield when it was clear that the public demanded action, and officers unable or unwilling to oblige did so at their own risk.

In response to a request from Commanding General of the Army Winfield Scott, during the first week of June McDowell drew up a plan for a campaign against forces the new-born Confederate States of America were deploying between Washington and Manassas Junction, Virginia. The latter was a critical point on the map, for there two operationally important railroads intersected. The Orange and Alexandria (O&A) Railroad was the obvious line of advance for any Union force marching south and west out of Washington; the Manassas Gap Railroad connected the O&A with the Shenandoah Valley. As a consequence of the need to defend both the line of the O&A and the agriculturally rich Shenandoah Valley, Confederate military authorities had divided their forces in northern Virginia between those two points, with the Manassas Gap Railroad providing a convenient means for shifting forces back and forth between them. After presenting his plan for attacking Manassas Junction to Lincoln, who hoped popular support in the South for independence would evaporate if the North could quickly win a significant battlefield victory, McDowell was directed to execute it.

On July 16 McDowell's army left its camps around Washington and marched south and west toward Manassas Junction. Although well aware of the Confederacy's ability to utilize the Manassas Gap Railroad to reinforce its defense of the O&A, McDowell was assured by Scott and Lincoln that a Union force in the Shenandoah Valley commanded by Brig. Gen. Robert Patterson would prevent this from happening by menacing the 11,000-man Confederate force in the Valley, commanded by Brig. Gen. *Joseph E. Johnston*. Defending Manassas Junction was the responsibility of Brig. Gen. *Pierre G. T. Beauregard*, the hero of Fort Sumter, who had approximately 22,000 men under his command. *Beauregard* posted all but one of his brigades behind Bull Run, a stream that offered the first good defensive line north and east of Manassas Junction. A few miles in front of Bull Run, Beauregard placed one brigade at Fairfax Court House.

As it marched west from Washington, McDowell had his army of about 35,000 men fan out across the northern Virginia countryside with an eye on attacking Fairfax Court House from three directions and capturing its garrison. Unfortunately, poor march discipline frustrated his plans and the Fairfax garrison easily managed to escape what was, on paper, a well-conceived plan. After occupying Fairfax Court House on July 17, McDowell directed his lead division, commanded by Brig. Gen. Daniel Tyler, to push forward toward Centreville and the Bull Run crossings. Tyler did so and then, ignoring explicit orders from McDowell not to heavily engage the enemy, pushed his infantry forward in the direction of Blackburn's Ford, where a Confederate brigade commanded by Brig. Gen. *James Longstreet* guarded the road from Centreville to Manassas Junction. In a brief but sharp fight in the afternoon of July 18, Tyler's lead brigade was thrashed by *Longstreet's* men with the aid of elements from Col. *Jubal Early's* brigade.

McDowell arrived on the scene as the fighting at Blackburn's Ford was winding down. For the next two days he concentrated his command at Centreville and ordered reconnaissances made of the Confederate position behind Bull Run, with particular focus on the area north of the Stone Bridge where the Warrenton Turnpike crossed the creek. *Beauregard* also planned to take the offensive. When news of McDowell's advance from Washington on July 16 reached Richmond, the Confederate government sent a message to *Johnston* in the Valley that led that officer to begin moving his command east to aid *Beauregard*. Upon receiving news of *Johnston's* move, which Patterson failed to prevent, *Beauregard* began drawing up plans for an offensive stroke against the Federal army at Centreville.

These came to nothing, as McDowell was able to launch his offensive first on the morning of July 21. Based on reports from his engineers, McDowell drew up plans to have one division demonstrate against the Stone Bridge and another brigade do the same against Blackburn's Ford. As this was going on, two divisions would cross Bull Run a few miles upstream from the Stone Bridge. The Federals would then push south toward Manassas Junction, roll up the Confederate army, and, it was hoped, end the Civil War before too much blood had been shed.

Henry Hill Visitor Center

The Henry Hill Visitor Center at Manassas National Battlefield Park is an excellent resource for students of the Civil War. It contains a gallery of exhibits and artwork focused mainly on the First Battle of Manassas (Second Manassas is the focus of the visitor center at the Brawner Farm, which is the first stop for study of that battle). In addition, there is a bookstore and a theater in which audiovisual programs are offered. Of particular interest is the electric map that shows the movements of the armies at First Manassas. After you have become acquainted with the Visitor Center, you are ready to begin your exploration of the Manassas Battlefield.

Optional Excursion Before visiting the scenes of the fighting of July 21, you may want to do the First Manassas Campaign Excursion, which covers the Union march to Manassas and first engagement with the Confederates at Blackburn's Ford.

General Pierre Gustav Toutant Beauregard, C.S.A. BLCW 1:77. From a photograph.

Overview of July 21, 1861

Both commanders planned to take the offensive on July 21, 1861. Federal commander Brig. Gen. Irvin McDowell developed a plan whereby part of his command would conduct demonstrations against Confederate positions along Bull Run at and below the Stone Bridge, while two divisions crossed the creek upstream at Sudley Ford and Poplar Ford and then moved south against the Confederate left and rear. For his part, Confederate Brig. Gen. *Pierre G. T. Beauregard* planned to have the forces on his right cross Bull Run and attack the Union left and rear at Centreville, which Brig. Gen. *Joseph E. Johnston* approved upon his arrival at Manassas Junction the day before.

McDowell roused his command and put his plan into motion early on July 21. One division advanced directly from Centreville to the Stone Bridge and began demonstrating against the Confederate position there. By the time the Federals crossed and began pushing south from Sudley Ford (they failed to find Poplar Ford), though, the commander of Confederate forces at the Stone Bridge, Col. *Nathan G. Evans*, had shifted the bulk of his command to Matthews Hill. A sharp fight then ensued on Matthews Hill that ended with the Confederates retreating south, during which *Beauregard* and *Johnston* abandoned their plans for an offensive and began shifting forces to deal with the threat to their left.

Rather than immediately following up his victory at Matthews Hill, McDowell decided to halt his offensive and consolidate his position. This gave the Confederates time to move forces to Henry Hill, the most important of which was the brigade commanded by Brig. Gen. *Thomas J. Jackson*. By the time McDowell resumed his offensive during the afternoon, he found a formidable Confederate force there that was able not only to resist his attacks—for which *Jackson* and his command would earn the nickname "Stonewall"—but force the Federals back from the hill. Meanwhile a Union brigade moved west to Chinn Ridge but found itself overwhelmed by reinforcements directed to that part of the field by *Johnston*.

Seeing that no more could be accomplished, McDowell ordered his command to fall back across Bull Run and rally at Centreville. However, Union organization disintegrated during the withdrawal, and McDowell was compelled to retreat all the way to Washington, enabling the Confederacy to claim a decisive victory in the first major battle of the Civil War.

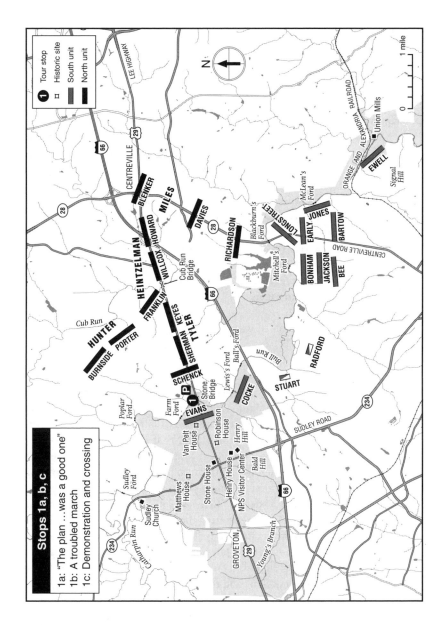

Stops 1a, b, c

1a: "The plan ...was a good one"
1b: A troubled march
1c: Demonstration and crossing

Legend:
- ① Tour stop
- ⊓ Historic site
- ▮ South unit
- █ North unit

STOP 1   Stone Bridge

Directions   Exit the parking area for the Henry Hill Visitor Center. *Turn right*
onto SUDLEY ROAD (VA 234) and proceed 0.4 mile to the inter-
section with LEE HIGHWAY (U.S. 29). *Turn right* at the intersection onto LEE HIGHWAY. *Proceed* 1.4 miles to the parking area for
Stone Bridge on the left side of the road. Exit your vehicle and
follow the trail at the end of the parking lot for 100 yards to the
overlook by the National Park Service (NPS) markers "Strategic
Crossing" and "Union Retreat," *or continue* for about another 100
yards on the trail across the bridge, then *turn right* and follow

the path for about 25 yards. *Stop here* and face east toward the bridge and Bull Run, which flows from left to right in front of you (right to left if you are doing the stand at the markers).

Orientation

The Stone Bridge is the point where the historic Warrenton and Alexandria Turnpike (modern U.S. 29) crossed Bull Run. The turnpike's intersection with Sudley Road is a little over 1 mile west from where you are standing. The point where U.S. 29 crosses Cub Run is about 2 miles east of you, while Centreville is about 4. Sudley Ford is approximately 2 miles upstream, while Union Mills is about 8 miles downstream.

NOTE: This is also the first stop for the First Manassas Campaign Excursion. If you would like to examine the operations that preceded the Battle of First Manassas in greater detail, turn to page 138.

STOP 1A

"The plan . . . was a good one," July 18–21, 1861

Directions

Face toward the bridge.

What Happened

McDowell's initial plan for dealing with the Confederate forces defending Manassas Junction was to try to cross Bull Run below their position and attack their right. The nature of the terrain, however, rendered that plan impracticable, and McDowell was unwilling to attempt a frontal assault, his reticence at doing so reinforced by the defeat Union forces suffered in a sharply fought skirmish at Blackburn's Ford on July 18. Thus he decided to investigate the possibility of crossing the creek upstream from the Confederates and directed engineer officers to reconnoiter the approaches to Sudley Ford.

Finally, late on July 20, McDowell called his subordinates together and explained to them the results of the reconnaissance missions and the plan he had developed in response. Three brigades from Brig. Gen. Daniel Tyler's division would advance along the Warrenton Turnpike toward the Stone Bridge. This was where Federal intelligence correctly reported the leftmost significant body of Confederate forces was posted. Marching out of Centreville behind Tyler would be the divisions of Col. David Hunter and Col. Samuel P. Heintzelman. After crossing Cub Run, Tyler would continue to advance along the turnpike toward the bridge, while Hunter and Heintzelman would turn north and follow farm roads to Sudley Ford and Poplar Ford. Tyler's move, it was hoped, would distract the Confederates sufficiently to enable Hunter to reach and cross Bull Run at Sudley Ford and its tributary Catharpin Run at Sudley Springs Ford unmolested, while Heintzelman used Poplar Ford to cross

Bull Run. Meanwhile a brigade detached from Tyler's division commanded by Col. Israel Richardson and the division commanded by Col. Dixon Miles would be positioned along the direct road between Centreville and Manassas Junction to cover the Federal rear and distract the Confederates from the movements further upstream.

Once across Bull Run, McDowell planned for Hunter and Heintzelman to push south and drive off any Confederates that might be found between the fords and the Warrenton Turnpike. If Tyler had not already done so, once this occurred his division might then cross and join the other two divisions for a push against Manassas Junction and the Manassas Gap Railroad.

Vignette

One of the brigade commanders in Tyler's division who attended the conference the night before the battle in which McDowell described his plan, Col. Erasmus Keyes, later recalled, "On the evening of July 21, I was encamped on the slope of the hill at Centreville. General McDowell called a council of war, and the movements for the next day were discussed. The plan of the intended battle, from all I could learn of the field and the position of the enemy, was a good one. I noticed no want of confidence in our commander, and but for the rawness of a large majority of the volunteers a victory might have been anticipated."

STOP 1B

A Troubled March, 2:30–9:30 a.m.

Directions

Remain in place.

What Happened

At 2:00 in the morning on July 21, 1861, Tyler rousted his men from their bivouacs and put them on the march. Leading the Federal march west along the Warrenton Turnpike that morning was Brig. Gen. Robert Schenck's brigade, with brigades commanded by Col. William T. Sherman and Colonel Keyes following behind. Five companies fanned out in front and advanced with such caution that it took them nearly an hour to reach Cub Run. Although their fears that the bridge might be defended proved unfounded, a quick examination led McDowell to conclude that he needed to call up his engineers to bolster the bridge so it could carry his army's wagons and artillery. Finally, around 5:30 a.m., Tyler's men were able to resume their march toward Bull Run.

The repair work on the bridge and excruciating slowness with which Tyler's men pushed forward along the turnpike before and after reaching Cub Run imposed delays on the two divisions following behind. When Hunter's men finally turned onto and began moving along the road that they were supposed to follow to Sudley Ford, they found that it was much narrower and rougher than had been reported. Thus Col. Ambrose Burnside, commander of the brigade leading the march, was compelled to call forward twenty-five men from the 2nd New Hampshire and put them to work widening and improving the road. When Tyler began his demonstration at the Stone Bridge at around 6:00 a.m. by firing three shots from a 30 pdr Parrott rifled artillery piece known as "Long Tom," Hunter's and Heintzelman's divisions were still a considerable distance from their designated crossing points.

Then, as if the roughness of the road were not enough, when Burnside reached a fork in the road, he took the advice of a guide assigned to him by Hunter and directed his brigade to take the wrong road, which had the effect of extending the march over 3 miles. It was not until 9:30 a.m. that Hunter finally reached Sudley Ford. Worsening matters, because no one was able to find a road to Poplar Ford, both Hunter's and Heintzelman's commands would end up using Sudley Ford to cross Bull Run, which further compromised McDowell's plan.

Analysis

Clearly the Federal high command made a number of errors in executing their operations for the morning of July 21. While McDowell conceived a good plan on paper, it was rooted in a fundamental misunderstanding of the terrain. The principal fault for this lay with an engineer officer, Maj. John G. Barnard, whom McDowell had assigned the task of reconnoitering the route to Sudley Ford. In the course of carrying out this task, Federal scouting parties that Barnard led personally encountered Confederate outposts. Deciding it was more important to avoid alerting the Confederates to what McDowell intended, the engineers turned back without fully checking the road, mistakenly believing they had seen enough to be able to tell their commander that it was sufficient for what he wanted to do. While their desire to preserve secrecy was understandable, it is clear that they erred and that, in trusting their assessments, McDowell also erred. Yet given the high reputation Barnard enjoyed in the army as an engineer before the war, it is hard to fault McDowell for doing so.

Vignette

One of the men who participated in the march to Bull Run as part of Burnside's command later wrote, "We were leading the brave, lighthearted division of Hunter in the direction of Bull Run. The plan of this day's work is, perhaps, better known than that of any other of the war. In a few words, it consisted of a strong demonstration upon the enemy's front, while the main attack was to be made upon the rear of his position which was to be gained by means of a road making a wide detour to the right, and coming upon the extreme left.

"The forenoon was by this time well advanced, and the sun was pouring his rays down fiercely upon the toiling columns. Far away to the left, in the direction of Manassas, clouds of dust were arising. . . . We got our first 'reliable information' of the prospects ahead from one of the natives, a female, who probably classed herself as one of the whites, and who possibly might have been after a vigorous use of soap and water. She stood in the door of a dilapidated log hovel, and took delight in informing us that there were enough Confederates a little ways ahead to whip us all out, and that her husband was among them. And hardly were we out of her sight before the roar of a heavy gun came from the direction the left column had taken. We all felt that this was the prelude of a conflict to come, and scores of watches were drawn to note the precise time when the first gun was fired."

STOP 1C   Demonstration and Crossing, 9:30 a.m.–12:00 p.m.

Directions   Remain in place.

What Happened   On the morning of July 21, the task of defending the Stone Bridge rested in the hands of Col. *Nathan "Shanks" Evans*. Evans had under him a small force composed of one South Carolina regiment, a Louisiana battalion, two troops of cavalry, and two pieces of artillery. From his headquarters on Van Pelt Hill, the high ground overlooking the creek north of the Warrenton Turnpike, Evans responded skillfully to news of Tyler's advance. He posted two companies of skirmishers along the creek to put up a show of resistance and kept the rest of his command concealed on the heights.

Evans's shrewd management of his command frustrated Tyler's efforts to quickly figure out what exactly he faced. Thus Tyler decided to push three regiments forward to the creek. This compelled *Evans* to commit five companies to the increasingly bitter skirmishing taking place around the bridge, and by 7:00 a.m. the low area around it was enshrouded in smoke.

At this point, Hunter's and Heintzelman's commands were still a considerable distance from Sudley Ford, and as the fight continued with no evidence that Tyler really intended to cross the creek, *Evans* began to suspect that what he faced was simply a feint. Then, around 8:00 a.m., the small band of pickets he had posted farther upstream began sending reports of a large Federal force moving toward Sudley Ford. By then Confederate signalmen posted on high ground farther downstream had caught a glimpse of the Federal flanking column and sent a message to *Evans* warning him, "Look out for your left." His suspicions confirmed, *Evans* responded decisively and wisely. Leaving 200 men at the creek to continue the fight with Tyler, he took the other 900 of his command north and west to Matthews Hill to confront the Federal flanking force.

Analysis

The skill with which *Evans* managed his command during the morning of July 21 was exceptional—especially in light of the lack of experience he, like all other officers who participated in this battle, had handling a command of this size. Given a tough assignment that necessitated the decisive exercise of independent judgment, he effectively responded to the actions of a far superior force throughout the morning along the creek, properly and prudently calibrating his movements against those of the enemy. Then he acted quickly and decisively in response to reports of the Federals crossing upstream. When the day was over, few officers on either side would merit more praise and credit for the shape and outcome of the first major battle of the Civil War than *Shanks Evans*.

Vignette

"The enemy made his appearance in line of battle on the east side of the stone bridge," *Evans* later wrote, "about fifteen hundred yards in front of my position, and opened their fire with rifled cannon at 5.15 a.m., which was continued at intervals for about an hour. Having my entire force covered by the crest of the hills on the west side of the bridge, I did not return the fire. Observing the enemy had deployed a considerable force as skirmishers in front of his line, and that they were advancing on my position, I directed the two flank companies of the Fourth Regiment South Carolina Volunteers and one company of Major [*Roberdeau*] *Wheat's* Special Battalion Louisiana Volunteers to advance as skirmishers, covering my entire front.

"The skirmishers were soon engaged, and kept up a brisk fire for about an hour, when I perceived that it was not the intention of the enemy to attack me in my present position, but had commenced his movement to turn my left flank. I at once decided to quit position and to meet him in his flank movement, leaving the skirmishers of the Fourth Regiment of South Carolina Volunteers, supported by the reserve of two companies, to keep him engaged. I sent word to Colonel *Philip St. George Cocke* that I had abandoned my position at the bridge, and was advancing to attack the enemy."

Further Exploration

If you would like to see the approximate point where Union brigades commanded by Col. William T. Sherman and Col. Erasmus Keyes crossed Bull Run during the late morning, *turn left* (if you did not cross the bridge in the course of doing at the stand, do so first to proceed to the stand on the west side of the creek) and resume walking along the path. At about 600 yards there will be a fork in the trail. *Take the right trail* to continue walking along the creek for about another 200 yards until you reach an NPS marker on the right that reads "Farm Ford."

Further Reading   Hennessy, *The First Battle of Manassas*, 26–46; Rafuse, *A Single Grand Victory*, 115–27; Gottfried, *The Maps of First Bull Run*, 20–23.

General Irwin McDowell.
BLCW 1:170. From a photograph.

STOP 2	Matthews Hill

Directions

Turn right onto LEE HIGHWAY (U.S. 29) upon exiting the parking area and proceed 1.4 miles to the traffic light at the intersection of LEE HIGHWAY and SUDLEY ROAD (VA 234). *Turn right* at the intersection onto SUDLEY ROAD and *drive north* for 0.6 mile until you reach a parking area on the right. *Pull into* the parking area. When you exit your vehicle you will clearly see the NPS wayside marker "First Contact" and a small "Matthews Hill Loop Trail" sign at the south side of the parking lot. *Follow the trail* for about 300 yards to the crest of the ridge, where you will see a line of cannon. *Turn left* and walk about 50 yards to the fourth cannon. *Turn right* to face south.

Orientation

You are standing on Matthews Hill, where the first major fighting of the First Battle of Manassas took place. In front of you the hill gradually slopes down toward the valley of Young's Branch, where the historic Warrenton Turnpike is. If you look to your left front, you will see traffic moving along Lee Highway just east of the Stone House, while the Sudley Road is to your right. Just before the Stone House, which is about 0.5 mile to the south, the Matthews Hill makes its final descent into the valley, with the last bit of high ground known as Buck Hill. On the other side of the Sudley Road, the high ground continues and is known as Dogan Ridge. From where you are standing, Henry Hill and the Visitor Center are clearly visible about 1 mile away. Sudley Church and the ford are about 1 mile north of you. The guns here mark the approximate location of Capt. William H. Reynolds's Rhode Island Battery during the fight for Matthews Hill. In front of you about 150 yards away is a marker that indicates the approximate location of the Confederate line on Matthews Hill.

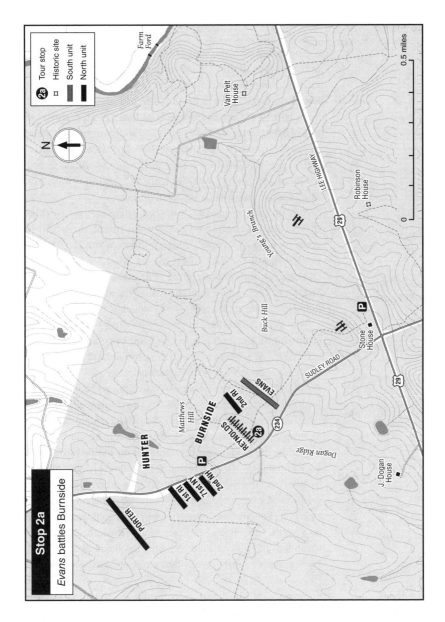

STOP 2A

Evans Battles Burnside, 9:30–10:00 a.m.

Orientation

You are standing on Matthews Hill.

What Happened

After leaving only a few hundred men at the Stone Bridge to deal with Tyler's demonstration, Evans moved the bulk of his small command here, to Matthews Hill. He then deployed his approximately 900 men with the left flank of Col. *J. E. B. Sloan's* 4th South Carolina at the Sudley Road and Maj. *Roberdeau Wheat's* 1st Louisiana Battalion to Sloan's right. Two guns from the Lynchburg Artillery supported Evans's line.

The first significant body of Federal troops that crossed Bull Run belonged to the brigade commanded by Col. Ambrose E. Burnside. As his men rested after crossing Bull Run at Sudley Ford and its tributary Catharpin Run at Sudley Springs Ford, Burnside and division commander Col. David Hunter dispatched two officers south to reconnoiter. Upon learning from them of *Evans's* presence on Matthews Hill, Burnside and Hunter immediately ordered their men to advance south along Sudley Road with five companies from Col. John Slocum's 2nd Rhode Island Infantry in the lead.

Slocum's skirmishers made contact with *Evans's* men on Matthews Hill at around 10:00 a.m. Accompanying them as they drove back *Evans's* skirmish line was Hunter, who directed Burnside to bring up the rest of the regiment. When Burnside arrived on the scene with the rest of the 2nd Rhode Island, he ordered Slocum to deploy his command east of the Sudley Road. Upon doing so, Slocum advanced toward *Evans's* line on Matthews Hill.

Heavy fire from *Evans's* infantry and artillery halted the Federal advance. Slocum's men began firing back, and a fierce but brief firefight erupted between the two lines as Capt. William Reynolds moved his six-gun battery from the 1st Rhode Island Light Artillery up to a rise between Slocum's right and the Sudley Road. The addition of Reynolds's guns to the Federal firing line, however, was not enough to break the stalemate.

Hunter then fell wounded and turned over the battle to Burnside. Burnside promptly ordered up the rest of his brigade and moved Maj. Joseph Balch's 1st Rhode Island Infantry up to extend the Federal line. Balch's men arrived just as *Evans* was attempting to break the stalemate by ordering a charge by *Wheat's* Louisianans. *Wheat's* assault, however, was shattered by Federal fire. *Wheat* fell, seriously (though not fatally) wounded, and his command fell back a considerable distance, leaving *Sloan's* South Carolinians alone on Matthews Hill.

Analysis

Evans and his command merit praise for the alacrity with which they moved to Matthews Hill and the tenacity with which they fought upon their arrival. However, their ability to hold off the advance of the far superior Federal force that had crossed Sudley Ford also owed much to the poor performance of Hunter in division command. Inexperienced in his duties, Hunter preoccupied himself with a task, the placement of skirmishers, that should have been left to others with narrower responsibilities. As a consequence, he failed to develop a broader tactical perspective and failed to exercise effective command over his entire division. Because of his decision to personally accompany the 2nd Rhode Island when it entered the battle and stay with it long enough to get wounded, the rest of his division did not move forward to join the fight seriously until over a half hour after it began. Consequently, instead of quickly overwhelming *Evans's* small command—something he had more than enough force to do— Hunter only committed a regiment and battery to the battle. After he was wounded and turned the battle over to his subordinates, the Federal effort became much more effective. Critical time had been lost, however.

Vignette

"When we arrived at the ford," Rhode Island artillerist Thomas Aldrich later recalled, "we were so tired and thirsty that we took the opportunity to fill our canteens with water. In two minutes the stream was a perfect mudpuddle; everybody rushed into it knee-deep to get water, and it was slow work and quite a little time elapsed before all our brigade had crossed the stream. We marched about a half mile on the edge of oak woods with openings on the right, two companies of the Second Rhode Island Regiment in the advance as skirmishers, and the remainder of the regiment following closely after. We halted on a stony road where the Second Regiment lay down to rest. Some of the men of our battery dismounted, the officers remaining in their saddles, when all of a sudden a cracking of guns and a singing of bullets began. Through my ignorance of warfare I thought it was fun, and I said to Lieut. William B. Weeden, who was on the opposite side of the gun from me, 'They are driving in the pickets, lieutenant!' In reply he said, 'I am afraid they are hard old pickets, Aldrich.' I thought his voice sounded strange, and I said to him, 'You are not afraid, are you?' when he smiled and said, 'No, it will not do to be afraid,' and, drawing his watch from his pocket, he said: 'It is ten minutes past ten.'

"In less time than it takes one to write this the command, 'Forward!' was given to the Second Regiment by General Burnside, and I never will forget the scene I then witnessed. Every man seemed to move at once, and all threw off their haversacks and blankets, which they were wearing across their shoulders, and away they went on a quick run over the hill. They had no more than started before the command, 'Forward your artillery!' by the same voice, and in an instant the battery was smashing through a rail fence on the right, the rails flying as the guns passed over them. It was a startling sight as the battery reached the hill to see men shooting at us less than two hundred yards away.

"How they ever let us get on the top of the hill is more than I can imagine. At our left was the farmhouse of Mathews, and sloping down from his house was a large cornfield. The view spread before us was very picturesque. Here the Second Regiment and the Second Battery drove the enemy back down the slope. Both the regiment and battery seemed to have been there about twenty minutes or more before any relief came.... General Hunter was wounded and his horse killed about this time. He then placed Colonel Burnside in command and soon afterwards left the field."

A Louisiana "Tiger". BLCW 1:196.

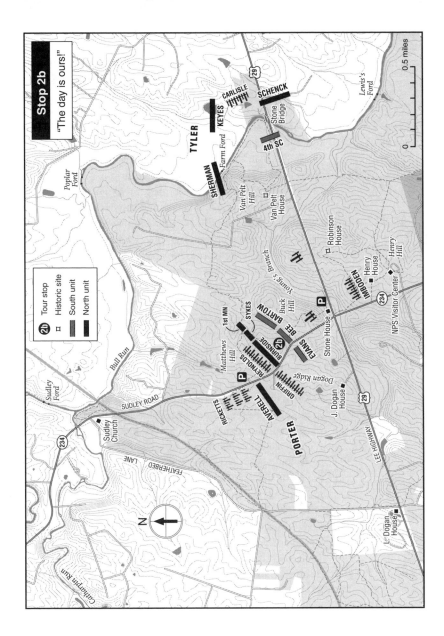

STOP 2B   "The day is ours!" 10:00–11:30 a.m.

Directions   Remain in place or *retrace your steps* toward the parking area for about 50 yards. At this point, instead of turning right, *turn left and proceed* about 175 yards to the NPS sign "Blocking the Union Advance" that marks the approximate location of the Confederate line on Matthews Hill. *Turn around* and face in the direction of the high ground on which the cannon are positioned.

What Happened

By the time *Evans* completed deploying his men and began engaging the Federals, help was already on the way. Brig. Gen. *Barnard Bee's* and Col. *Francis Bartow's* brigades from *Johnston's* army had just reached Henry Hill about 1 mile to the south of Evans's position, as had a battery of four guns commanded by Capt. *John D. Imboden*. As *Evans* began exchanging fire with the Federals on Matthews Hill, *Bee* eagerly exulted to *Imboden*, "Here is the battlefield, and we are in for it!"

Fortunately for the Confederates, it was not long after the repulse of *Wheat's* attack that *Bee's* and *Bartow's* brigades began arriving on Matthews Hill. *Bee* immediately began posting his brigade to the right of *Sloan's* regiment, while *Bartow* extended the Confederate right from *Bee's* command into a thicket of woods. This not only boosted the strength of the Confederate line on Matthews Hill but placed its right beyond the Union left, which *Bartow's* men took advantage of to inflict severe punishment on the Federals.

As the fighting escalated, Burnside and Col. Andrew Porter, the commander of the other brigade in Hunter's division, moved to put more Federal troops into the fight. Porter ordered his command to push southwest of the Sudley Road toward Dogan Ridge in order to turn the Confederate left at Matthews Hill. In response to a request from Burnside, Porter also dispatched the battalion of regulars commanded by Maj. George Sykes to the east side of Sudley Road. After passing behind Burnside's battle line, Sykes's command reached the Federal left and joined the battle there, effectively checking the Confederates' advantage on that end of the field.

As Sykes's command entered the battle, Porter's 3,700-man brigade, accompanied by six pieces of artillery commanded by Capt. Charles Griffin, was moving toward Dogan Ridge. Then, shortly after 11:00 a.m., the vanguard of Col. Samuel Heintzelman's division arrived on the field. Heintzelman promptly pushed forward his lead regiment, Col. Willis A. Gorman's 1st Minnesota, to further extend the Union left, while Capt. James B. Ricketts's six guns moved over to join Griffin on Dogan Ridge. Facing the danger of their battered and badly outnumbered commands being completely annihilated and believing they had done all they possibly could, at around 11:30 a.m. *Evans, Bee*, and *Bartow* ordered them to retreat from Matthews Hill. As the Confederates fled the battlefield, an ecstatic McDowell and his subordinates rode over the field shouting, "They are running! . . . The day is ours!"

Analysis

Although driven from the field, the Confederates on Matthews Hill had accomplished a great deal. Through stout defensive fighting, *Evans* and his men were able to arrest the momen-

tum of the Federal advance from Sudley Ford and buy sufficient time for *Bee's* and *Bartow's* commands to reach the field.
But even with *Bee's* and *Bartow's* men on hand, the Federal
advance ultimately proved too powerful for the Confederate
defenders. However, during the hour and a half of fighting
on Matthews Hill, *Johnston* and *Beauregard* were persuaded to
drop their plan for taking the offensive on July 21 and begin
shifting forces north, to Henry Hill. By doing so, they set the
conditions for the fight that would bring the day to a trium-
phant close for the Confederacy.

Vignette   After the war, *William Robbins* of the 4th Alabama published
a vivid account of his experience on Matthews Hill. "Mount-
ing the hill and entering the copse of timber north of the
Stone House," he wrote, "we began to hear a sharp crackling
of musketry ahead of us—a collision between the Federals and
some small bodies of Confederates we had not known were
there before, among them . . . *Wheat's* Louisiana Tigers, wearing the zouave uniform.

"As we emerged from the little wood we caught sight of
these Tigers, utterly overwhelmed and flying pell-mell . . . their
zouave uniform, which we had never before seen, but had
heard some of the enemy wore, for a minute caused us to mistake these 'Tigers' for Federals, and as they were flying in disorder, some of our men set up a loud yell and shout of victory,
supposing the enemy were already routed and retreating, where-
upon one ardent fellow of the Fourth Alabama, with his fin-
ger on the trigger and anxious to pull down on somebody
before they all got away, burst out with: 'Stop your darned hol-
lerin' or we won't get a shot!' But the mistake was discovered
just in time to prevent our firing on friends. A little way further up the hill beyond the timber and we struck the enemy
and no mistake. Their long advancing line, with the Stars and
Stripes waving above it (which made some of us feel sorry),
began to peer over the crest, eighty yards in our front, and
opened a terrific fire, which at first went mostly over us. . . .
On receiving the enemy's first fire we lay down and waited
until we could see their bodies to the waist, when we gave
them a volley which was very effective, firing uphill. The Federals fell back and disappeared behind the crest. After some
interval they advanced another and longer line; but the result
was the same as before, only they held on longer this time and
their fire hurt us badly.

"A third time they came on in a line which extended far
beyond both our flanks, and now the conflict became bloody
and terrible to us, their balls coming not only from the front
but from the right and left oblique, cutting down our colonel

(*Egbert Jones*) and stretching lifeless many a familiar form so recently full of hope and gayety. Then war began to show us his wrinkled front. But we thought of what they would say at home if we flinched and how ashamed we should feel if after all the big talk about whipping the enemy we let them whip us at the first chance. . . . Besides, it looked like they could hardly help killing every one of us if we got up and tried to run away . . . so from sheer desperation, as much as anything, we kept to it, until after awhile, to our great joy, the enemy fell back once more behind the crest, and their fire lulled. Our general, seeing we would be certainly overwhelmed at the next onslaught, gave us the order to retire, which we did before another attack. . . . But nearly one third of the Fourth Alabama had gone down in the effort and were left on the ground, including the colonel, mortally wounded."

Further Reading   Hennessy, *First Battle of Manassas*, 46–62; Rafuse, *A Single Grand Victory*, 123–39; Gottfried, *The Maps of First Bull Run*, 25–35.

NOTE: If you are studying both battles today, you will be visiting the Stone House during your study of Second Manassas. Thus, to save time and avoid redundancy, it is suggested that you go ahead and do the next stop, Stone House, here. Simply face toward the Visitor Center on Henry Hill and begin reading the Stone House section of the guide.

STOP 3   Stone House

Directions   *Turn left* on exiting the parking area and proceed 0.6 mile on
                             SUDLEY ROAD (VA 234) to the intersection with LEE HIGHWAY
                             (U.S. 29). *Turn left* onto LEE HIGHWAY. Upon doing so, you will
                             almost immediately see on your left the parking area for the
                             Stone House. *Pull in here* and exit your vehicle. *Follow the paved
                             path* from the parking area for about 100 yards, then *turn left*
                             and walk for about 50 yards around the house until you reach
                             its southwest corner near an old well. *Stop here* and face south
                             toward U.S. 29.

Orientation   From where you are standing, the Visitor Center on top of
                             Henry Hill, which is directly in front of you on the other side
                             of Young's Branch, is about 0.5 mile away. About 1.2 miles to
                             your left is the Stone Bridge crossing over Bull Run, while Cen-
                             treville is about 5 miles away. Gainesville is 4.5 miles west of
                             you. Sudley Church is a little over 1.5 miles north of you.
                             Manassas Junction is about 6 miles south of you.

On the skirmish line. BLCW 1:465.

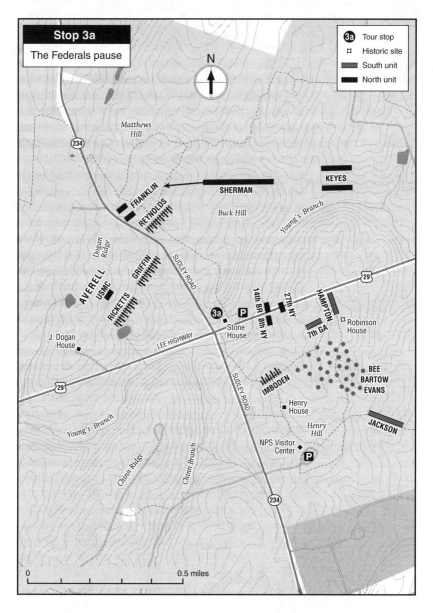

STOP 3A   The Federals Pause, 11:30 a.m.–12:30 p.m.

What Happened   With the collapse of the Confederate line on Matthews Hill, the Federals began pushing south toward the valley through which the Warrenton Turnpike passed and the turnpike's intersection with the Sudley Road. The only noteworthy resistance they faced at that point came from the four guns of *Imboden's* battery, which were posted on the northern slope of Henry Hill overlooking the intersection. *Imboden* put up a determined resistance, but McDowell had more than enough men available to overrun his position.

McDowell, however, decided at this point to call a halt to offensive operations. Instead, while his artillery on Dogan Ridge and Matthews Hill kept up long-range fire on Henry Hill, he would spend about two hours consolidating the Federal forces on this side of Bull Run. This included, in addition to the divisions of Hunter and Heintzelman that had been engaged on Matthews Hill, two brigades from Tyler's division that had crossed Bull Run using a ford located just upstream from the Stone Bridge. The lead brigade, commanded by Col. William T. Sherman, had arrived on the field just as the Confederate line on Matthews Hill was collapsing.

Without authorization from McDowell, though, elements from Porter's brigade (now commanded by Lt. William Averell) of Hunter's division pushed forward to clear the area around the Stone House intersection of Confederates. Col. Henry W. Slocum's 27th New York then began moving east along the Warrenton Turnpike in response to fire from *Imboden's* guns. Slocum's advance soon came into contact with Confederates posted in and around the lane linking the home of James Robinson, a free black man, on Henry Hill with the turnpike. These troops belonged to a 600-man force of South Carolinians commanded by Col. *Wade Hampton.* The Hampton Legion (so-called because it was organized as a mixed force of infantry, artillery, and cavalry, though its cavalry element was not on the field) waited until Slocum's New Yorkers were less than 200 yards from their line before opening a devastating fire into their ranks that led Slocum to order his command to withdraw north, up the slopes of Buck Hill.

Meanwhile *Imboden,* low on ammunition, had withdrawn his guns from the slope of Henry Hill. This led Averell to push forward two New York regiments, which then proceeded to follow in Slocum's footsteps by advancing east along the turnpike toward *Hampton's* line. *Hampton,* however, this time aided by artillery that had just arrived on Henry Hill accompanied by a fresh brigade of infantry commanded by Brig. Gen. *Thomas J. Jackson,* was able to once again thwart the Federal advance.

Analysis

In retrospect, McDowell's decision to halt his command was clearly a serious mistake. At the time, only *Imboden's* artillery, *Hampton's* command, and the remnants of the forces that had been so roughly handled on Matthews Hill stood between the Federal army and possession of Henry Hill, which proved to be the key to the battle and whose value as a piece of terrain could not have escaped the attention of the Federal high command. Yet the fog of war hung heavily over the Federals during the late morning and early afternoon of July 21. They had little idea what was on Henry Hill or beyond, in part because

McDowell lacked adequate cavalry to scout ahead and could reasonably assume that the morning delays had given the Confederates plenty of time to respond to the situation. Moreover, any fair analysis of McDowell's decision must take into account the exhausted condition of much of the Federal army, which had been up since well before sunrise and had covered several miles just to reach the battlefield. Thus while McDowell's commands were generally well in hand, given the rawness of the Federal troops the usual arguments for a tactical pause to allow a full regrouping before resuming the fight undoubtedly seemed more compelling than usual, something Averell's and Slocum's easily thwarted advances underscored.

Vignette   *Imboden* later recalled his experience on the slope of Henry Hill during the late morning of July 21, "My little battery was under a pitiless fire for a long time. Two guns from an Alexandria battery—[*Capt. H. G.*] *Latham's*, I think—took part in the conflict on the north side of Young's Branch to our right and across the turnpike, so long as *Bee*, *Bartow*, *Evans*, and *Wheat* were on that side, we firing over their heads; and about 11 o'clock two brass 12-pounder Napoleons from the New Orleans Washington Artillery unlimbered on our right, retiring, however, after a few rounds. . . .

Ricketts had 6 Parrott guns, and Griffin had as many more, and, I think, 2 12-pounder howitzers besides. These last hurt us more than all the rifles of both batteries, since the shot and shell of the rifles, striking the ground at any angle over 15 or 20 degrees, almost without exception bored their way in several feet and did no harm. It is no exaggeration to say that hundreds of shells from these fine rifle-guns exploded in front of and around my battery on that day, but so deep in the ground that the fragments never came out. After the action the ground looked as though it had been rooted up by hogs."

Further Exploration   The Stone House, an important landmark for both of the Manassas battles, was built by the Carter family, a large landowning family in Prince William County, who completed construction on it in 1828 using local red and yellow sandstone. In part it was built to provide a point where travelers on the Warrenton Turnpike (modern Lee Highway, U.S. 29), a major macadamized road in which the Carters were investors and on which initial construction was completed in 1815, could find lodging and food. During the First Battle of Manassas, soldiers from both sides sought refuge from the fighting under its protection and availed themselves of the water in its well. By the time the battle was over, it had been converted to a field hospital, a function it also served during the Second Bat-

tle of Manassas. Two injured Federal soldiers from that battle, Privates Charles E. Brehm and Eugene P. Geer, carved their
initials into the floorboards on the second floor. These are
still visible today.

In 1912, after it had passed through a number of owners,
George Hawks Ayres and his wife acquired the Stone House.
Ayres built a restaurant and cabins on the property with an
eye to exploiting its potential as a tourist attraction. It was
probably Ayres who embedded the five artillery shells that are
visible in the house's outside walls. After Ayres's death, the
house was sold to the U.S. government in 1949. During the
summer, the National Park Service frequently opens it up to
visitors, with rangers on site to interpret its history.

Further Reading   Hennessy, *First Battle of Manassas*, 64–68; Rafuse, *A Single Grand
Victory*, 143–45, 146–48; Gottfried, *Maps of First Bull Run*, 36–
39; Michael D. Litterst, *The Stone House: Silent Sentinel at the Crossroads of History*, NPS pamphlet.

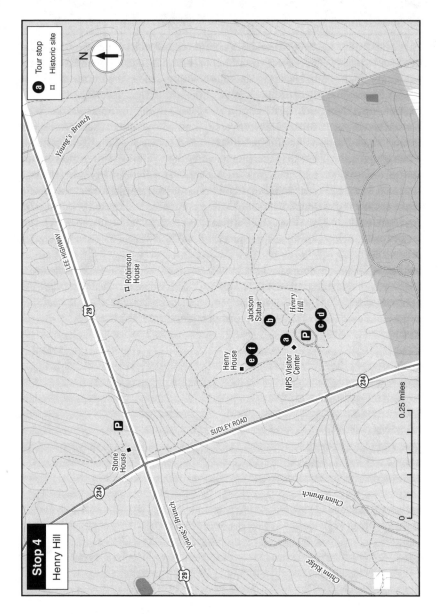

STOP 4   Henry Hill

Directions   Upon exiting the Stone House parking area, *turn right* onto
LEE HIGHWAY and proceed to the traffic light. *Turn left* at the
light onto SUDLEY ROAD and drive 0.4 mile to the entrance
to the Manassas National Battlefield Visitor Center on the left.
Turn here and proceed up the driveway to the parking area. (If
you did the Stone House stand at Matthews Hill, *turn left* out
of the parking area onto SUDLEY ROAD and proceed 1.1 miles
to the entrance to the Manassas National Battlefield Visitor
Center.)

This section offers three options for touring Henry Hill. The first involves doing the entire fight for Henry Hill at a single location. The second will take you to four points on Henry Hill. The final option includes, in addition to these four stops, an excursion that takes you along the Confederate position to study the fighting of July 21 a bit more in depth. All three begin at the same point, the eastern side porch of the Visitor Center, which is located just outside the bookstore. At this point, you will be oriented to the major landmarks on Henry Hill to help you follow the action regardless of which option you choose for studying the battle.

An orderly at headquarters.
BLCW 2:406.

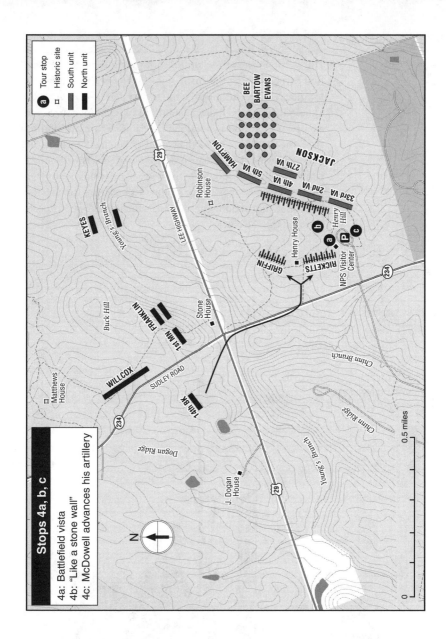

Stops 4a, b, c

4a: Battlefield vista
4b: "Like a stone wall"
4c: McDowell advances his artillery

Legend:
- ⓐ Tour stop
- ▫ Historic site
- South unit
- North unit

Map labels: BEE, BARTOW, EVANS, JACKSON, HAMPTON, 5th VA, 4th VA, 2nd VA, 27th VA, 33rd VA, Robinson House, LEE HIGHWAY, KEYES, Young's Branch, Henry House, Henry Hill, GRIFFIN, RICKETTS, NPS Visitor Center, Buck Hill, FRANKLIN, 1st MN, Stone House, WILLCOX, Matthews House, SUDLEY ROAD, 14th BK, Dogan Ridge, J. Dogan House, Chinn Branch, Chinn Ridge, Young's Branch, 234, 29, 0.5 miles, N

STOP 4A   Battlefield Vista

Directions   Exit the Visitor Center from the bookstore. To your left you will see a stone compass on top of the wall of the porch and a large statue of a general on a horse directly in front of you. That is a monument to Brig. Gen. *Thomas J. "Stonewall" Jackson.* Stand at the northeast corner of the porch with the two-story building (the Henry House) and red stone monument to your left front and the *Jackson* monument to your right front.

Orientation

Start by looking to your left rear, where you see the Sudley Road on the other side of the Visitor Center. From here, scan to your right. You will see six cannon posted in a row between the Visitor Center and the Henry House. These mark the location of Capt. James B. Ricketts's battery, which became the focal point of the fight for Henry Hill on July 21, 1861. Between the third and fourth cannon, look up. About 1 mile away, you will see a mostly cleared ridge. That is Dogan Ridge. Beyond that, on a clear day you will see the Bull Run Mountains, which are about 10 miles away. Next note the Henry House, which in 1861 was a much smaller, single-story structure. Right next to it you will see a red stone obelisk. That is the Bull Run Monument, which was constructed by Union soldiers and dedicated in 1865.

In the distance beyond the monument and house, there is a large cleared hill about 1 mile away on the other side of the Young's Branch valley where Sudley Road and the historic Warrenton Turnpike (modern Lee Highway, U.S. 29) intersect at the Stone House. That hill is Matthews Hill. If you continue panning to the right until you are looking straight ahead, you may be able to see some fence lines that mark the boundaries of what in 1861 was the property of James Robinson, a free black man. (The house fell victim to arson in 1993, leaving only the foundation.) On your right front is the *Jackson* monument. To the left of it is a small stone marker next to a tree that is the monument to Col. *Francis Bartow*, who was killed during the fight for Henry Hill. To the right of *Jackson's* monument is a stone monument to Brig. Gen. *Barnard Bee*, who was also killed on Henry Hill. Beyond those monuments, you will see a line of artillery and tree line. That is where *Jackson* posted his command on arriving on the field. Portici, where Brig. Gen. *Joseph E. Johnston* had his headquarters during the battle, is about 0.75 mile beyond that. As you pan farther to your right, you will see two cannon on the other side of the parking lot to the Visitor Center. Those mark the approximate location of the position held by Capt. Charles Griffin's two Federal guns at a critical point in the battle for Henry Hill.

STOP 4B

"Like a stone wall," 11:30 a.m.–2:00 p.m.

Directions

For those with limited time or mobility issues, you can do the rest of the stand from this spot. Otherwise, walk over to the *Jackson* monument, located about 100 yards from the porch.

What Happened

As *Hampton's* command was dealing with the Federals venturing east from the Stone House intersection, the five regiments of Brig. Gen. *Thomas J. Jackson's* brigade reached Henry Hill shortly before noon. Upon reaching the hill, *Jackson* encountered artillerist Capt. *John Imboden* as he was pulling back from his position overlooking the Stone House intersection in order to refill his caissons. *Jackson* directed *Imboden* to halt his guns in front of the woods on the southeastern end of the plateau at the top of Henry Hill and pledged to provide him with infantry support. *Jackson* then went to work rounding up more artillery and deploying his command under the shelter of the woods at the edge of the plateau. After gathering about a dozen pieces of artillery, *Jackson* authorized *Imboden* to let his gunners depart so they could refill their empty limber chests.

As *Jackson* established his position on Henry Hill, *Johnston* and *Beauregard* arrived on the scene. They and *Jackson* went to work encouraging the men and rallying the remnants of *Bee's*, *Bartow's*, and *Evans's* commands. By around 1:00 p.m. the situation had stabilized enough that *Beauregard* proposed to *Johnston* that he return to Portici, the plantation house where army headquarters was located, and assume responsibility for forwarding units to the field while *Beauregard* managed the situation on Henry Hill. Seeing *Beauregard* and *Jackson* had matters well in hand, *Johnston* agreed to do so.

Analysis

Jackson demonstrated a keen eye for terrain in positioning his command. He took advantage of the ground to position much of his infantry on the reverse slope of the hill and under the cover of the trees. This provided them with some protection from Federal artillery fire, the main menace to their position during the early afternoon, and concealed the strength of the Confederate line from the Federals. *Jackson's* artillery had a clear field of fire in their front as well.

Vignette

As Confederate and Union artillery exchanged fire during the afternoon, near the Robinson House, Brig. Gen. *Barnard Bee* rode among the men of his brigade as they tried to recover from their ordeal on Matthews Hill. Upon encountering members of the 4th Alabama, *Bee* asked them, "Will you follow me back to where the fighting is going on?" One of the men assured the general they would "go wherever you lead and do whatever you say." *Bee* then pointed to his left and shouted, "Yonder stands *Jackson* like a stone wall; let's go to his assistance." *Bee's* words were widely reported after the battle, resulting in *Jackson* and his brigade henceforth being known as "Stonewall." *Bee* was mortally wounded shortly after he said these words and thus never explained exactly what he meant by his reference to *Jackson* on Henry Hill. Most historians then and since have interpreted his words as complimentary toward *Jackson*, who was in fact turning in a superb performance that was critical to Confederate victory. Still, the evidence that this was the case is not conclusive enough to have prevented a considerable number of people from arguing that *Bee* was actually complaining that, at the time, *Jackson* seemed willing only to fight on the defensive on Henry Hill.

Further Exploration   If you wish to study the fighting on Henry Hill in greater depth, turn to page 149 for the directions for the *Jackson's* Line Excursion.

STOP 4C   McDowell Advances His Artillery

Directions   Remain in place or, if you did the last stand at the *Jackson* statue, walk about 200 yards to the two guns located on the other side of the parking lot. Face in the direction in which they are pointing. If you did the *Jackson's* Line Excursion, this is the point where you again pick up the main Henry Hill tour.

What Happened   At around 2:00 p.m., McDowell decided to resume the offensive. Henry Hill, due to the nature of the terrain and the fact that the Confederates had clearly determined to make a stand there, would be the key to the battle and the target of his attack. McDowell decided the first step would be to soften up the Confederate position with artillery. Thus he directed Maj. William Barry, his chief of artillery, to move the batteries commanded by Capt. James B. Ricketts and Capt. Charles Griffin that had been firing at long range from Dogan Ridge forward to Henry Hill.

When Ricketts and Griffin received their orders, both immediately expressed concern about what McDowell planned to provide in the way of infantry support. Griffin suggested the infantry go forward first to secure a position before the artillery moved. Barry, however, insisted on strict compliance with McDowell's instructions, though he assured Griffin that orders were at that moment being sent to a New York regiment to follow the batteries to Henry Hill and support them. This did little to reassure Griffin, a long-serving officer in the regular army who had a low opinion of the ninety-day volunteers that made up the bulk of the Federal army.

Griffin and Ricketts then dutifully hitched up their guns and moved south along the Sudley Road. Ricketts was the first to turn off the road and onto the farm lane that traveled up a slope from the road to the Henry House. Upon reaching the top of the slope near the house, Ricketts was able to clearly see the Confederate line only 300 yards away on the other side of the plateau. As his crews began deploying the battery's six guns to the right of the Henry House, they came under fire from Confederate sharpshooters in the building. Ricketts immediately, in his words, "turned my guns upon the house and literally riddled it." The Confederates promptly evacuated the house, but eighty-five-year-old Judith Henry, who was also inside it along with three other members of the Henry household, was mortally wounded—the only civilian casualty of the battle.

Meanwhile Griffin moved five guns up from the Sudley Road and placed them north of the Henry House to the left of Ricketts's battery. The Federal gunners then turned their attention to the Confederates on the other end of the plateau and engaged them in an artillery duel on top of Henry Hill. As they did so, Ricketts and Griffin looked nervously over their shoulders for the infantry support Barry had promised would be sent to them.

Analysis

McDowell clearly was taking a risk sending his two batteries forward before he could be certain that infantry would be able to support them when they went into action. In doing so, he was acting fairly in line with early nineteenth-century tactical doctrine, according to which artillery was placed in front of infantry—a method that had worked effectively for American forces during the Mexican-American War. *Jackson* too followed this practice, placing his infantry behind his artillery when he arrived on Henry Hill.

Confederate types. BLCW 1:548.

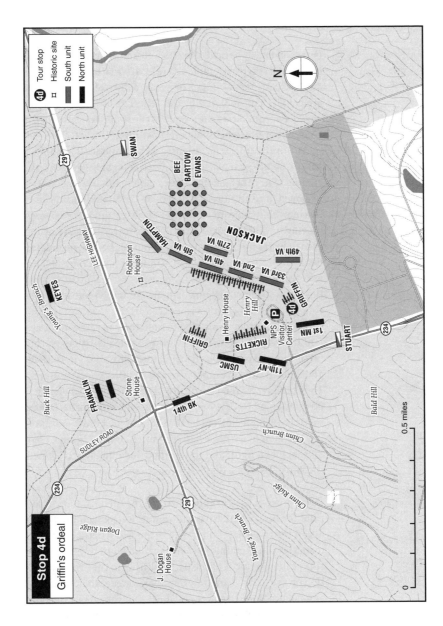

STOP 4D   Griffin's Ordeal, 2:00–2:30 p.m.

Directions   Remain in place.

What Happened   As Ricketts and Griffin led their guns up to Henry Hill, Barry
and McDowell went to work rounding up infantry support.
When the infantry reached Henry Hill, though, it took only
a few rounds of fire from the Confederates to drive them away,
to the intense dismay of Ricketts and Griffin. Especially nota-
ble was the ease with which a battalion of U.S. Marines, composed largely of raw recruits, that was sent to Ricketts's sup-

port abandoned the field. The 11th New York, a unit distinctively clad in red shirts, attempted to rally after falling back to the Sudley Road. As they did so, however, a force of 150 Confederate cavalry commanded by Col. *James E. B. Stuart* suddenly appeared from out of the woods to the south and launched a charge that overwhelmed their position.

As the effort to send infantry to his support floundered, shortly before 3:00 p.m. Griffin moved two of his guns north, circling around behind Ricketts's position, to a rise from where he hoped to be able to enfilade *Jackson's* left flank. Shortly after reaching his new position, Griffin spotted an unidentified force moving toward his position. Griffin was certain it was hostile, even though a number of the men were clad in blue, and ordered his men to fire on it. Then, Griffin later complained, Major Barry rode up and told him the force was Federal infantry moving up to support his guns. Griffin disagreed but unwisely yielded to his superior's wishes.

As Griffin ordered his men to hold their fire, the unidentified force closed to within 100 yards of his position. At this point the men of the approaching force leveled their muskets and opened fire at point-blank range on the Federal gunners. The Confederate forces, Col. *Arthur Cummings's* 33rd Virginia, possibly aided by Col. *William Smith's* 49th Virginia Battalion, then charged. Decimated by the shock of the Confederate volley, the men of Griffin's battery were in no condition to put up much of a fight, and those who tried quickly abandoned the two guns to the Confederates.

Analysis

The capture of Griffin's guns marked the turning point of the fight for Henry Hill. Up to this point, it had been the Federals on the offensive, and the question was whether the Confederates could maintain their position on Henry Hill. After this point, the focus of the battle shifted to the Federal position on the plateau and whether the Confederates could take and hold it. Moreover, every moment that passed saw the Confederates growing stronger as forces from other points along the Confederate line moved to the battlefield and units arrived on the scene from the Shenandoah Valley during the afternoon. In truth, while there remained more than a fair share of twists and turns in the contest yet to be played out, the capture of Griffin's guns probably marked the point at which whatever hopes the Federals had for a truly decisive, potentially war-winning victory at Manassas had passed.

Vignette

"We started for the hill," Griffin later recalled, "and halted once or twice. Once I went to Major Barry and told him I had no support, that it was impossible to go there without support. He told me that the Fire Zouaves would support us. . . . I told them they would not support us. He said they would. He said 'Yes, they will; at any rate, it is General McDowell's order to go there.' I said, 'I will go; but mark my words, they will not support us.' . . . We got on the hill and fired for about half an hour, when I moved two of my pieces to the right of Ricketts's battery . . . and commenced firing. After I had been there for about five minutes, a regiment of confederates got over a fence on my front, and some officer (I took it to be the colonel) stepped out in front of the regiment, between it and my battery, and commenced making a speech to them. I gave the command to one of my officers to fire upon them. He loaded the cannon with canister, and was just ready to fire upon them, when Major Barry rode up to me and said, 'Captain, don't fire there; those are your battery support.' I said, "They are confederates; as certain as the world, they are confederates.' He replied, 'I know they are your battery support.' I sprang to my pieces and told my officer not to fire there. He threw down the canister. . . .

"After the officer who had been talking to the regiment had got through, he faced them to the left, and marched them about forty yards towards us, and then opened fire upon us, and that was the last of us. . . . Before this occurred I started to limber up my pieces, so thoroughly convinced was I that they were the confederates. But as the chief of artillery told me they were my battery support, I was afraid to fire upon them. . . . I never delivered the fire, for we were all cut down. The Zouaves were about twenty yards to the rear of us; they were sitting down. I begged them to come up and give them a volley and then try the bayonet. They did not run at first, but stood as if panic stricken. . . . And after they had received three, perhaps four, volleys from this regiment of confederates, they broke and ran. I went down the hill and found Major Barry at the stream watering his horse. I stopped to water my horse also. Said I, 'Major, do you think the Zouaves will support us?' 'I was mistaken,' he said. Said I, 'Do you think that was our support?' 'I was mistaken,' he said. 'Yes,' said I, 'you were mistaken all around.'"

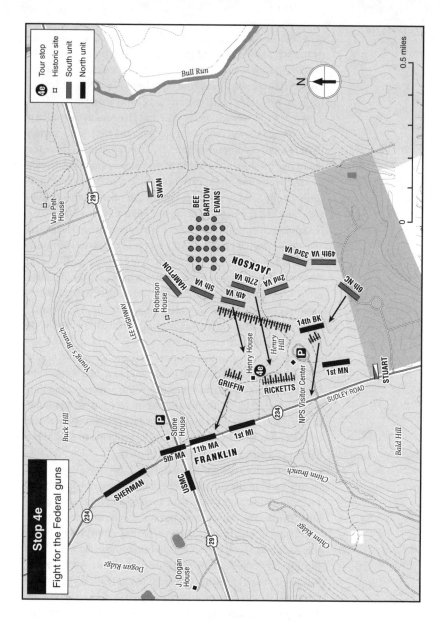

STOP 4E   Fight for the Federal Guns, 2:30–2:45 p.m.

Directions   Remain in place or, if at Griffin's guns, walk over to and beyond the Visitor Center for about 200 yards until you reach the Henry House. *Turn right* and face across the plateau toward the *Jackson* monument.

What Happened   The Confederates did not get to savor their capture of Griffin's guns for long. Shortly after driving off Griffin's men, they were greeted with the sight of Col. A. M. Wood's 14th Brooklyn advancing toward them. Their organization and discipline broken down as a consequence of their excitement over the capture of Griffin's guns, the Virginians were in no condition to put up much of a fight when Wood attacked. After unleashing a fierce volley, the Federals charged forward, drove off the Confederates, and reclaimed Griffin's guns. Seeing *Cummings's* men give way, the commander of the next regiment in *Jackson's* line, the 2nd Virginia, ordered the three companies on his left to pull back so they could face the Federals. However, the order miscarried, and efforts to correct the mistake fell apart when the commander of the 2nd Virginia, Col. *James Allen*, was injured when a limb from a tree that had been struck by artillery fire hit him in the face. An officer watching the scene rode over to *Jackson* and exclaimed, "General, the day is going against us." "If you think so, sir," *Jackson* replied, "you had better not say anything about it."

Wood attempted to sustain the momentum of his attack. But as his men approached the position held by the two regiments in the center of *Jackson's* line, the 4th and 27th Virginia, the Confederates unleashed a storm of artillery and infantry fire with *Jackson* watching closely. The momentum of Wood's advance was arrested, and within a few minutes his men were retreating back toward the Sudley Road.

As Wood's command fell back, *Jackson* sensed the time had come to take the offensive. He called out, "We'll charge them now, and drive them to Washington!" With *Jackson's* directive to "yell like Furies" ringing in their ears, the 4th and 27th Virginia advanced across Henry Hill toward Ricketts's guns. Ricketts's men were able to get off only a few rounds before the Confederates were on them. Those who could fell back to the Sudley Road as *Jackson's* men claimed possession of their guns.

Meanwhile the men of Col. *Charles Fisher's* 6th North Carolina, which had just reached the field, rushed forward to recapture Griffin's guns from the few men from the 14th Brooklyn still clinging to them. However, *Fisher's* men then came under fire from the woods to their left, where Federal troops belonging to Col. Samuel Heintzelman's division had taken refuge. Their fire mortally wounded *Fisher* and compelled the North Carolinians to fall back, which made it possible for Federal troops to remove Griffin's two guns from the field.

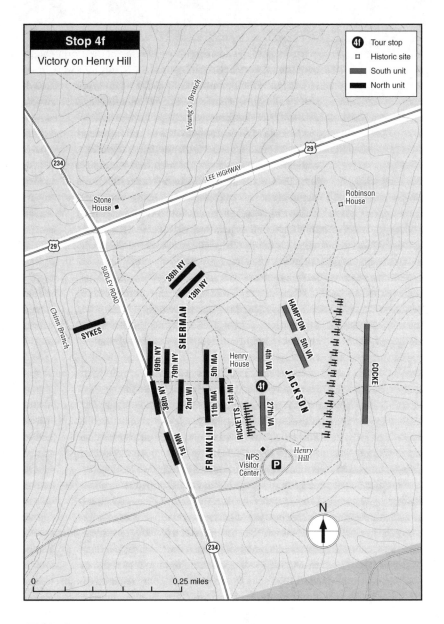

4f Tour stop
◻ Historic site
▬ South unit
▬ North unit

Young's Branch

29

234

LEE HIGHWAY

Stone House ■

Robinson House ◻

29

SUDLEY ROAD

Chinn Branch

SYKES

38th NY

13th NY

SHERMAN

HAMPTON

5th VA

69th NY

79th NY

5th MA

Henry House ■

4th VA

COCKE

38th NY

2nd WI

11th MA

1st MI

RICKETTS

4f

27th VA

JACKSON

1st MN

FRANKLIN

NPS Visitor Center

P

Henry Hill

N

0 ———————— 0.25 miles

STOP 4F   Victory on Henry Hill, 3:00–5:00 p.m.

Directions   Remain in place.

What Happened While the 6th North Carolina was coming to grief, the two
regiments from *Jackson's* brigade that had captured Ricketts's
guns endeavored to consolidate their position in anticipation
of a Federal effort to recapture the guns. The first Federal
attempt to do so, a fumbling attempt by the 1st Michigan,
failed, but then two Massachusetts regiments belonging to
Col. William B. Franklin's brigade reached the Sudley Road

at the bottom of the slope leading to the Henry House. After taking the time to carefully deploy them into line, Franklin ordered his men forward. Firing as they advanced, they quickly reached the top of the hill, forced *Jackson's* men to fall back, and reclaimed possession of Ricketts's guns.

Their success would be short-lived, for at this moment *Beauregard* personally led a charge by the 5th Virginia and Hampton Legion that drove Franklin's men back down the slope to the Sudley Road. As Franklin's men fell back, McDowell turned to the brigade commanded by Col. William T. Sherman and ordered it into the fight. Sherman's first two attempts to recapture Ricketts's guns failed, as he made each of them with only a single regiment. His third attempt succeeded, thanks to the fact that a regiment from Col. Orlando Willcox's brigade also participated in the attack.

Once again, though, the Federal success would be short-lived, for before they could consolidate their position or haul away Ricketts's guns, another Confederate force charged across the plateau on top of Henry Hill. This one consisted mainly of two regiments from Col. *Philip St. George Cocke's* brigade, and once again the Federals were driven back to the Sudley Road. Having no more fresh troops on hand to throw into the fight, McDowell's men began pulling back north to the low ground through which Young's Branch flowed, their retreat covered by a battalion of U.S. regular troops commanded by Maj. George Sykes. As they did so, Confederate infantry pushed forward to the Sudley Road, ending the fight for Henry Hill.

Analysis

The Federals' effort to regain their position on Henry Hill was compromised by a lack of coordination, with the consequence that at no point in the fight did the Federals put more than two regiments into the fight at the same time. As with Hunter on Matthews Hill, this can largely be attributed to the inexperience of McDowell and his subordinates. Although his presence where the fight was going on might have had some positive effect on the men's morale, McDowell probably would have served his cause better by being farther back from the fight so he could take a broader perspective on the tactical situation as he handled his troops. At the same time, he was not particularly well served by Sherman. It was Sherman who sent his regiments into the fight for Ricketts's guns one at a time, and it was only when McDowell was personally present that Sherman's final stab at the position was assisted by elements from other commands.

Sherman's efforts were also compromised by cases of mistaken identity that would be comic had they not had such tragic results. The first of his regiments to attack Henry Hill, the 2nd Wisconsin, was clad in gray uniforms, which caused its efforts to falter due to fire from both friend and foe. This was followed by the advance of the 79th New York, which lost momentum when the men paused on catching sight of a Confederate flag, which was similar to the U.S. flag at this point in the war. This gave the Confederates time to pour a killing fire into their ranks that mortally wounded Col. James Cameron, brother of the secretary of war, and compelled the Federals to fall back to the Sudley Road.

In contrast, *Jackson* and *Beauregard* effectively managed their forces and timed the commitment of them to the fight for Henry Hill well. This ensured they could take advantage of Federal mistakes, prevent the Federals from consolidating positions around the guns, and force them to finally give up the fight for the hill. One of the reasons they were able to do this was *Johnston's* willingness to swallow his ego and leave the field. Consequently, unlike on the Union side, there was someone in charge of the larger tactical situation beyond Henry Hill, which would do much to ensure that when Confederate forces arrived on the field at Manassas during the afternoon of July 21, 1861, they would be at the right place and the right time.

Further Reading Hennessy, *First Battle of Manassas*, 68–108; Rafuse, *A Single Grand Victory*, 148–82; Gottfried, *Maps of First Bull Run*, 41–65.

STOP 5 Chinn Ridge

Directions Drive to the Visitor Center driveway's intersection with SUD-LEY ROAD (VA 234). *Continue straight on* to the one-way park road, then *proceed* 0.3 mile to where the park road runs along the base of a high, clear ridge on your right. Find a convenient spot to pull over far enough to enable other vehicles to pass around you. Exit your vehicle and face toward the cleared ridge.

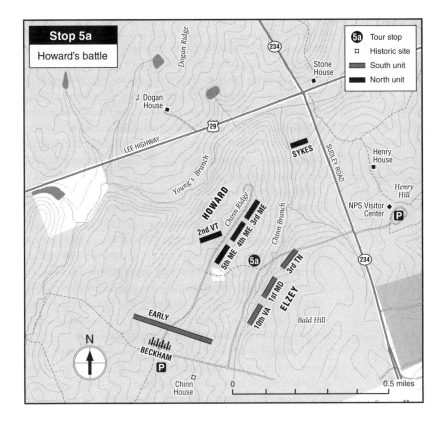

Stop 5a

Howard's battle

🅐	Tour stop
���	Historic site
▰	South unit
▰	North unit

STOP 5A   Howard's Battle, 3:00–4:30 p.m.

Orientation   You are standing in the valley of Chinn's Branch, which sep-
arates Chinn Ridge in front of you from Bald Hill behind you.
East of you, on the other side of Bald Hill, is Sudley Road and
Henry Hill, the crest of which is about 800 yards from where
you are standing.

What Happened   As the battle for Henry Hill raged, both McDowell and John-
ston attempted to extend their line west. The critical piece of
terrain in this effort would be Chinn Ridge. McDowell assigned
the task of securing it to Col. Oliver Otis Howard's brigade of
Heintzelman's division. Howard's had been the last unit in
the Federal army to make the march from Centreville to the
battlefield via Sudley Ford and were in reserve on Matthews
Hill when orders arrived at around 3:00 p.m. to move to Chinn
Ridge. Upon reaching the ridge, Howard deployed his brigade,
which since beginning a very hard march that morning had
shed nearly half of its strength.

          Meanwhile, as forces arrived during the day at Manassas
Junction from the Shenandoah Valley, from his headquarters
at Portici, *Johnston* ordered them west. As Howard deployed his

men on Chinn Ridge, Brig. Gen. *Edmund Kirby Smith's* brigade, the last from *Johnston's* force to arrive from the Valley, approached the battlefield. Just before they reached the Sudley Road, *Smith* was wounded by a batch of isolated Federal troops. Command then passed to Col. *Arnold Elzey*, who led the brigade across the Sudley Road to Bald Hill.

As *Elzey* deployed his infantry, Col. *Jubal Early's* brigade of *Beauregard's* command began arriving on the scene and took up a position on *Elzey's* left. Supported by four guns from Lt. *Robert Beckham's* Culpeper Artillery, *Elzey* ordered his men to advance on Howard's position. Fire from the Confederate artillery quickly began to wreak havoc on Howard's green troops. Howard responded by bringing up his reserves and ordering some of his men to pull back a bit to reform their lines. Before he knew it, though, his entire line had begun falling back. At this point, *Elzey* ordered his men to cross Chinn Branch and seize Chinn Ridge. The combination of *Beckham's* artillery and *Elzey's* infantry advancing on their front, and the fact that *Early's* command was moving on their right flank, was too much for Howard's green and exhausted troops to bear. Within minutes all order in the brigade disintegrated as the men began a headlong retreat back to Sudley Ford.

Howard's collapse, along with the defeat of the final effort to recapture Ricketts's guns on Henry Hill, convinced McDowell that nothing more could be accomplished west of Bull Run on July 21. Orders went out to his subordinate commanders, many of whose men were already doing so, to fall back, recross Bull Run, and make their way back to Centreville.

Vignette

"Colonel *Elzey*," a member of *Elzey's* command later recalled, "moved us first to the left oblique in column across open ground and then forward in line of battle through a wood, the Maryland regiment now in the centre, and when about twenty or thirty yards from its further edge we received an unexpected volley and saw a line drawn up on high ground.... All peered anxiously through and under the foliage which partly obstructed the view. After looking through his glass for a few moments, *Elzey* dropped his hand, his eye lighted up—I was a few feet directly in front of him—and he hastily cried, 'Stars and Stripes! Stars and Stripes! Give it to them, boys!'

"The words were scarcely out of his mouth, the men seeming to take the command from his eye, when a rolling volley was poured into the enemy. Once or twice we loaded and fired, or many did, and we had the satisfaction of seeing the line disappear behind the crest in confusion.... The order was now given to charge bayonets (only our two right companies . . .

had bayonets), and we pressed forward with a cheer, not in a very regular line but each one striving to be foremost.

"But in passing over the stubble or pasture field we discovered it bore an abundant crop of blackberries, and being famished with hunger and our throats parched with thirst, the temptation was too strong to be resisted, the men stopped with one accord and the charging line of battle resolved itself into a crowd of blackberry pickers. Officers swore or exhorted, according to their different principles, and presently succeeded in getting the line to move on. Still, whenever an unusually attractive bush was passed over, we reached down without stopping and stripped off berries, leaves and briers, which we crammed into our mouths; for days afterwards I was occupied extracting the thorns from the palms of my hands. Just before reaching the top of the ridge we were halted and Colonel *Elzey* ordered Lieutenant *T. O. Chestney* of his staff to ride forward. . . . No enemy was to be seen and he waved us forward and we advanced some distance over the open ground until near a pine wood in front, or a little to the left oblique.

"At this moment an irregular fire was poured into this wood by a part of our line, it being supposed that the enemy had halted there and some asserting that from it a fire had been first opened on us. Our fire was presently stopped by the exertions of the officers, but the entire line, consisting of the 1st Maryland, 10th Virginia and 3d Tennessee, was halted while the Newtown Battery, Captain *Beckham*, attached to our brigade, from the extreme left shelled the woods for some time. When this ceased we again advanced and had scarcely entered the woods when we saw abundant evidence of the place having been occupied by the enemy and of our execution, both from artillery and small arms. . . .

"I was startled by hearing a voice calling me and discovered a man lying with his head and shoulders propped against a tree. Walking over to him, I saw that he evidently had but a short time to live, an hour or two at most, being horribly torn about the waist by a shell. He belonged to a Maine regiment, was a fine looking man of middle age, having a heavy dark beard, and belonging to a respectable class in society. I told him I was sorry to see him in such a condition—was there anything I could do? 'Yes,' he replied in a perfectly composed manner, 'you can do one thing for me, and I wish you to do it—for God's sake, take your bayonet and run me through, kill me at once and put an end to this.' I replied that I could not do that, and remembering what I had read of the sufferings of wounded men on battlefields, asked if he did not want some water. He answered, yes, but that made no matter, and reiterated his request to be put out of misery. I told him he had but a few more hours to live, and recommended him to make his preparation for death. He said he was ready to die and earnestly, but without excitement, begged me to run my bayonet through his heart.

"Having no canteen, I ran back to the company where I found *Thomas H. Levering* with one full of water and got him to go back with me. He drank eagerly but still begged us to kill him and as we moved away his voice followed us until we were out of hearing."

Further Reading   Hennessy, *First Battle of Manassas*, 109–16; Rafuse, *A Single Grand Victory*, 183–89; Gottfried, *Maps of First Bull Run*, 67–69.

NOTE: If you are studying both battles today, it is suggested that you go ahead and do the next stop, Sudley Church, here to save time and avoid redundancy. (You will be visiting Sudley Church as part of your study of Second Manassas. Moreover, doing the stop here will spare you a trip through what can be a decidedly aggravating Sudley Road–Lee Highway intersection.) Simply remain in place and begin reading the Sudley Church section of the guide.

To reach the first stop for Second Manassas from Chinn Ridge, resume driving on the park road to a T intersection. *Turn left* and proceed 0.6 mile to SUDLEY ROAD (VA 234). *Turn left* onto SUDLEY ROAD and drive 0.9 mile. At the intersection of SUDLEY ROAD and LEE HIGHWAY (U.S. 29), *turn left* and, after traveling 2.5 miles, *turn right* onto PAGELAND LANE. *Proceed* 0.4 mile and then *turn right* to enter the driveway leading to the parking area for the Brawner Farm. Exit your vehicle at the parking area and follow the 300-yard marked path leading to the Brawner Farm Interpretive Center.

STOP 6   Sudley Church

Directions   To reach Sudley Church from Chinn Ridge, resume driving on
                      the park road to a T intersection. *Turn left* and proceed 0.6 mile
                      to SUDLEY ROAD (VA 234). *Turn left* onto SUDLEY ROAD and drive
                      2.4 miles to the parking area for Sudley Church. Exit your vehi-
                      cle and face toward Sudley Road with the church on your left.

STOP 6A   The Federal Retreat, 4:30–7:00 p.m.

What Happened   The Federal retreat from the battlefield started out relatively
                      well, considering the greenness of McDowell's army. As the
                      various elements of his command made their way to and across
                      the Bull Run crossings at Sudley Ford and Farm Ford, although
                      organization within the various commands had broken down,
                      there seemed to be little sense among the Federals that they
                      had been routed or, with Sykes's battalion of regulars and
                      Capt. Richard Arnold's battery covering their rear, that there
                      was any cause for panic. Once they reached Centreville, McDow-
                      ell and his subordinates would place them on good ground
                      holding the heights. They could then recover their offensive
                      spirit and await reinforcements that would allow them to
                      take another shot at the Confederates.

                      The Confederate high command, of course, was eager to
                      expand on their victory. *Johnston* directed Col. *R. C. W. Radford*
                      to take a battalion of cavalry across Bull Run at Lewis Ford
                      (located about .75 mile downstream from the Stone Bridge) to
                      see what he could accomplish. *Radford* did so and led his cav-
                      alry to a point on the Warrenton Turnpike near the Spindle
                      House. There, seeing a large number of Federals trying to draw
                      water from a well, he ordered a charge that resulted in the
                      capture of several guns and dozens of prisoners. Perhaps more
                      significant than the physical effect of *Radford's* charge was the
                      psychological effect it had on the Federals. Rumors that the
                      dreaded Confederate "Black Horse Cavalry" had made an appear-
                      ance quickly spread in the Union ranks, further frazzling the
                      nerves of those who had eluded *Radford's* grasp but had yet to
                      reach the bridge over Cub Run.

                      Meanwhile two regiments of South Carolinians that *Beau-
                      regard* had ordered to cross the creek managed to capture a
                      U.S. congressman. They quickly pushed forward to a plateau
                      from where they could see the Federals jammed up on the
                      turnpike as they approached the bridge over Cub Run. Col.
                      Joseph Kershaw then called up two pieces of Capt. *Delaware Kem-
                      per's* artillery and ordered the gunners to fire on the bridge.
                      Kemper's very first shot knocked over a wagon on the bridge.
                      With the road blocked in their front, artillery exploding all

around them, and rumors of the Black Horse Cavalry lurking in their rear, terror swept through the Federal ranks. All order and discipline evaporated as panic seized the Federal soldiers. "There is no alternative but to fall back to the Potomac," McDowell informed Washington, "and I shall proceed to do so."

Analysis

During and after the war, the question of who was responsible for the failure of the Confederate army to follow up their victory by continuing offensive operations to further damage McDowell's badly shaken command and possibly even capture Washington would provoke considerable debate. Yet the prospects for the Confederate high command accomplishing even more than they did in the First Manassas Campaign were not especially great. Effective pursuits are rare in military history, even when undertaken by veteran forces. Moreover the haste with which the Federals pulled back to Washington made it unlikely that *Johnston's* and *Beauregard's* green troops, many of whom were exhausted from combat and undoubtedly satisfied just to have survived and prevailed at Manassas, could have even caught them. Indeed *Johnston* later conceded that at the end of the battle his "army was more disorganized by victory than that of the United States by defeat."

Vignette

"In the final struggle for the Henry hill," John L. Rice of the 2nd New Hampshire later recalled, "just before the stampede of the Union army, I went down with a musket ball through my lungs. My comrades bore me off in the wake of our retreating forces toward Sudley Church, where our surgeons had established a hospital. In a short time, being closely pursued by the enemy, and finding that I was apparently dead, they laid me under a fence and made their escape. Some two days after the battle I recovered consciousness, but was unable to move. The blood from my wound soon putrified and attracted swarms of flies, whose larvae in a short time were wriggling under my clothing and into my wound in constantly increasing numbers.

"In this condition I was found by *Amos Benson* and his wife.... The Confederate medical staff at that time was very poorly prepared for the emergency of a battle, especially for the care of the wounded of both armies. Had it not been for the efforts of the Bensons and the few other people living in the vicinity of the battlefield, our wounded would have had little food or attention during the first days following the battle. Benson, discovering life in me, brought an overworked surgeon from the church, who, however, turned away with the remark that he had no time to spend on so hopeless a case. Mrs. Benson meanwhile brought me food from her house, while her husband removed my clothing and scraped away the vermin that were preying upon me. They continued to feed and care for me till, at the end of ten days, I was so far revived that the surgeons were persuaded to remove me from under the fence to more comfortable quarters in a freight car at Manassas Junction, whence in a few days I was carried to Richmond and consigned to Libby prison."

A little over two decades later, Rice visited Washington and, in the words of the regimental historian, "carried out a long cherished purpose to visit his kind benefactors. He found both still living, and it would be hard to tell whether he was more pleased to see them or they to see him. To Rice's assurance that he hoped to be able in some way to repay their kindness, they refused any recompense for themselves; but Mrs. Benson replied: 'If you want to do that, you can help us poor people here pay for our little church yonder. It was destroyed during the war, and it cost us a severe struggle to rebuild it. We owe two hundred dollars on it yet, which in this poor country is a heavy burden.' Rice promised to send her a contribution. When he reached home he related this to the editor of the *Springfield Republican*, who published the story with a request for contributions. Within two or three days $235 had been subscribed."

STOP 6B   The Cost of the Battle

Directions   Remain in place.

What Happened   Sudley Church served as a field hospital during and after the battle of July 21, 1861. Victory had cost the Confederacy approximately 1,900 casualties, of which 378 were killed, 1,489 wounded, and 30 missing. McDowell's command lost 460 killed, 1,124 wounded, and 1,312 missing, for a total of 2,896 casualties.

Vignette   During the fighting on Matthews Hill, Maj. Sullivan Ballou was leading the men of the 2nd Rhode Island when cannon fire tore off his right leg. Brought back to the vicinity of Sudley Church, where Federal surgeons had set up a hospital, Ballou was left behind when the Federals retreated from the field; he died on July 28. On July 14, two days before the campaign began, he had written a long letter to his wife, Sarah: "Our movements may be of a few days duration and full of pleasure— and it may be one of severe conflict and death to me. Not my will, but thine, O God be done. If it is necessary that I should fall on the battle field for my Country, I am ready.... But, my dear wife, when I know that with my own joys, I lay down nearly all of your's, and replace them in this life with cares and sorrows, when after having eaten for long years the bitter fruits of orphanage myself, I must offer it as their only sustenance to my dear little children. . . . Sarah my love for you is deathless, it seems to bind me with mighty cables, that nothing but Omnipotence could break; and yet my love of Country comes over me like a strong wind, and bears me irresistibly on with all those chains, to the battle field.

"The memories of all the blissful moments I have spent with you, come creeping over me, and I feel most gratified to God and you that I have enjoyed them so long. And how hard it is for me to give them up and burn to ashes the hopes of future years, when, God willing we might still have lived and loved together, and seen our boys grow up to honorable manhood around us. I have, I know, but few and small claims upon Divine Providence, but something whispers to me—perhaps it is the wafted prayer of my little Edgar, that I shall return to my loved ones unharmed. If I do not, my dear Sarah, never forget how much I love you, and when my last breath escapes me on the battle field, it will whisper your name. . . . O Sarah! if the dead can come back to this earth and flit unseen around those they loved, I shall always be near you; in the gladest days and the darkest nights, advised to your happiest scenes and gloomiest hours, always, always; and if there be a soft breeze upon your cheek, it shall be my breath, or the cool air cools your throbbing temple, it shall be my spirit passing by. Sarah do not mourn me dead; think I am gone and wait for thee, for we shall meet again."

Lamentably, when officials from Rhode Island arrived in the area in March 1862 to recover Ballou's body, they learned that Confederate soldiers had exhumed, burned, and mutilated it. With the assistance of local residents, though, they were able to locate a few of Ballou's remains to send back to Rhode Island, along with reports of what they had learned, which sparked outrage throughout the North.

Further Exploration The trail that begins on the other side of Sudley Road from the parking area is part of a loop trail that runs along the unfinished railroad to bluffs overlooking Bull Run, then turns left to follow the stream to where Catharpin Run flows into it and then to the Sudley Springs Ford crossing of Catharpin Run. (The crossing of Bull Run is inaccessible.) From the ford, the trail follows the original trace of the road through the woods, passing a structure that was once the Sudley Post Office and at the time of the battle was the home of the Thornberry family, back to the parking area. If you look to your left, on the other side of the road from the church you will see a fence line that indicates where the historic Sudley Road meets up with the modern road.

Further Reading   Hennessy, *First Battle of Manassas*, 117–23; Rafuse, *A Single Grand Victory*, 191–98; Gottfried, *Maps of First Bull Run*, 70–73.

To reach the first stop for the Second Manassas tour, exit the parking area and *turn left* onto SUDLEY ROAD (VA 234). Drive 0.1 mile, then *turn left* onto FEATHERBED LANE. *Proceed* 2.2 miles on FEATHERBED LANE to the intersection with LEE HIGHWAY (U.S. 29). *Turn right* onto LEE HIGHWAY, and after traveling 1.4 miles, *turn right* onto PAGELAND LANE. *Proceed* 0.4 mile and then *turn right* to enter the driveway leading to the parking area for the Brawner Farm. Exit your car and follow the 300-yard marked path leading to the Brawner Farm Interpretive Center.

To return to the Henry Hill Visitor Center: Exit the parking area and *turn right* onto SUDLEY ROAD (VA 234). Drive 2.0 miles south, then *turn left* to enter the driveway leading to the Visitor Center.

"Captured by Stonewall Jackson himself."
BLCW 2:360.

Second Manassas

Starke's brigade fighting with stones near the "Deep Cut." BLCW 2:534.

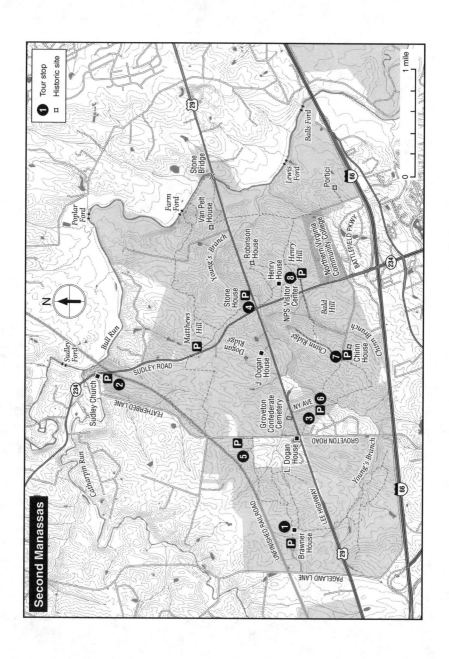

Second Manassas

Tour stop ●1
Historic site ⌑

Sudley Ford

Catharpin Run

Poplar Ford

Bull Run

Sudley Church

234

Farm Ford

Van Pelt House

SUDLEY ROAD

FEATHERBED LANE

UNFINISHED RAILROAD

PAGELAND LANE

Matthews Hill

Young's Branch

Stone House

Dogan Ridge

J. Dogan House

Groveton Confederate Cemetery

J.L. Dogan House

LEE HIGHWAY

Brawner House

GROVETON ROAD

NY AVE

Young's Branch

Robinson House

Henry House

Henry Hill

NPS Visitor Center

Bald Hill

Chinn Ridge

Chinn House

Chinn Branch

Northern Virginia Community College

BATTLEFIELD PKWY

Stone Bridge

Balls Ford

Lewis Ford

Portici

29

66

234

66

29

N

0   1 mile

The Road to Second Manassas

In the year following the Confederate victory at First Manassas, the Confederate States of America was driven to the brink of defeat, as during the first half of 1862 Federal armies won victories in North Carolina, Kentucky, Arkansas, Tennessee, and Virginia that carried them deep into Confederate territory and depressed Confederate morale. With public attention largely focused on events in the East, the most compelling military campaign was the one that took a massive Union army commanded by Maj. Gen. George B. McClellan to within 10 miles of Richmond by June. McClellan's efforts were greatly hampered, though, by the withholding of what he believed to be essential forces and by directives from Washington issued in response to defeats at the hands of Confederate forces commanded by Maj. Gen. *Thomas J. "Stonewall" Jackson* in the Shenandoah Valley. Of equal significance to the ability of the Confederacy to thwart McClellan's effort to capture Richmond was the appointment on June 1 of Gen. *Robert E. Lee* to command the South's principal army in Virginia. During the last week of June, *Lee* initiated a massive offensive that drove McClellan's Army of the Potomac back in a series of engagements that became known as the Seven Days' Battles.

Even as the Seven Days' Battles were being fought, President Lincoln had already set in motion the sequence of events that would culminate in a second Confederate victory at Manassas. On June 26 he ordered that the three separate commands that had floundered about in the Shenandoah Valley and north of Richmond be consolidated into a single, three-corps Army of Virginia. To command this army, Lincoln turned to Maj. Gen. John Pope, an ambitious and rather pompous, though capable, officer whose close friendship with the president and with Republicans in Congress contrasted sharply with the acrimonious relationships they had with McClellan.

This was evident in several ways. One was Pope's public pledge to conduct aggressive operations and willingness to do so along the overland route between Washington and Richmond, which accorded with Lincoln's sense of how the war should be conducted and contrasted sharply with McClellan's. "I hear constantly," Pope pompously complained in a widely circulated message to his men shortly after taking command, "of 'taking strong positions and holding them,' of 'lines of retreat,' and of 'bases of supply.' Let us discard such ideas.... Success and glory are in the advance." Pope was also determined upon assuming command to make war on Southern civilians. McClellan firmly believed that the best way to persuade Southerners to come back to the Union was with a policy of conciliation in which Southern property and liberties—above all their right to own slaves—would be respected. That the war, and the Lincoln administration's policy toward the South, was taking a harder turn was evident in Pope's decision to issue a series of general orders in July that promised a tougher hand against Southern civilians. It was also evident in Congress's passage of a new Confiscation Act in the aftermath of the Seven Days Battles and Lincoln's private announcement to his cabinet during the second half of July that he intended to issue a proclamation emancipating the slaves of the rebels if they did not come back to the Union. However, he decided to heed the counsel of one of his cabinet members to wait until after a battlefield victory to take this step.

Lincoln also decided in July 1862 to appoint a new general-in-chief of all the Union armies and selected Maj. Gen. Henry W. Halleck for the job. Halleck's first big task upon assuming his new post in late July was to help Lincoln figure out what to do about the situation in Virginia. McClellan's army was posted east of Richmond at Harrison's Landing, on the James River, while Pope was in the process of consolidating his widely scattered command in northern and central Virginia along the Orange and Alexandria Railroad. Neither Halleck nor Lincoln liked the idea of McClellan and Pope operating along separate lines, with the main Confederate army concentrated between them around Richmond. Thus they ordered McClellan to abandon Harrison's Landing and return to northern Virginia to join his command with Pope's.

Lincoln and Halleck's decision was a godsend to *Lee*. Angered by Pope's promise of rougher treatment of Southern civilians, *Lee*, who scorned Pope and considered him a "miscreant" that needed "to be suppressed," very badly wanted to strike a blow at the new Federal commander. Moreover, he recognized that the Army of Virginia's scattered condition and lengthy railroad line of operations offered good prospects for successful maneuver. The same could not be said of McClellan's well-entrenched camp at Harrison's Landing, which in addition to being unassailable posed a danger to Richmond of such magnitude that *Lee* had no choice but to make it his first priority.

Despite the constraints imposed by the Federal presence at Harrison's Landing, the fact that Pope was within striking distance of the critical railroad that connected Richmond and the Shenandoah Valley via Gordonsville compelled *Lee* to send Maj. Gen. *Thomas J. "Stonewall" Jackson* north in mid-July with two divisions. When evidence of the Federal decision to evacuate Harrison's Landing reached *Lee*, he immediately began sending more of his command north.

Lee first dispatched an additional division to *Jackson's* aid. *Jackson* responded by crossing the Rapidan River and advancing on Culpeper Court House, where Pope was concentrating his command, hoping to strike a blow. On August 9, though, it was *Jackson* himself who was surprised when a Federal force commanded by Maj. Gen. Nathaniel Banks aggressively moved south to confront the Confederates. Upon reaching *Jackson's* position near Cedar Mountain, Banks launched a powerful attack that caught the Confederates unprepared. However, *Jackson* was able to personally rally his men, and they managed to fight off the Federal assault. Banks then fell back toward Culpeper, where the rest of Pope's army was completing their concentration. This frustrated *Jackson's* hopes that he would be able to follow up his victory at Cedar Mountain with a successful pursuit and compelled him to fall back across the Rapidan.

In mid-August *Jackson* was joined by the rest of the Army of Northern Virginia, which *Lee* had ordered north to the Rapidan and organized into two wings: one commanded by *Jackson* and the other by Maj. Gen. *James Longstreet*. Upon arriving at the Rapidan, *Lee* immediately hatched plans for an offensive. He correctly assumed Federal authorities planned to combine Pope's and McClellan's armies, with Pope's Army of Virginia maintaining a position along the Orange and Alexandria Railroad, while the units of McClellan's army disembarked around Fredericksburg after traveling by water from the York-James Peninsula, and then moved west up the Rappahannock River to link up with Pope. *Lee* also saw that Culpeper Court House, where Pope had concentrated his army, was between two rivers, the Rappahannock to the north and the Rapidan (a tributary of the Rappahannock) to the south.

Lee hatched a plan whereby his two wings would cross the Rapidan south and east of Culpeper to attack Pope's left and drive his army away from Fredericksburg. Meanwhile Confederate cavalry commanded by Maj. Gen. *James E. B. Stuart* would move to cut off Pope's retreat across the Rappahannock. Unfortunately for *Lee*, delays concentrating his command gave an enterprising band of Union cavalry the opportunity early on August 18 to launch a raid on the hamlet of Verdiersville, where *Stuart* had his camp. Although unable to capture *Stuart*, the Federals managed to secure a copy of the orders outlining *Lee's* plan. Alerted to the danger, Pope evacuated Culpeper Court House and pulled back across the Rappahannock. A frustrated *Lee* ordered his army across the Rapidan and advanced to the banks of the Rappahannock. He then made a series of attempts to push *Jackson's* command across the river to attack Pope's right flank. The Federals, however, were able to effectively thwart these, all the while buying time for units from McClellan's army to move to the front.

While these were going on, during the evening of August 21–22, *Stuart's* cavalry crossed the river upstream from both armies to conduct a raid against Pope's communications. On reaching Catlett's Station, *Stuart* managed to capture documents laying out the position of the various Federal units and brought them to *Lee*. Learning from these just how fast the window of opportunity was closing for dealing with Pope before McClellan's entire army joined him, and out of room to continue maneuvering along the Rappahannock, *Lee* decided on a bold plan. He directed *Jackson* to replicate *Stuart's* maneuver, but on a grander scale. While *Longstreet* held Pope's command in place along the Rappahannock, *Jackson's* three divisions would maneuver around them and fall on his communications along the Orange and Alexandria Railroad.

On August 26 *Jackson's* command, after covering over 50 miles in less than two days of marching, managed to reach the railroad at Bristoe Station, then pushed north to seize the Federal supply depot at Manassas Junction. Pope responded by ordering his army and the three corps that had arrived from the York-James Peninsula to move north and east in the direction of Centreville and Manassas Junction, with the goal of achieving no less than the complete destruction of *Jackson's* command. Two corps operating under the command of Maj. Gen. Irvin McDowell would move along the Warrenton Turnpike to a position from which it could block *Jackson's* escape route to the west. Meanwhile the rest of the army, four corps under Pope's direct command, would move north and east toward Manassas Junction directly.

Pope's hopes that his plan would result in the crushing of *Jackson's* command would not be realized. Confederate forces commanded by Maj. Gen. *Richard S. Ewell* managed to hold off the advanced units of Pope's force moving up along the railroad long enough on August 27 to enable the rest of *Jackson's* command to engage in an orgy of looting and destruction at Manassas Junction and then depart unmolested that evening. The possibility that the elements from McClellan's army that had been directed to disembark at Alexandria instead of near Fredericksburg might threaten *Jackson* from the direction of Washington was also thwarted on the morning of August 27, when *Jackson's* men thrashed a small force that had been dispatched to the scene from Alexandria near where the Orange and Alexandria Bridge crossed Bull Run.

Nonetheless, on the morning of August 28, Pope fully believed a decisive victory over *Jackson's* force at Manassas Junction was within his grasp. However, during the night of August 27–28, *Jackson's* three divisions left Manassas Junction. Consequently, when the vanguard of Pope's command reached the junction on August 28, they found only a few stragglers and reports that *Jackson's* command had marched to Centreville. Based on these reports, during the afternoon Pope ordered his command to set their sights on Centreville. By the time he issued orders to McDowell to follow the Warrenton Turnpike all the way to Centreville instead of turning off at Gainesville to move on Manassas Junction, though, all but two of the divisions in his wing of the army had turned off the turnpike so long ago that there was no point calling them back.

One of those two divisions belonged to Brig. Gen. James Ricketts. It had already received orders from McDowell to turn off the turnpike in the opposite direction from Manassas Junction and move toward Haymarket. McDowell issued these out of concern that *Longstreet's* wing of the Army of Northern Virginia was much closer than Pope suspected. This was a wise decision. *Lee* and *Longstreet* had put the latter's command on the march a few days earlier and on the night of August 27–28 had it in bivouac only a few miles west of Thoroughfare Gap in the Bull Run Mountains. Ricketts's command was far too small, however, to defend the gap against *Longstreet's* far superior force. Although his men put up a stiff fight, by the time night fell on August 28 Ricketts's men were in full retreat. Thus the way was cleared for *Lee* to reunite *Longstreet's* and *Jackson's* commands.

It was in part due to its convenience to Thoroughfare Gap that *Jackson* chose Groveton, located on the Warrenton Turnpike just east of Gainesville and west of the First Manassas Battlefield, as the destination for his command's march during the night of August 27–28. In addition, north of Groveton there was an unfinished railroad bed, which provided a convenient place for *Jackson* to post his command.

Pope, however, believed *Jackson* had gone to Centreville. Thus Brig. Gen. Rufus King, whose division had just turned off the Warrenton Turnpike to move on Manassas Junction but had not gone so far that it could not quickly return to the road, received orders from McDowell to march back to the turnpike and follow it to Centreville. To reach Centreville, however, King's command would have to pass through Groveton, where, unbeknownst to anyone in the Union high command, *Jackson* was resting his three divisions and itching for an opportunity to strike.

When he learned King's isolated division was moving his way, *Jackson* ordered his men to engage them. The Second Battle of Manassas had begun.

Overview of August 28, 1862

When the sun rose on August 28, John Pope was confident he had issued the orders that would bring about the defeat of *Stonewall Jackson*. Pope had developed a plan for the day in which one wing of his army, composed of two corps operating under the direction of Maj. Gen. Irvin McDowell, would continue their march along the Warrenton Turnpike until they reached Gainesville on the Manassas Gap Railroad. McDowell's command would then turn right and follow the railroad, blocking *Jackson's* route of escape in that direction. While McDowell did this, the rest of the army would continue following the Orange and Alexandria Railroad toward Manassas Junction. With *Jackson's* force trapped between these two forces, its destruction seemed assured.

Pope's plan, however, rested on two false assumptions. The first was that *Jackson* was at Manassas Junction. In fact, during the night of August 27–28, *Jackson* had ordered his three divisions to leave Manassas Junction and move to Groveton, a small hamlet on the Warrenton Turnpike less than 4 miles east of Gainesville. Although two of *Jackson's* divisions would, due to a mix-up in orders, march to Centreville instead of taking the direct road to their destination (a development that would have significant ramifications for Federal movements), by midmorning all three had reunited and were settling into positions *Jackson* had selected for them near Groveton. This placed *Jackson's* command in relatively close marching distance to Thoroughfare Gap in the Bull Run Mountains.

Pope's second false assumption was that *Jackson's* command was completely isolated from the rest of *Lee's* army. *Longstreet's* wing of the Army of Northern Virginia, Pope believed, was too far away to help *Jackson* and thus not a concern. In fact that morning *Longstreet's* wing was at White Plains, less than 10 miles from Thoroughfare Gap and less than a good day's march from Groveton.

Pope was disabused of his first assumption when the vanguard of the Federal force marching along the Orange and Alexandria Railroad reached Manassas Junction around noon and reported that the Confederates were gone. As Pope digested this information, as well as conflicting reports of *Jackson's* movements during the night (a consequence of the mismanaged Confederate march), McDowell's wing was pushing east along the Warrenton Turnpike. On reaching Gainesville, Maj. Gen. Franz Sigel's corps dutifully turned right and began moving along the railroad toward Manassas Junction. McDowell, however, was not as sanguine as Pope was about the prospect of the rest of *Lee's* command making an unwelcome appearance and recognized the importance of Thoroughfare Gap. Consequently, as the corps following Sigel's moved along the turnpike, McDowell decided to detach from it the division commanded by Brig. Gen. James B. Ricketts and send it to Haymarket to watch Thoroughfare Gap.

Meanwhile Pope ordered the rest of his command to begin moving toward Centreville in response to reports that *Jackson's* command had marched there during the night. By the time the orders arrived, though, all but two of the divisions in McDowell's wing had already moved so close to Manassas Junction that there was no point ordering them back to the turnpike. One of those other divisions was Ricketts's; the other was Brig. Gen. Rufus King's. After directing King to march to Centreville in accordance with Pope's orders, McDowell departed and began riding cross-country in an effort to find Pope.

In fact the rest of the Confederate army was much closer than Pope thought it was. *Lee* and *Longstreet* did not exercise particular haste in their movements during the morning of August 28. Nonetheless, upon reaching the entrance to Thoroughfare Gap at around 2:00 p.m., they were able to compel a band of Federal cavalry to fall back with relative ease. As the Federal cavalry pulled back, *Longstreet's* men encountered Ricketts's division moving up from Haymarket. Ricketts's command then established a strong position about 0.5 mile from the eastern end to the gap. There they fought a fierce engagement with units belonging to the Confederate division commanded by Brig. Gen. *David R. Jones.* Ricketts, however, had too few troops to hope to hold off *Longstreet's* entire command for long. When *Longstreet* moved forces onto high ground on Pond Mountain to the south and Mother Leathercoat to the north, Ricketts had no choice but to retreat and ordered his men to fall back to Gainesville.

Meanwhile *Jackson* finished posting his three divisions north of the Warrenton Turnpike with his line roughly conforming to an unfinished railroad bed. As his men rested during the afternoon, *Jackson* kept an anxious eye out for the Federals. He badly hoped to bring Pope to battle before the Federals had crossed Bull Run. Once Pope's army was across, *Jackson* understood it would be close enough to the Washington defenses and reinforcements that prospects for a truly decisive Confederate battlefield success would decline precipitously.

Thus it was a source of no little relief to *Jackson* when he learned of King's march along the Warrenton Turnpike. As the head of King's column reached Groveton at around 6:00 p.m., *Jackson* ordered the Stonewall Brigade forward to engage them. Unaware of what exactly was in front of him, Brig. Gen. John Gibbon moved forces from his brigade north from the turnpike to accept *Jackson's* challenge. This touched off a fierce two-hour engagement near the Brawner Farm that ended in a tactical stalemate.

Pope reacted just as *Jackson* hoped: he abandoned his plans to move his army across Bull Run. Delighted to have finally found *Jackson* and determined to fulfill hopes he expressed in an earlier order to McDowell that "we shall bag the whole crowd," Pope directed King to hold his position in order to block *Jackson's* escape route to the west and ordered the rest of the army to the old Manassas battlefield. King and his brigade commanders, however, had already decided to withdraw their battered commands. They did so in part due to information received from Ricketts about his fight with *Longstreet*. Realizing he was facing far more than his command could handle, King ordered his men to fall back to Manassas Junction during the night, while Ricketts had his men do the same in the direction of Bristoe Station.

Thus August 28 ended with the Confederates having achieved both of their goals for the day: Pope had stopped his movement across Bull Run and was moving to give battle, while *Longstreet* now had a clear road to march to *Jackson's* assistance. As he planned for August 29, Pope eagerly anticipated positive results from the first development—and was oblivious to the second.

Major-General John Pope. From a photograph taken since the war. BLCW 2:453.

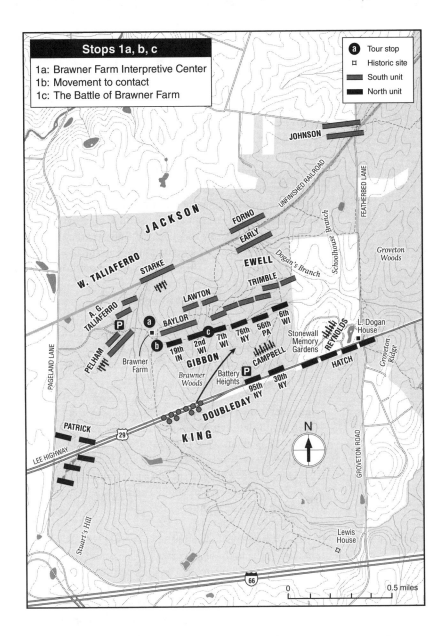

STOP 1   Brawner Farm

Directions   From the Henry Hill Visitor Center, exit the parking area, *turn right* onto SUDLEY ROAD (VA 234), and drive 0.4 mile to the traffic light. At the light, *turn left* onto LEE HIGHWAY (U.S. 29). After traveling 2.5 miles, *turn right* onto PAGELAND LANE. *Proceed* 0.4 mile and then *turn right* to enter the driveway leading to the parking area for the Brawner Farm. Exit your vehicle at the parking area and follow the 300-yard paved path leading to the Brawner Farm Interpretive Center.

STOP 1A   Brawner Farm Interpretive Center

Orientation   Although smaller than the Henry Hill Visitor Center, the
                       Brawner Farm Interpretive Center, which is open from March
                       1 through November 30, is nonetheless an excellent place to
                       begin your study of Second Manassas. At the time of the Civil
                       War, the property was owned by Augusta Douglas, who leased
                       it to John Brawner. The building has recently been restored
                       by the National Park Service and contains exhibits discuss-
                       ing such topics related to the Second Manassas Campaign as
                       the Fitz John Porter court-martial, the Emancipation Procla-
                       mation, and the 5th New York Zouaves. Of particular interest
                       is the electronic map, which, like the one in the Henry Hill
                       Visitor Center, provides a brief visual account of the battle.

STOP 1B   Movement to Contact, August 28, 1862

Directions   Walk to a spot on the south side of the Brawner Farm Inter-
                       pretive Center next to the NPS marker "Jackson Opens Fire"
                       and face south toward the historic Warrenton Turnpike, which
                       today is U.S. 29 (LEE HIGHWAY).

Orientation   From where you are standing, the Stone Bridge that carries
                       U.S. 29 over Bull Run is about 3.5 miles to the east (your left).
                       Gainesville is about 2.5 miles west of you, while Manassas
                       Junction is about 6 miles to the south and east. To your right
                       front, you will see a cleared spot on a hill across U.S. 29. That
                       is Stuart's Hill, where *Lee* established his headquarters on
                       arriving on the field on August 29.

What Happened   Having wrongly concluded that, after leaving Manassas Junc-
                       tion during the night of August 27–28, *Stonewall Jackson* had
                       marched his command to Centreville, Pope ordered his army
                       to concentrate there. In line with Pope's wishes, McDowell
                       directed King's division to march east along the Warrenton
                       Turnpike toward the Bull Run crossing at the Stone Bridge.
                       By 6:00 p.m., King's lead brigade, commanded by Brig. Gen.
                       John P. Hatch, had reached the small hamlet of Groveton,
                       while the rear brigade, commanded by Brig. Gen. Marsena
                       Patrick, was in the vicinity of the turnpike's intersection with
                       modern Pageland Lane.

                       King's line of march carried him across the front of *Jackson's*
                       three divisions, which were posted in concealed positions north
                       of the Warrenton Turnpike. *Jackson* was eager to engage the
                       Federals before they reached the Bull Run crossings and upon
                       learning of King's approach had ordered his men to move into
                       position to do so. At around 6:00 p.m., *Jackson* ordered his artil-

lery to begin firing on King's command. At that point, the brigade behind Hatch in the Union line of march, Brig. Gen. John Gibbon's, had just about finished passing through a large woodlot known as Brawner's Woods.

Gibbon responded by riding up to a rise north of the pike and concluded, based on what he had been told about *Jackson's* whereabouts and the sight of a seemingly isolated battery moving into position, that the Federals had merely come across some Confederate horse artillery. After consulting with Brig. Gen. Abner Doubleday, the commander of the next brigade in the Federal line of march, Gibbon ordered Col. Edgar O'Conner's 2nd Wisconsin to move north under the cover of Brawner's Woods to eliminate what he believed to be only a minor nuisance.

Analysis *Jackson's* decision to engage King's command completely transformed the situation on August 28, 1862. Pope's movements up to that point would in all likelihood have resulted in his command being safely across Bull Run, close enough to the Washington defenses and reinforcements to all but eliminate whatever prospects there might be for *Lee's* forces to engage them successfully. To be sure, forcing the Federals all the way back from the Rapidan to Bull Run, eliminating their presence from a large area of Virginia, was in itself a significant accomplishment. However, Pope's response to the engagement at Brawner Farm, to reorient his forces in an attempt to seize what he perceived to be an opportunity to finally engage and possibly "bag" *Jackson*, gave the Confederate high command something more. Namely, it gave them the opportunity to also inflict a decisive battlefield defeat on the Federals.

Vignette "The Pike passed within a quarter of a mile of our troops in the woods," cavalryman *William Blackford* later recalled, "who had now been resting quite long enough to refresh them after their labors of the march, and were burning with enthusiasm. . . . *Jackson* rode out to examine the approaching foe, trotting backwards and forwards along the line of the handsome parade marching by, and in easy musket range of their skirmish line, but they did not seem to think that a single horseman was worthy of their attention. . . . We could almost tell his thoughts by his movements. Sometimes he would halt, then trot on rapidly, halt again, wheel his horse and pass again along the front of the marching column, or rather along its flank. About a quarter of a mile off, troops were now opposite us. . . . Presently General *Jackson* pulled up suddenly, wheeled and galloped towards us. 'Here he comes, by God,' said several, and *Jackson* rode up to the assembled group as calm as a May morning and, touching his hat in military salute, said in as soft a voice as if he had been talking to a friend in ordinary conversation, 'Bring out your men, gentlemen!' Every officer whirled round and scurried back to the woods at a full gallop. The men had been watching their officers with as much interest as they had been watching Jackson, and when they wheeled and dashed towards them they knew what it mean, and from the woods arose a hoarse roar like that from cages of wild beasts at the scent of blood."

STOP 1C   The Battle of Brawner Farm, 6:00–9:00 p.m.

Directions   *Turn left* and hike about 150 yards to the NPS marker "2nd Wisconsin Infantry." *Stop here* and *turn left* to face the fence line at the top of a small rise. This fence line marks the location of the Stonewall Brigade on August 28 and gives you a good sense of just how close the two lines were during the fighting at Brawner Farm.

What Happened   Upon reaching the northern edge of Brawner's Woods, Gibbon and his men were greeted with the sight of lines of Confederate infantry moving toward them. He and O'Conner rapidly deployed their men in line of battle to face Col. *William Baylor's* Stonewall Brigade, which in the year since it won fame at Manassas under *Jackson's* command, had seen hard and distinguished service on numerous battlefields. In contrast, O'Conner's command had only a poor performance at First Manassas on its record, while the rest of Gibbon's command—known as the "Black Hat Brigade" for their distinctive headgear—had yet to see any significant action at all.

Nonetheless O'Conner's men did not flinch, and within a few minutes both sides were pouring fire into each other less than 100 yards apart. Recognizing he was badly outnumbered, Gibbon immediately ordered up the rest of his brigade. Within a half hour he had all of his regiments up and engaged. As their men exchanged fire at point-blank range in almost perfectly dressed ranks, both *Jackson* and Gibbon searched for further assistance. King, however, had been stricken with an epileptic seizure shortly after the battle begun. Thus Gibbon was able to secure only the assistance of two regiments from Doubleday's brigade, raising the strength of the Federal firing line to about 2,500 men. Hatch's command was pinned down in the open area around Groveton by Confederate artillery fire, while Patrick refused to go to Gibbon's assistance without orders from King.

Jackson, meanwhile, despite having well over 20,000 men in his command, committed only about 3,600. At around 7:30 p.m. *Jackson* ordered a series of frontal assaults by Brig. Gen.

Isaac Trimble's and Brig. Gen. Alexander Lawton's brigades. Gibbon's and Doubleday's men easily and bloodily repulsed them. Jackson then ordered Col. A. G. Taliaferro's brigade and Capt. John Pelham's artillery to attempt to turn the Federal left. The regiment on the Union left, though, Col. Solomon Meredith's 19th Indiana, effectively responded to Jackson's move, pulling back to a rail fence behind which they were able to fight off the Confederates.

The fighting finally ended about two hours after it began, as darkness made it impossible for either side to see what they were doing very well. Gibbon and Doubleday then pulled their men back toward the turnpike. In just two hours of fighting, approximately 1,150 Federals and 1,250 Confederates had fallen. Among the wounded were two Confederate division commanders, including Jackson's most trusted and capable subordinate, Maj. Gen. Richard Ewell, who suffered a gruesome wound that would result in the amputation of much of his left leg.

After consulting with his subordinates, an exhausted and shaken King initially wanted to hold his position or continue the march to Centreville. Then, however, he began receiving exaggerated reports regarding the size of Jackson's command that had been gleaned from Confederate prisoners. After digesting these, King and his subordinates agreed they had no choice but to fall back to Manassas Junction and began doing so around 1:00 a.m.

Analysis

The bitter fight at the Brawner Farm marked the baptism of fire for most of Gibbon's command and one of the relatively rare occasions in the Civil War when the two sides faced each other in a stand-up fight. While the men on both sides performed admirably, the same could not be said of many of their commanders. The fine performance of Gibbon's men was a consequence of the strict discipline and rigor their commander had instilled in them during the months prior to the fight. Nonetheless Gibbon merits censure for impetuously committing his men to a fight on August 28 when he had a decidedly incomplete picture of what he was facing. As if this were not bad enough, King's physical incapacitation precluded effective commitment of the rest of his division to the fight. Fortunately Gibbon was spared the potentially catastrophic consequences of his decision to commit to the battle by Doubleday's willingness to assist him, the performance of his men, and the equally poor performance of the Confederate high command.

Despite having over 20,000 men on hand, more than enough to annihilate Gibbon's command—and possibly King's entire division as well—Jackson failed to commit sufficient strength to the battle. Moreover, not until it was too late in the battle to really accomplish anything decisive, did he make an attempt to break the stalemate through assaults or maneuver. Consequently the fight at the Brawner Farm ended with both sides battered and little to show for their efforts and sacrifice. Yet the fact that the fight happened would have significant consequences for the overall campaign. It led Pope to commit to battle on the Manassas side of Bull Run, believing that he had *Jackson* isolated and fixed in place. This conviction and the idea that he had an opportunity for a decisive success before him would shape Pope's conduct for the next two days. He would not shake them until it proved too late for himself and his command to avoid defeat at Manassas.

Vignette

Maj. Rufus Dawes later recalled how he and other members of the 6th Wisconsin were moving "along the turnpike on that quiet summer evening as unsuspectingly as if changing camp. Suddenly the stillness was broken by six cannon shots fired in rapid succession by a rebel battery, point blank at our regiment. . . . Battery 'B,' 4th U.S. artillery, now came down the turnpike on a gallop. Quickly tearing away the fence, they wheeled into position in the open field, and the loud crack of their brass twelve pounders echoed the rebel cannon. Thus opened our first real battle. . . . No sooner had the 2nd Wisconsin shown its line in the open field, than there burst upon them a flame of musketry, while Confederate batteries distributed along about a mile of front opened with shell and round shot. . . . Captain J. D. Wood, of Gibbon's staff, came galloping down the turnpike with an order for the sixth to move forward into action. . . .

"The regiment advanced without firing a shot, making a half wheel to the left in line of battle as accurately as if on the drill ground. Through the battle smoke into which we were advancing, I could see a blood red sun, sinking behind the hills. I cannot account for our immunity from the fire of the enemy while on this advance. When at a short range, Colonel [Lysander] Cutler ordered the regiment to halt and fire. The seventh Wisconsin now came forward. . . . Our united fire did great execution. It seemed to throw the rebels into complete confusion, and they fell back into the woods behind them. We now gave a loud and jubilant cheer throughout the whole line of our brigade. Our regiment was on low ground which, in the gathering darkness, gave us great advantage over the enemy, as they overshot our line. . . . It was quite dark when the enemy's yelling columns again came forward, and they came with a rush. Our men on the left loaded and fired with the energy of madmen, and the sixth worked with an equal desperation. This stopped the rush of the enemy, and they halted and fired upon us their deadly musketry. During a few awful moments, I could see by the lurid light of the powder flashes, the whole of both lines. I saw a rebel mounted officer shot from his horse at the very front of their battle line. It was evident that we were being overpowered and that our men were giving ground. The two crowds, they could hardly be called lines, were within, it seemed to me, fifty yards of each other, and they were pouring musketry into each other as rapidly as men could load and shoot. Two of General Doubleday's regiments (56th Pennsylvania and 76th New York,) now came suddenly into the gap on the left of our regiment, and they fired a crashing volley. Hurrah! They have come at the very nick of time. The low ground saved our regiment, as the enemy overshot us in the darkness. Men were falling in the sixth, but our loss was small compared to that suffered by the regiments on the left. I rode along our line and when near Colonel Cutler, he said, 'Our men are giving ground on the left, Major.' 'Yes, Sir,' said I. I heard a distinct sound of the blow that struck him. He gave a convulsive start and clapped his hand on his leg, but he controlled his voice. He said, 'Tell Colonel Bragg to take command, I am shot.' . . . I rode quickly to Lieut. Colonel [Edward] Bragg and he at once took command of the regiment. There was cheering along our line and it was again standing firmly.

"General Doubleday's two regiments by their opportune arrival and gallant work, aided much in turning the battle in our favor. The 'Little Colonel' (Bragg) always eager to push forward in a fight, advanced the regiment several rods. But soon the enemy came on again just as before, and our men on the left could be seen on the hill, in the infernal light of the powder flashes, struggling as furiously as ever. . . . Our regiment was suffering more severely than it had been; but, favored by the low ground, we kept up a steady, rapid, and well aimed fire. . . . Our line on the left gradually fell back. It did not break but slowly gave ground, firing as savagely as ever. The rebels did not advance. Colonel Bragg directed our regiment to move by a backward step, keeping up our fire and keeping on a line with our brigade. . . . The other regiments of the brigade fell back to the turnpike. After an interval of quiet, Colonel Bragg called upon the regiment to give three cheers. No response of any kind was given by the enemy."

Further Exploration   You can continue walking along the trail from the 2nd Wisconsin marker to follow the 1.2-mile-long loop trail that takes you along the length of both the Union and Confederate lines at Brawner Farm. Alternatively you can do a much shorter loop trail. To do this, *turn right* and walk from the 2nd Wisconsin marker about 100 yards to a point where you see another trail to your left. *Turn here* and proceed 150 yards to another fork and *turn left*. Walk about 125 yards to the marker "First Brigade (The Stonewall Brigade)." (*En route* you will pass five cannon, which face east and north, next to which is the NPS marker "Shooting Gallery," which explains the role this position played in the fighting of August 30, 1862.) From the Stonewall Brigade marker, *continue* on the trail for about 200 yards to return to the Brawner Farm Interpretive Center.

Further Reading   Hennessy, *Return to Bull Run*, 161–93; Gaff, *Brave Men's Tears*; Hennessy, *Second Manassas Battlefield Map Study*, 4–14, 29–36.

Major-General Fitz John Porter.
From a photograph.
BLCW 2:333.

Overview of August 29, 1862

Believing that *Jackson's* command was isolated north of the Warrenton Turnpike, Pope's plan for the day was for a force of three divisions under the command of Maj. Gen. Fitz John Porter to march from Manassas Junction to Gainesville on the Manassas Gap Railroad. Upon reaching Gainesville, Porter's command would be in a position to cut *Jackson* off from the west and then attack the Confederate right, which the previous evening's battle indicated was located near the Brawner Farm. Meanwhile the rest of Pope's command would concentrate on the First Manassas Battlefield and attack *Jackson's* line along the unfinished railroad to keep the Confederate commander's attention focused on his front and distracted from Porter's move.

Porter dutifully led his men forward during the morning. However, as his vanguard approached a small stream known as Dawkins's Branch, it received evidence of the arrival on the scene of *Longstreet's* wing of the Army of Northern Virginia. *Lee* posted *Longstreet's* command to the right of *Jackson's*, in a line that ran south across the Warrenton Turnpike and extended down to the Manassas Gap Railroad. His advance to Gainesville blocked, Porter, with the approval of McDowell, decided to halt his march at Dawkins's Branch.

Unaware of *Longstreet's* arrival, Pope launched a series of assaults on *Jackson's* line. The first attacks were made during the morning by units from Sigel's corps that were fought off by the Confederates. On the other side of the field, *Lee* proposed launching an immediate counterattack but was dissuaded from doing so by *Longstreet*, who suggested that to do so would be prohibitively hazardous in light of the fact that Porter's command would then be in a position to attack his own flank.

During the afternoon an attack by Brig. Gen. Cuvier Grover's brigade managed to find a gap in the Confederate line and achieve a penetration; however, the Confederates were able to rally and drive his command back. Pope then ordered IX Corps commander Maj. Gen. Jesse Reno to send part of his command forward against Jackson's line. An attack by Brig. Gen. James Nagle's brigade was able to briefly penetrate the Confederate line, but in doing so Nagle exposed his left flank to a counterattack that forced his men back to Dogan Ridge.

After sending orders again to Porter demanding that he "push forward into action at once on the enemy's flank, and, if possible, on his rear," which arrived too late for Porter to execute and remained unfeasible due to *Longstreet's* presence on the field, Pope then ordered yet another assault on *Jackson's* position. Launched shortly after 5:00 p.m., Brig. Gen. Philip

Kearny's powerful attack pushed back Maj. Gen. *A. P. Hill's* command, and for a moment *Jackson's* entire line was in severe peril. *Jackson* responded by sending a fresh brigade to *Hill's* assistance, which blunted Kearny's advance and restored the Confederate line.

Nonetheless, after receiving reports of enemy wagons moving west on the Warrenton Turnpike, Pope concluded that the Confederates had had enough and were retreating. Thus he ordered Brig. Gen. John Hatch's division to push west along the turnpike in pursuit. Hatch's men, however, promptly ran into a division *Longstreet* had sent forward on a reconnaissance in force. In the sharp twilight engagement that followed, Hatch's men got the worst of it and were forced to fall back to Dogan Ridge.

Lieutenant-General
Ambrose P. Hill, C.S.A.
From a photograph.
BLCW 2:626.

STOP 2   Unfinished Railroad

Directions   Upon exiting the parking area for Brawner Farm, *turn left* onto
PAGELAND LANE and proceed 0.4 mile to the intersection
with LEE HIGHWAY (U.S. 29). *Turn left* onto LEE HIGHWAY and
drive 2.6 miles to the intersection with SUDLEY ROAD (VA 234).
Turn left and proceed north for 1.5 miles on SUDLEY ROAD to
a small parking area on the left side of the road. Park here
and, after exiting your vehicle, walk over to the NPS marker
"The Unfinished Railroad."

STOP 2A   Pope's Plan for August 29

Orientation   From where you are standing, Henry Hill is a little over 1.5
miles to the south, while Manassas Junction is about 6 miles
south of that. Gainesville is about 5 miles to the west.

What Happened   When he learned during the afternoon of August 28 that King's
command was engaged with *Jackson*, Pope ordered his army
to stop moving toward Centreville. Instead he directed McDowell and King to keep the latter's command where it was so it
could block *Jackson's* ability to move west. However, McDowell could not be found, and before the orders arrived King was
already moving south toward Manassas Junction.

Upon learning of King's retreat, Pope sent him orders to
return to Gainesville. In addition to King's division, Pope decided
to send Maj. Gen. Fitz John Porter's corps, which was just arriving at Manassas Junction, to Gainesville as well. Meanwhile
Pope labored to concentrate the rest of his army on the old
Manassas battlefield (with the exception of Maj. Gen. Nathan-
iel Banks's corps, which received the task of guarding Federal
stores) in order to attack *Jackson's* position near Groveton. Maj.
Gen. Franz Sigel's corps managed to reach Henry Hill and Chinn
Ridge in time to spend the night of August 28–29 there, but
Maj. Gen. Philip Kearny refused to march his division over from
Centreville until the morning.

When Pope's orders reached Manassas Junction, McDowell
was there and wrote back to Pope asking for clarification of
his personal role that morning, as King's division (command
of which King had just turned over to Brig. Gen. John P. Hatch)
belonged to his corps. McDowell waited in vain until 10:00
a.m. for a response before releasing Porter and Hatch to begin
their march on the Manassas-Gainesville road with Maj. Gen.
George Morell's division of Porter's corps in the lead.

All this gave *Jackson* plenty of time during the morning of
August 29 to prepare his three divisions, posted in a line that
followed the bed of an unfinished railroad, for battle. The line

began near Sudley Church with Maj. Gen. *A. P. Hill's* division and extended south and west from there to the vicinity of the Brawner Farm, with Brig. Gen. *Alexander Lawton's* division (formerly *Ewell's*) holding the center and Brig. Gen. *William E. Starke's* (formerly *W. B. Taliaferro's*) on the right. Meanwhile *Longstreet* had begun his march from Thoroughfare Gap at 6:00 a.m.

Analysis   Pope's plan for August 29 was based on a belief that *Jackson* was isolated, his western flank was vulnerable, and a march from Manassas to Gainesville could be made unimpeded to either strike *Jackson's* flank or serve as the anvil for the hammer of Sigel's command. All of these assumptions were rendered invalid by the failure the previous day to block the passage of *Longstreet's* command through Thoroughfare Gap and its arrival during the late morning to take up a position blocking the road from Manassas Junction to Gainesville. Not aware of *Longstreet's* arrival, Pope grew increasingly exasperated as the day passed and it became evident that Porter would not be at Gainesville as expected. Pope, suspicious of Porter due to Porter's closeness to McClellan, whose contempt for Pope was matched only by Pope's disdain for him, would see to it that he would be subsequently court-martialed for his failure to obey orders. On January 10, 1863, Porter was found guilty by the court and sentenced "to be cashiered, and to be forever disqualified from holding any office of trust . . . under the Government of the United States." In 1879 a commission headed by John Schofield, aided by evidence that the original court did not have available, exonerated Porter, and a few years later Congress passed a law restoring him to his 1863 rank as a colonel in the U.S. Army.

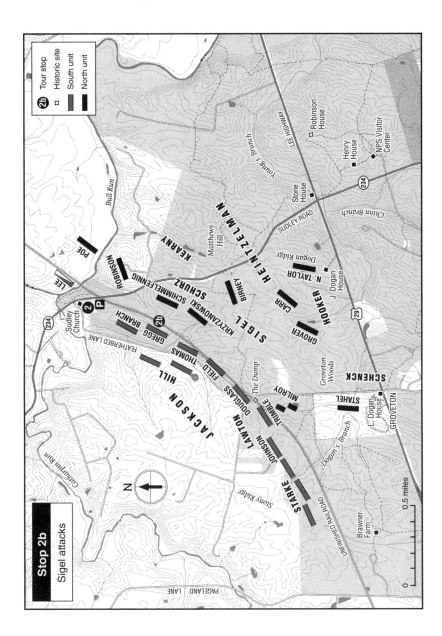

STOP 2B   Sigel Attacks, 10:00 a.m.–1:00 p.m.

Directions   You can remain in place and do the rest of the substops here or take what will be a roughly 1.5-mile-long round-trip hike to various points along the unfinished railroad. To reach the first stop, *turn right* at the NPS "Unfinished Railroad" marker and walk about 700 yards along the bed of the unfinished railroad to the NPS marker "Gregg's Brigade." *Stop here and turn left* to face south.

During the early morning of August 29 Pope sent orders to Sigel directing him to attack *Jackson*. Sigel then spent the early morning examining what was in front of him before hatching a plan in which the two brigades of Brig. Gen. Carl Schurz's division on the Union right would advance following the Manassas-Sudley Road with Col. Wladimir Krzyzanowski's brigade west of the road and Col. Alexander Schimmelfennig's east of it. A brigade commanded by Brig. Gen. Robert Milroy would operate on Krzyzanowski's left. Meanwhile the two brigades of Brig. Gen. Robert Schenck's division, supported by Brig. Gen. John Reynolds's division south of the turnpike, were directed to follow the Warrenton Turnpike west to search for *Jackson's* right.

Reynolds's and Schenck's efforts produced little of consequence. Milroy, however, impetuously ordered an attack against the unfinished railroad near the point where it crossed the Groveton-Sudley Road (modern Featherbed Lane). One of his regiments, Col. James Cantwell's 82nd Ohio, managed to hit the point in *Jackson's* lines west of the road where *Lawton's* and *Starke's* divisions were separated by a 100-yard gap known as "the Dump" and achieve a penetration of the Confederate line. However, there were no friendly troops nearby to support their efforts, and, shortly after Cantwell fell mortally wounded, the Ohioans were compelled to fall back. The rest of Milroy's command was not fortunate enough to find a gap in the Confederate line and within a few minutes after beginning their attack had suffered such terrible casualties that they were compelled to retreat.

Meanwhile Krzyzanowski's advance carried him into a patch of woods that covered the section of *Jackson's* line held by Brig. Gen. *Maxcy Gregg's* brigade of *Hill's* division. Upon receiving word from skirmishers of Krzyzanowski's advance, *Gregg* pushed three South Carolina regiments forward to meet the Federals. When the two lines met each other a fierce hour-long battle ensued in the woods. Finally, at around 11:00 a.m., Sigel ordered Schimmelfennig's brigade to move to the west side of the Sudley Road to assist Krzyzanowski. Seeing Schimmelfennig's brigade approaching, Col. *Dixon Barnes* of the 12th South Carolina, the regiment holding Gregg's left flank, ordered his men to charge.

The shock of *Barnes's* attack shattered the center of Schurz's line and enabled the South Carolinians to advance to the edge of the woods. Any hopes they had of pushing farther, though, were abruptly dashed by bursts of artillery fire from five guns belonging to a New York battery commanded by Capt. Jacob Roemer. This made it possible for Schurz to rally two New York regiments, but by the time they were able to resume their advance the 1st South Carolina Rifles had moved up on *Barnes's* left, and together they drove the Federals back yet again.

Gregg then ordered his command to pull back. On seeing this, Schurz directed his men to once again advance. As he did so, he learned Sigel had directed Kearny's division to advance on his right. Krzyzanowski's and Schimmelfennig's men were then able to drive *Gregg's* command back and advance to the railroad cut. Schurz was content for his men to remain there and exchange fire with the Confederates because he believed Kearny was about to join the battle. Instead, however, Kearny, in a fit of pique against Sigel, failed to carry out his role in the battle and wasted his energies on what proved to be a pointless foray across Bull Run. Finally, shortly after 1:00 p.m., the arrival of reinforcements on the field enabled Schurz to break off his fight at the railroad cut and pull his exhausted command back to Dogan Ridge.

Vignette
In his memoirs, General Schurz used the events of August 29 to provide "a Division Commander's personal experience in a battle." "I receive the order to advance and attack," he wrote, "Not the slightest sign of the enemy is to be seen. He is supposed to be posted in the woods yonder, but just where and in what strength, nobody knows. . . . At a brisk pace the skirmishers pass the detached groups of timber and enter the forest. The line of battle follows at the proper distance. No sign of the enemy. A quarter of an hour elapses. Perfect stillness all around. Are the enemy there at all? But hark!—two musket shots in rapid succession, apparently near the spot where my skirmishers are to join Milroy's. I hear the clear ringing of those two shots now. Then a moment's silence, followed by a desultory rattle of musketry along the line. No more doubt; we have struck the enemy.

"The rattle is increasing in liveliness and volume, but the enemy's skirmishers seem to be falling back. 'Seem to be'—for we can see very little. The woods are thick, permitting no outlook to the front nor to the right or left, beyond a few paces. Moreover, they are soon filled with white powder smoke. I am impatient to advance my line of battle with greater energy. But the troops, having marched forward through thick forest with tangled underbrush, the ranks are broken up into irregular little squads. The company officers, shouting and waving their swords, do their utmost to hold their men together. Still they press on. I cannot see anything except what is immediately around me. . . . The rattling fire of skirmishers changes into crashes of musketry, regular volleys, rapidly following each other. We have evidently struck *Jackson's* main position. Now, 'Steady, men! Steady! Aim low; aim low!' My men still advance, although slowly. . . . The rebels make a vicious dash against my center and throw it into confusion. But we succeed soon in restoring order, and with a vigorous counter-charge, we regain the ground we had won before. . . .

"I hear a tremendous turmoil in the direction of my center—the rebel yell in its most savage form, and one crash of musketry after another. I conclude that the rebels are making another and more furious charge. I order the commander of the artillery to load his pieces with grape-shot, and the Twenty-ninth New York, held in reserve, to be ready for action. Not many minutes later, three of my regiments, completely broken, come tumbling out of the woods in utter confusion. A rebel force in hot pursuit, wildly yelling, gains the edge of the forest and is about to invade the open, when the artillery pours into them one discharge after another of grape, and the Twenty-ninth New York, volley after volley of musketry. The rebels are stopped, but still hold the edge of the woods. . . . Sword in hand, we rally the broken regiments. The routed men present a curious spectacle: some fierce and indignant at the conduct of their comrades; some ashamed of themselves, their faces distorted by a sort of idiotic grin; some staring at their officers with a look of helpless bewilderment, as if they did not understand what had happened, and the officers hauling them together with bursts of lively language, and an incidental slap with the flat of their blades. But the men are quickly rallied and reformed under their colors. A few encouraging words revive their spirits. 'Never mind, boys! Such things may happen to the best of soldiers. Now, forward with a hurrah!' The hurrah is given, we rush upon the enemy, and the line we had occupied is promptly regained. On my right, Schimmelfennig's brigade remained perfectly firm, and Krzyzanowski's left had yielded but little.

"Presently an officer of the corps staff comes at a gallop, he hands me a letter addressed by General Sigel to General Kearney, which I am to read and forward. Sigel requests Kearney to attack at once with his whole strength. . . . Construing Sigel's request as implying an instruction for myself, I order a general advance of my whole line, and put in every man I have. It is gallantly executed with a hurrah. . . . On my left the fight comes to a stand at an old railroad embankment, nearly parallel with my front, which the enemy use as a breastwork, and from behind which they pour a galling fire. On my right, Schimmelfennig's brigade, by a splendid charge, gains possession of this embankment, and goes even beyond it, but is received there with so murderous a cross-fire of artillery and infantry that it has to fall back; but it holds the embankment firmly in its grip. General Sigel sends me two small mountain howitzers, which I put at once into the fire-line of my left brigade. With the aid of their effective short-range fire, that brigade, too, reaches the embankment and holds it. The enemy repeatedly dashes against it, but is hurled back each time. . . .

"It is about two o'clock of the afternoon, and the fight about my railroad embankment has dwindled into a mere exchange of shots between skirmishers, when I am advised by General Sigel that my division is to be relieved. . . . The men still in the ranks have well nigh reached the point of utter exhaustion. Their stomachs are as empty as their cartridge boxes. The water in their tin flasks has long given out, and for hours they have been tortured by that agonizing thirst which nobody knows who has not, on a hot summer day, stood in the flaming fireline of a battle without a drop of water to moisten his tongue."

Major-General Franz Sigel.
From a photograph.
BLCW 1:286.

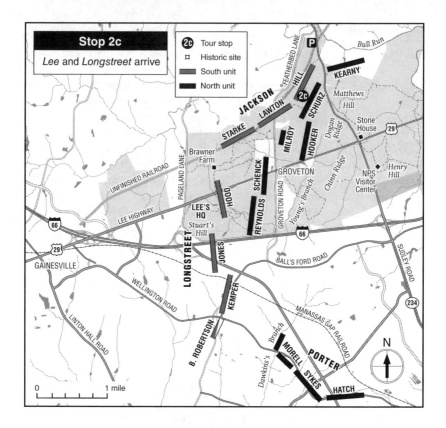

STOP 2C *Lee* and *Longstreet* Arrive, 10:00 a.m.–12:00 p.m.

Directions Remain in place.

What Happened As *Jackson* was fighting off Sigel's attacks, *Lee* and *Longstreet* led the rest of the Army of Northern Virginia to the field. Near Gainesville they encountered Maj. Gen. *James E. B. Stuart* and gave his cavalry the task of screening *Longstreet's* right as it advanced to the field. At around 10:00 a.m., *Lee* was riding ahead of the column when a bullet grazed his cheek. "A Yankee sharpshooter," a seemingly unfazed *Lee* remarked to his staff, "came near killing me just now." Shortly thereafter he and *Longstreet* met with *Jackson* along the Warrenton Turnpike. Upon receiving a report from *Jackson* laying out the situation and deployment of his command, *Lee* directed *Longstreet* to begin deploying his command in accordance with suggestions from *Jackson*. The first of *Longstreet's* divisions to arrive, Brig. Gen. *John B. Hood's* was posted astride the turnpike with its left near the Brawner Farm.

Meanwhile *Stuart's* cavalry rode out about 3 miles on the Manassas-Gainesville road and picked up evidence of Porter's advance. With no infantry support nearby, *Stuart* directed his subordinates to drag brush along the road to kick up dust and give the Federals the impression that a much larger force was in front of them. When Porter and McDowell reached the ridge overlooking Dawkins's Branch and caught sight of the dust, they halted the march and pushed out skirmishers. This gave time for some of *Longstreet's* infantry to arrive, blocking the Federal march to Gainesville and securing the Confederate right.

Meanwhile *Lee* and *Longstreet* deployed the rest of the latter's command to fill the mile or so between *Hood* and the forces on the Manassas-Gainesville road. *Lee* told *Longstreet* he wanted to immediately attack the Federals. *Longstreet*, however, disagreed and argued that with what *Stuart* was reporting to be a strong force just off to the south and east, an attack at that time carried too much risk and too little prospect of truly decisive success. *Lee* reluctantly—but wisely—deferred to his subordinate's judgment.

Analysis

Longstreet's ability to persuade *Lee* not to launch an attack on August 29 has been criticized by a number of historians, most prominently *Lee's* great biographer Douglas Southall Freeman. Freeman saw this episode as foreshadowing problems at Gettysburg, where *Longstreet's* execution of *Lee's* battle plan on the second day of battle was grudging and problematic. "The moment was an important one in the military career of *Lee*," Freeman argued in his analysis of *Lee's* actions on August 29, "important less in its effect on the outcome of the battle than in its bearing on *Lee's* future relations with *Longstreet*. In all the operations since *Lee* had taken command of the Army of Northern Virginia he had not shown any of the excessive consideration for the feelings of others that he had exhibited in West Virginia. . . . Now it appeared again. The seeds of much of the disaster at Gettysburg were sown in that instant—when *Lee* yielded to *Longstreet* and *Longstreet* discovered that he would." In fact *Longstreet* was correct to argue against launching an attack and *Lee* correct to accept his judgment. Although Porter's command was not acting with much energy, its presence on the Confederate right could not be ignored. Moreover it must be kept in mind that when *Longstreet* did attack on August 30, the situation south of the turnpike was quite different. The Federals had a much more significant body of troops there on August 29. While probably insufficient on their own to stop an assault by *Longstreet's* men, they would have been enough of an obstacle that it is unlikely that such an attack would accomplish nearly as much as the attack on August 30, which, it should be noted, still fell short of achieving all that *Lee* and *Longstreet* hoped for.

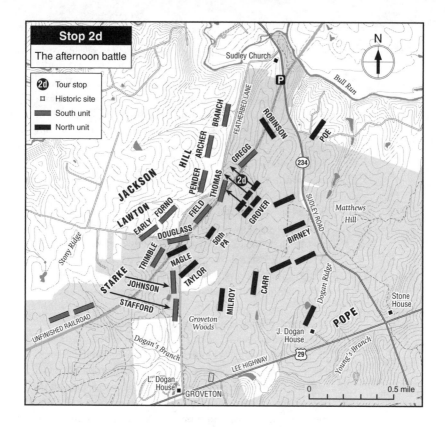

STOP 2D

STOP 2D

The Afternoon Battle, 10:00 a.m.–4:30 p.m.

Directions

Resume walking along the unfinished railroad for about 200 yards to a fork in the trail. *Take the left fork* and walk for about 200 yards to the NPS marker on the right side of the trail "1st Massachusetts Infantry." *Turn right* and face toward the unfinished railroad.

What Happened

Pope was oblivious to *Longstreet's* arrival when the Federal commander finally reached the battlefield early in the afternoon of August 29. Shortly before then, he had sent an order to Porter and McDowell reiterating his wishes that they advance to Gainesville to turn *Jackson's* left. The order reached Porter and McDowell just as they were processing reports of a substantial body of Confederates in their front. In addition, McDowell had just received a report from cavalry officer Brig. Gen. John Buford that a large body of enemy infantry had been seen passing through Gainesville. Pope's order also stated, "It may be necessary to fall back behind Bull Run at Centreville to-night. I presume it will be so" and informed Porter and McDowell, "If any considerable advantages are to be gained by departing from this order it will not be strictly carried out. One thing must be kept in view," the order further declared, the "troops must occupy a position from which they can reach Bull Run to-night or tomorrow morning." Upon digesting Pope's order and the information before them, McDowell told Porter he was "too far out already; this is no place to fight a battle." Leaving Porter's command to hold the position at Dawkins's Branch, McDowell then decided to take Hatch's and Ricketts's divisions (the latter at that moment moving up from Bristoe Station) to the main battlefield.

Pope, however, believed that he had sent unambiguous orders to Porter and McDowell to advance on Gainesville and, unaware of *Longstreet's* arrival, that there was nothing to prevent their doing so. To prevent *Jackson's* command, which Pope presumed to be isolated, from reacting to Porter's advance by leaving its position north of the Warrenton Turnpike, shortly after 2:00 p.m. Pope ordered the forces posted near his headquarters on Dogan Ridge to continue to engage the Confederates. Preliminary to this, Schurz was permitted to pull back his exhausted division and orders were sent to Maj. Gen. Joseph Hooker to attack *Jackson's* line.

To spearhead his division's assault, Hooker selected the brigade commanded by Brig. Gen. Cuvier Grover. Grover promptly moved his command into Groveton Woods, where he found Milroy still engaged with the Confederates. Grover then conducted a reconnaissance that convinced him to shift his command to the right so he could advance under the cover of thick woods. This placed his command in front of a gap of about 125 yards in the Confederate line between *Gregg's* right and the left of Col. *Edward Thomas's* brigade. Grover then finished deploying his 1,500 men, posting three regiments in his front line and two in support, and directed them to charge with the bayonet.

After shaking off a volley of fire from *Thomas's* command, Grover's men quickly overwhelmed the Confederate defenders of the unfinished railroad. As the 1st Massachusetts on Grover's right poured into the gap in the Confederate line, the rest of his command crushed *Thomas's* brigade and drove it from the field. As they surged forward into the breach in the Confederate line, though, Grover's men became disordered. Worse, the brigade Kearny sent to support Grover's attack did nothing when it came up on Grover's right.

Thus *Gregg* was free to reorient the units of his brigade so they could pour an intense fire into the ranks of the 1st Massachusetts. Meanwhile *Hill* and *Thomas* rallied with the assistance of a brigade commanded by Brig. Gen. *William Dorsey Pender*. The momentum of Grover's attack was lost as his men began taking fire in front and on both their flanks. Unable to accomplish anything more, Grover had no choice but to retreat. The

Confederates pursued until they reached the edge of the woods and their efforts were brought to a halt by the powerful artillery position the Federals had established on Dogan Ridge.

Meanwhile Pope had sent orders to Reynolds to push his division forward south of the Warrenton Turnpike to probe for *Jackson's* right and rear. Reynolds dutifully complied by advancing two of his brigades. Their advance was quickly brought to a halt by artillery and small arms fire from *Longstreet's* command. Reynolds called his men back and sent a messenger back to Pope warning him of the presence of a large body of Confederates south of the turnpike.

Pope, however, brushed off the warning. Instead he turned to IX Corps commander Maj. Gen. Jesse Reno and directed him to clear some woods in his front. Reno selected a brigade commanded by Col. James Nagle for the assignment. Nagle led his command forward to strike the unfinished railroad where it crossed the Groveton-Sudley Road (modern Featherbed Lane) and was defended by Brig. Gen. *Isaac Trimble's* (commanded by Capt. *W. F. Brown* after *Trimble* was wounded) and Col. *Marcellus Douglass's* brigades of *Lawton's* division.

Upon reaching the front of the cut, Nagle's men poured a vicious fire into the Confederates defending it, drove them away, and then pushed about 100 yards beyond. Like Grover earlier, though, Nagle made his attack unsupported. Thus the Confederates were able to bring up a brigade, commanded by Col. *Bradley Johnson*, from *Starke's* division to hit Nagle's unsupported left. As Nagle's men began falling back, Col. *Leroy Stafford* ordered his brigade to advance on *Johnson's* right. Together *Johnson* and *Stafford* not only drove Nagle away but also overwhelmed a brigade commanded by Brig. Gen. Nelson Taylor that had moved up to assist Nagle and a West Virginia regiment Milroy ordered up in response to Nagle's initial success.

As the Confederates surged forward into Groveton Woods, though, Milroy managed to locate Capt. R. B. Hampton's battery and position sections of it south and west of the woods. From these positions, Hampton was able to put up enough of a fight to buy time for Federal officers to assemble a strong line of infantry east of the woods. Deciding that they had accomplished enough, *Starke* ordered *Johnson* and *Stafford* to fall back to the unfinished railroad.

Analysis

Federal attacks on *Jackson's* line suffered from a lack of coordination and support throughout the day on August 29. Consequently even when they succeeded in achieving a penetration of the Confederate line, *Jackson's* men were able to contain the damage and drive the Federals back. It is easy to criticize the Federals for this. Still, it must be kept in mind that for

Pope, the purpose of these attacks was not to achieve decisive success on their own (though Pope would have no doubt been happy if they had) but to keep *Jackson's* command engaged in front so it would be unable to deal with Porter's move against what Pope believed to be the Confederate right.

Moreover, even had the attacks been better coordinated and supported, it would have been difficult for them to achieve a great deal more than they did. In large part this was due to a fundamental problem with frontal assaults. In order to achieve anything truly decisive with a frontal assault, some means to exploit a successful penetration of the enemy line is necessary. It is rare for infantry even in the best of circumstances to be able to exploit a penetration (and given the roughness of the terrain around the unfinished railroad, this was not the best of circumstances) faster than defenders can seal it. Consequently, in the nineteenth century the task of exploiting penetrations was performed by heavy cavalry (in the twentieth century it was achieved using motor vehicles), kept in reserve for such moments. Neither army at Manassas had such a force, in part due to the fact that the greater range of the weaponry Civil War soldiers carried largely neutralized the effectiveness of heavy cavalry as a shock force. (Attempts to use heavy cavalry in the Franco-Prussian War a few years later resulted in heavy carnage.) Moreover heavy cavalry was only really effective operating over relatively level, clear terrain. Consequently, even had it been on hand, the broken terrain over which it would have had to operate would have considerably diminished its ability to enable the Federal assaults on August 29 to achieve more than they did.

Capture of a Confederate battery. BLCW 1:527.

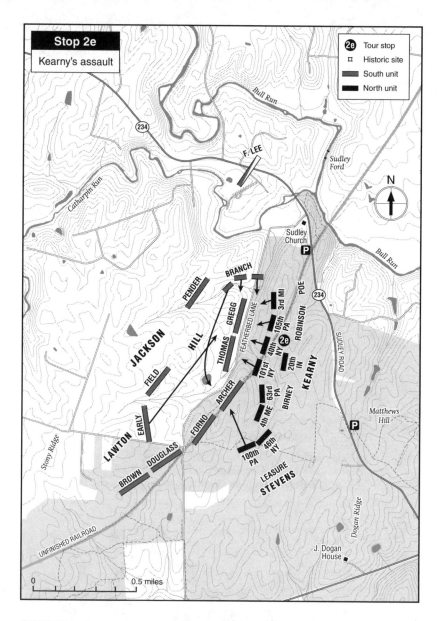

Stop 2e

Kearny's assault

2e Tour stop
▫ Historic site
South unit
North unit

N

STOP 2E   Kearny's Assault, 4:30–6:30 p.m.

Directions   *Retrace* your steps about 200 yards to the fork in the trail. From here, *continue* walking in the direction of Sudley Church for about 150 yards to the NPS marker on the left side of the trail for "4th Maine Infantry; 40th New York Infantry; 101st New York Infantry" from Brig. Gen. David Birney's brigade. *Stop here* and face left.

What Happened   As *Johnson's* and *Stafford's* men fell back, *Jackson* and Pope both took stock of the situation. So far *Jackson's* men had been able to handle everything Pope had thrown at them, although there had to be concern about the fact that the Federals had managed to penetrate their lines on three occasions. Especially troubling was the condition of *Gregg's* brigade. In the course of fighting off Schurz and assisting in the repulse of Grover, *Gregg's* men had nearly exhausted their ammunition and energy. *Hill* sent a staff officer to *Jackson* to explain the situation and express concern about *Gregg's* ability to handle another attack. *Jackson* responded by personally riding over to *Hill's* command post. As *Jackson* explained to *Hill* why nothing could be done to relieve him, the sound of another Union attack reached their post. "Here it comes," *Hill* shouted as *Jackson* prepared to leave. "I'll expect you to beat them," *Jackson* replied.

At 4:30 p.m. Pope, furious that Porter had apparently failed to comply with his orders to advance to Gainesville, dictated an order directing him to "push forward into action at once on the enemy's flank, and, if possible, on his rear." He then called Kearny to headquarters and ordered him to assault the Confederate left near Sudley Church. Kearny quickly organized an assault force of about 2,700 men from Brig. Gen. John C. Robinson's and Brig. Gen. David Birney's brigades, supported by three batteries of artillery.

Kearny opened his attack at around 5:00 p.m. by personally leading the 63rd Pennsylvania forward through the woods toward the section of the unfinished railroad held by Brig. Gen. *James Archer's* brigade. *Archer's* men were able to fight off the Pennsylvanians; however, just to the north the regiment holding *Gregg's* left flank was driven from their position facing a cornfield south of Sudley Church by the 105th Pennsylvania and 3rd Michigan. Exhausted from all they had already been through that day and with their left flank collapsing, *Gregg's* men were in no condition to handle the advance of the 40th and 101st New York against their front. "Forward boys; we're driving them," the commander of the 101st New York shouted as his men surged forward, crossed the unfinished railroad, and shoved *Gregg's* and *Thomas's* commands back across the Groveton-Sudley Road. Making matters worse for *Hill*, as this was going on, Kearny gave orders to Col. Daniel Leasure to throw his small brigade from Brig. Gen. Isaac Stevens's division into the fight against *Archer*. Leasure promptly did so, and within a few minutes the 100th Pennsylvania had driven back part of *Archer's* command and seized possession of a section of the unfinished railroad.

Fortunately for *Archer*, *Gregg*, and *Thomas*, help was on the way. The first came from Brig. Gen. *Lawrence O'Bryan Branch's* brigade, whose commander sent one of his regiments to *Gregg's* aid directly and then led two regiments forward in a way that brought them onto the right flank of Kearny's command. Their appearance touched off a fierce fight that arrested the momentum of the Federal advance, while two regiments *Branch* dispatched to *Archer's* assistance helped bring Leasure's advance to a halt.

Meanwhile, at around 5:30 p.m. *Lawton* released his reserve brigade, Brig. Gen. *Jubal Early's*, to be sent to *Hill's* assistance. When *Early* arrived on the scene, he immediately pitched his 2,500 men into the battle. After passing through the lines of *Hill's* exhausted commands, *Early's* men slammed into Kearny's weary force and drove it back. After falling back from the woods, Kearny and Stevens managed to rally their commands and turn back *Early's* attempt at a pursuit. As *Early's* men then fell back through the woods to bring the battle to an end, *Hill* dispatched an officer to *Jackson* to report that his division had held. "Tell him I knew he would do it," *Jackson* replied.

Vignette

"Ten hours of actual conflict had exhausted all the romance of the battle," a member of the 1st South Carolina later wrote. "Our feet were worn and weary, and our arms were nerveless. Our ears were deadened with the continuous roar of the battle, and our eyes were dimmed with the smoke. . . . But Kearny was pitiless. It mattered not to him that we were tired. . . . The enemy pressed on, crossed the cut, and slowly but steadily compelled us, step by step, to yield the long coveted position—the position, on the extreme left, a little in advance of *Hill's* line, with which, early in the morning, our brigade had been entrusted, and which we had maintained all day. But we would not give it up without a struggle. Now again the same hand to hand fight we had with Grover, we renewed with Kearney—we were not, however, entirely without help. General *Branch* came to our assistance with one of his regiments, and, literally, with coat off, personally took part in the affray. With his aid we made a stand on the top of the knoll, and there, over the bodies of our dead and wounded comrades, we struggled on. . . . But Stevens, who was supporting Kearney, was on hand to make one more last effort of the day. We heard the cheers of his men as he ordered them in—telling us our work was not yet done.

"It was at this time that an officer rode up to *Gregg*, with a message from General *Hill*, asking if he could hold the position any longer; and then was his famous reply, that his ammunition was exhausted, but 'he thought he could still hold his position with the bayonet.' . . . Having sent word to *Hill* that he had no ammunition, but would hold the position with the bayonet, General *Gregg* drew up the remnants of his five regiments, now reduced to a mere handful in two lines. . . . We were upon the top of the hill, the point to which we had been driven back by Kearney, some two or three hundred yards from the railroad excavation. Here General *Gregg* formed us to await the assault of the enemy, whose cheers we heard as they were ordered forward. I can see him now, as with his drawn sword, that old Revolutionary scimitar we all knew so well, he walked up and down the line, and hear him as he appealed to us to stand by him. . . . 'Let us die here, my men, let us die here.' And I do not think that I exaggerate when I say that our little band responded to his appeal, and were ready to die, at bay, there if necessary. The moment was, indeed, a trying one—a trying one to men who had shown themselves no cowards that day. We could hear the enemy advancing, and had not a round with which to greet them, but must wait the onslaught with only our bayonets. On they came. They had nearly reached the railroad, and were about to cross to the charge when a shout behind paralyzed us with dread. Was all the glorious fight we had made that livelong day to end in our capture by an unseen movement to our rear? Terror stricken we turned, when lo! There were our friends coming to our assistance, and not the enemy to our attack . . . rushing up, comparatively fresh for the work, and cheering as they advanced on either side of our little band, waited not the assault . . . but with a wild Confederate yell, rushed upon Stevens as he was in the confusion of crossing to our attack. The Federals halted, turned and fled, our friends crossing the railroad and pursuing them."

Further Reading   Hennessy, *Return to Bull Run*, 194–267; Hennessy, *Second Manassas Battlefield Map Study*, 147–57, 166–67, 172–73, 188–90, 194–96.

STOP 3   Groveton

Directions   Return to your vehicle. (If you did the walk along the unfinished railroad, the parking area is about 800 yards from the
NPS marker where you studied Kearny's Assault.) Exit the parking area and *turn right* onto SUDLEY ROAD. Drive south for 1.5
miles on SUDLEY ROAD to the intersection with LEE HIGH-
WAY (U.S. 29). *Turn right* and drive 0.9 mile, then *turn left* onto
NEW YORK AVENUE and pull into the parking area on the
right. Exit your vehicle and walk about 150 yards up to the
top of the ridge with the monument to the 14th Brooklyn
(84th New York) and cannon on top of it. Walk around to the
other side of the monument and face west (the direction the
cannon are pointing) toward the Groveton crossroads.

Major-General Philip Kearny.
From a photograph.
BLCW 2:492.

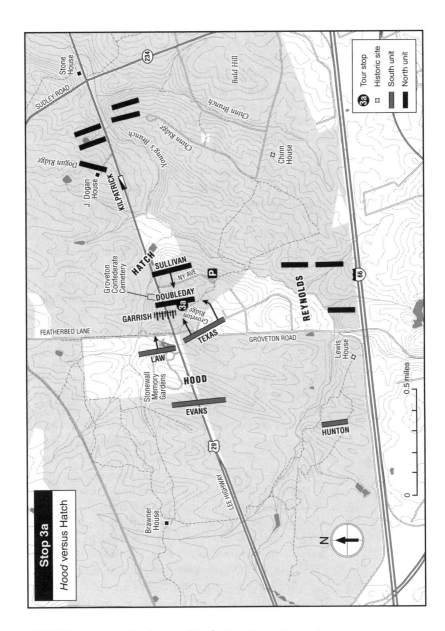

Stop 3a

Hood versus Hatch

STOP 3A Hood versus Hatch, 6:00–8:00 p.m.

Orientation From where you are standing, Gainesville is a little over 3 miles west of you, while the Stone House intersection is about 1 mile east of you.

What Happened Although Kearny's attack had been repulsed, he reported to Pope that he had been able to drive back the enemy and had inflicted severe casualties. This and the sight of Confederate wagons moving west along the Warrenton Turnpike led Pope to suspect that the enemy might be retreating from the field.

Thus he sent orders to McDowell, who had just arrived on the field with two divisions, to send one of them west on the turnpike to pursue the Confederates. Even though it had been heavily engaged the previous evening, it was Hatch's command that got the assignment.

Meanwhile, shortly before Kearny began his attack, *Longstreet* and *Stuart* reported to *Lee* that it appeared the Federal force along the Manassas-Gainesville road had diminished in strength. (*Longstreet* gleaned this from clouds of dust Hatch's command kicked up when McDowell marched it to the main battlefield.) *Lee* immediately wanted to push *Longstreet's* command forward to attack the Federals south of the Warrenton Turnpike. *Longstreet*, however, argued it was too late in the day for such a major effort and instead won permission from *Lee* to conduct a reconnaissance in force to lay the groundwork for an assault the following morning. Brig. Gen. *John B. Hood*, *Longstreet* directed, would advance his division, following the Warrenton Turnpike, with Brig. Gen. *Evander Law's* north of the road and the Texas Brigade south of it.

As his command approached the Groveton crossroads with Doubleday's brigade in the lead, Hatch ordered the 2nd U.S. Sharpshooters forward to serve as skirmishers. Upon reaching high ground overlooking Groveton, the sharpshooters saw a considerable Confederate force moving toward them. Hatch then ordered a battery of four guns commanded by Capt. George Garrish to the top of the ridge and Doubleday to deploy his three regiments south of the turnpike in support.

Doubleday's men got into position just in time to see the Texas Brigade advancing toward them—and the fact that the Confederate line extended far enough to the south to overlap their left flank. Hatch then ordered Col. Timothy Sullivan to move his brigade up to assist Doubleday. However, instead of moving up next to Doubleday to extend the line to the south, Sullivan's command attempted to pass through Doubleday's ranks, throwing both units into confusion. Nonetheless they were able to put up sufficient resistance to compel the Texas Brigade, unable to take advantage of the exposed Union left due to the darkness, to fall back. North of the turnpike, *Law's* command faced only fire from Garrish's guns and a few companies that had been detached from the 95th New York as it moved forward through the darkness.

It was not until the commander of the Texas Brigade shifted the bulk of his command into the woods to the south, where Doubleday's and Sullivan's left flank was located, that the Federal line began to unravel. When the 76th New York fired into the dark woods, some of the Confederates in them called out, "Don't shoot here! You are firing on your friends." The Federals responded by holding fire, which enabled the Confederates to unleash a ferocious volley into the Union left and front. Despite the best efforts of their officers, the two regiments on the Union left quickly fell apart, and their efforts to flee the field threw the rest of the Federal line south of the turnpike into further disorder. Meanwhile *Law* crossed a regiment to the south side of the turnpike to join the 1st Texas in a charge up the ridge. After a brief but vicious fight at short range at the top of the ridge, the rest of Doubleday's and Sullivan's commands broke and began fleeing the scene. Meanwhile Garrish's gunners blasted *Law's* advancing Confederates with canister and held them off long enough to enable the crews, aided by some of the infantry, to remove three of his guns from the field and join the flight back to Dogan Ridge. News of Hatch's repulse quickly reached Reynolds, whose division had spent the past several hours south of Groveton gathering evidence of the arrival of *Longstreet's* command and led Reynolds to pull his three brigades back toward the Sudley Road.

As Doubleday and Sullivan went to work reassembling their commands in the darkness, Lt. Col. Judson Kilpatrick ordered a squadron from his cavalry regiment to ride west along the pike to charge the Confederates. As they approached the Confederates of *Law's* brigade, their advance was clearly audible. *Law* happily left a gap in his line for Kilpatrick's men to ride through, knowing that they would soon run into Brig. Gen. *Nathan Evans's* brigade. *Evans's* men waited until Kilpatrick's men were nearly right on top of them, then fired a volley at point-blank range that shattered the momentum of the Federal advance. As the Federals turned around and raced back to their own lines, they were compelled to ride back through *Law's* command, who subjected them to yet another destructive fusillade. When Kilpatrick's horsemen finally reached the safety of Union lines, fewer than a dozen were left.

Vignette Having participated in the fight the previous evening at Brawner Farm, then marched all the way back from there to Manassas Junction, from Manassas Junction toward Gainesville in support of Porter, then to the main battlefield, the men of the 76th New York had already had more than their fair share of excitement at Manassas when they were "hurried some two miles, mostly at double-quick, to a point on the brow of a hill, to check the advancing enemy. On the way up, the Regiment passed General McDowell, who inquired: 'What regiment is this?'

"'The Seventy-sixth New York,' was the reply.

"'Well, boys,' said he, 'you are following a retreating foe! Push 'em like h—l!'

"The men gave a shout, and one of those yells of triumph which no one can appreciate until he hears it in battle, and on they went over the rolling ground, until they came to a hill larger than the others, and a mile in advance of the main army. They had nearly reached the summit, when they received a destructive volley from the enemy on the other side of the ridge. Doubleday's Brigade was in the advance, and this unexpected attack by the 'retreating foe,' produced considerable confusion for a moment. The Brigade finally swung into line and commenced firing. . . . Our line now extended from the road on the right, to a piece of woods on the left. The rebels were sheltered and hidden from sight by the woods, stone walls, and natural rifle pits, from which, while protected, they poured a most destructive fire.

"There may be sport, at least there is fair play, in standing up and fighting an open enemy equally exposed with yourself; but to stand a target, in an open field, for a concealed and protected enemy, has more of the disagreeable than the pleasing. . . . In the hottest of the fight, as the colors of the Seventysixth fell, they were seized by Colonel [William] Wainwright, who rushed to the front, and by his manly and timely exhibition of courage, infused new spirit into his men. Close to the left flank there was a dense wood, from which there had been no firing. Orders were at length given to fire into this wood, to ascertain whether the enemy were there, when the cry came,—

"'Don't shoot here! You are firing on your friends!'

"Supposing our skirmishers had probably entered there, and were being fired upon, the firing was ordered to cease. Silence reigned for a moment, when suddenly a terrific volley was poured from the wood, making sad havoc in our ranks.

"Nothing is so demoralizing to troops as an unexpected attack on the flank and rear. Men who can face a foe without an emotion, will often break in confusion when attacked by an unseen foe, from an unexpected quarter. It was soon ascertained that instead of pursuing a retreating foe, the alternative was presented to the Union troops to retreat or be annihilated. From every quarter the unseen foe poured the deadly volley—front, flank, rear! No army could stand in such a deathangle . . . one grand effort was made to push forward and prevent a stampede. Colonel Wainwright requested the officers, by an exhibition of personal courage, to inspire their men. . . . But the pressure of the retreating brigades was too strong, and soon the whole advance was retreating to the main line in wild confusion."

Further Reading   Hennessy, *Return to Bull Run*, 288–302; Hennessy, *Second Manassas Battlefield Map Study*, 203–9, 216–22.

Overview of August 30, 1862

Despite the battering Hatch's command had suffered in its clash with *Hood's* men along the Warrenton Turnpike the previous evening and a slew of reports from front-line commanders that suggested it was not just *Jackson's* command in front of him, throughout the morning of August 30 Pope refused to accept reports that indicated *Longstreet's* wing had reached the field and gone into position south of the Brawner Farm. Instead he became convinced that the Confederates were retreating from the battlefield and, shortly before noon, ordered his command to launch a pursuit. The pursuit ended almost as soon as it began, when the lead elements encountered such stiff resistance that Pope had no choice but to accept the fact that the Confederates were still holding their position along the unfinished railroad.

Pope reacted by ordering a massive assault against *Jackson's* line by Maj. Gen. Fitz John Porter's corps and a division from McDowell's corps. Porter dutifully ordered his men forward from Groveton Woods at around 3:00 p.m., and despite having to cross open ground under heavy artillery and small arms fire, some managed to reach the Confederate front line. However, the Federals were ultimately unable to overcome the combination of *Jackson's* infantry firing into their front and Confederate artillery positioned near the Brawner Farm pouring fire into their left flank. Less than an hour after they began their attack, Porter's men were retreating back through the woods toward Dogan Ridge.

As Porter's men fell back, McDowell ordered the only division then south of the Warrenton Turnpike over to Dogan Ridge to help secure the Federal position there against a possible counterattack by *Jackson's* command. This left only two regiments in the immediate front of *Longstreet's* forces south of the Warrenton Turnpike when its commander and *Lee*, upon seeing Porter's men fall back, decided to launch a counterattack with *Longstreet's* command. *Longstreet's* men quickly overwhelmed the two regiments just east of Groveton and then surged forward across Young's Branch and up the slopes of Chinn Ridge. Fortunately the lone Federal brigade there put up enough of a fight to give Pope and McDowell time to move more forces south of the turnpike. Although these too would be driven from Chinn Ridge by *Longstreet's* men, they bought further time for Pope, which he used to establish a defensive line at Henry Hill to cover the army's line of retreat to the Stone Bridge over Bull Run.

Pope's efforts to respond to *Longstreet's* attack were aided materially by the fact that *Jackson's* command north of the Warrenton Turnpike did little after repulsing Porter's attack.

Thus Pope was able to position enough forces on Henry Hill to fight off a series of determined attacks by *Longstreet's* command and preserve his army's line of retreat. Nonetheless when night fell on August 30, 1862, there was no denying that the day, and the battle, had produced, in *Lee's* words, a "signal victory" for the Confederacy.

Headquarters in the field.
BLCW 1:398.

STOP 4   Buck Hill

Directions   Drive to the intersection of NEW YORK AVENUE and LEE HIGH-
                          WAY (U.S. 29). *Turn right* onto LEE HIGHWAY and proceed 1 mile
                          to the parking area for the Stone House, which will appear
                          on the left side of the road just after you pass through the
                          traffic light at the intersection with SUDLEY ROAD (VA 234).
                          Exit your car and walk over to the Stone House. You can then
                          do the stand at the house or *turn right* just before reaching the
                          fence line (located about 75 yards from the parking area) and
                          hike about 150 yards to the NPS marker "Visions of Victory"
                          at the top of the ridge just north of the Stone House.

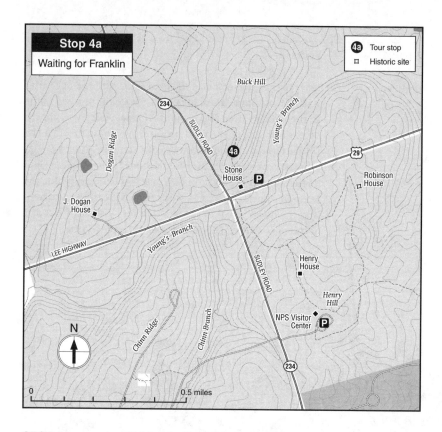

Buck Hill

234

SUDLEY ROAD

Young's Branch

Dogan Ridge

4a

Stone
House P

29

Robinson
House

J. Dogan
House

Young's Branch

LEE HIGHWAY

SUDLEY ROAD

Henry
House

Henry
Hill

Chinn Ridge

Chinn Branch

NPS Visitor
Center P

N

234

0   0.5 miles

STOP 4A Waiting for Franklin, August 28–30, 1862

Orientation The high ground north of the Stone House is known as Buck Hill. It was the site of Pope's headquarters on August 30, 1862.

What Happened While Pope's command battered *Jackson's* line along the unfinished railroad, Maj. Gen. Henry Halleck, general-in-chief of all the Union armies, was trying to send reinforcements out to him. Two corps, the Sixth and Second from the Army of the Potomac, had arrived at Alexandria, located just across the river from Washington, from the Peninsula on August 26 and 28, respectively. There they came under the control of Maj. Gen. George B. McClellan, who was still titular commander of the Army of the Potomac. McClellan was wary about sending the two corps out to Pope as a consequence of what happened the morning of August 27, when a brigade sent out to Manassas Junction had been mauled by *Jackson's* command. McClellan preferred to keep the corps around Washington to ensure the capital's security and believed that, instead of his sending Pope reinforcements from Washington, Pope should fall back toward the capital to meet them.

On the evening of August 28, though, McClellan responded to repeated orders from Halleck to send Maj. Gen. William

Franklin's Sixth Corps to Pope's assistance by assuring that he would do so the next day. Franklin put his men on the march early on August 29, but McClellan continued, as he had been doing ever since he reached Alexandria, badgering Halleck. In light of uncertainty over what the enemy was doing, McClellan argued that Franklin's command should not advance past Annandale, which was not even 10 miles beyond Alexandria, until they had more information about what was in front of them. Finally, at 3:00 p.m., Halleck wrote back that McClellan only need push Franklin far enough out to gather information and that a halt at Annandale might be sufficient to do so. Franklin, with McClellan's blessing, halted at Annandale.

When he learned of this, Halleck blasted McClellan on the grounds that the decision to halt Franklin at Annandale was "all contrary to my orders." For his part, President Lincoln was infuriated at McClellan over a letter the general sent him on August 29 declaring, "I am clear that one of two courses should be adopted: First, to concentrate all our available forces to open communications with Pope; Second, to leave Pope to get out of his scrape, and at once use all our means to make the capital perfectly safe."

Finally, on August 30 Franklin marched to Centreville. That same day, the Second Corps left Alexandria. By the time they reached Pope, though, it was too late. His army had already been beaten.

Major-General William B. Franklin.
From a photograph. BLCW 2:377.

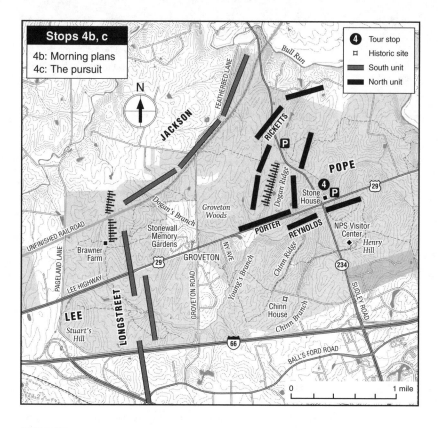

STOP 4B Morning Plans, 7:00–11:30 p.m.

Directions Remain in place.

What Happened As McClellan and Washington haggled over Franklin's movements, Pope was focusing his energies on the Confederates. At around 7:00 a.m. on August 30, he summoned his subordinates to his headquarters on Buck Hill to discuss the situation. Despite the results of Doubleday's fight with *Hood*, Pope had not shaken his belief from the night before that the Confederates were either retreating or preparing to do so. His subordinates did not agree and instead appealed for another attack over the ground where Kearny had fought the day before.

Shortly after this meeting, Porter reached Buck Hill after leading his corps to the field. Pope refused to believe his reports, or those of John Reynolds, regarding the presence of a large Confederate force south of the Warrenton Turnpike. Porter then, at Pope's direction, moved to Dogan Ridge. His command consisted of two divisions, minus a brigade that had fallen behind on the march, taken a wrong turn, and was en route to Centreville. As Porter moved to Dogan Ridge, Reynolds advanced his division forward, south of the Warrenton Turnpike, and pushed *Hood's* Confederates back from the Groveton crossroads. Meanwhile, on the other end of the Federal line, Ricketts's division of McDowell's corps moved up to relieve Kearny's command. Ricketts then pushed his lead brigade forward toward the unfinished railroad. They managed to reach and cross the railroad bed, but encountered stiff resistance from the Confederates that brought their advance to a halt. Ricketts promptly reported this to Pope.

Pope, however, remained convinced that the Confederates were preparing to withdraw. He authorized McDowell and Heintzelman to conduct a reconnaissance of the ground near Sudley Church. The two officers seem to have neither probed very far, nor to have talked with any of the Federal troops that had been engaged earlier that morning in the area, as they came away from their reconnaissance having found no evidence that the enemy was still on the field in force. Before they made their way back to Pope's headquarters, though, a Union soldier who Porter had sent back to headquarters stated that he had spent the previous evening within the enemy's lines and that they were in fact retreating. Pope immediately accepted the man's story, ignoring a note that Porter, whose skirmishers were then actively engaged with the Confederates, sent along with him, stating, "I regard him either as a fool or designedly released to give a wrong impression and no faith should be put in what he says."

By 11:30 a.m. Pope was so convinced that his next task was to organize a pursuit of the retreating enemy that he did not even bother to listen to what McDowell or Heintzelman might have to say when they returned to headquarters.

Analysis   Despite the failure to break *Jackson's* line and the arrival of *Longstreet's* command the previous day, Pope's command was still in good condition when August 30 began. It had the option of going over to the defensive and awaiting the arrival of reinforcements from Washington or pulling back across Bull Run to be closer to those reinforcements. Yet taking either of these courses of action, whatever their real military merits, would have been contrary to the more aggressive spirit Pope promised Washington he would inject into the Union war effort in Virginia. Indeed Pope's thinking on August 30 was undoubtedly shaped as much by intertwined political and personal considerations as by the situation on the ground. Upon taking command, Pope had won the hearts of the Lincoln administration and Republicans in Congress by publicly disparaging the officer corps of the eastern armies for their lack of aggressiveness and being too preoccupied about their lines of retreat. To retreat across Bull Run, after pulling back from Culpeper to the Rappahannock and then from the Rappahannock after the sack of Manassas Junction, would have been a severe blow to Pope's prestige and that of the administration that looked to him to chart a course in Virginia that was contrary to McClellan's. His dismissal of reports that *Longstreet's* command posed a significant menace and embrace of reports that confirmed his belief that the Confederates were retreating, while clearly in error, are also more understandable in this context. The fact that objections to his belief in *Jackson's* retreat and warnings of *Longstreet's* presence came from officers Pope believed—and not without some justification—were more solicitous of the interests of General McClellan than his own undoubtedly colored his response to their reports. Moreover the attacks of August 29 had inflicted significant punishment on *Jackson's* command, and it was not unreasonable for Pope to surmise that the Confederates might have had enough or that one more strong push might be enough to bring a decisive victory.

Vignette

Years after the war the mood at army headquarters and the state of Pope's mind on the morning of August 30 were still fresh for brigade commander John Gibbon, who recalled that it was "comparatively quiet for many hours and everyone seemed to be asking the question 'What next?' As the morning wore on I paid a visit to General Pope's Headquarters, nothing more than a position on the line just in rear of where I was. There were no tents, nothing to mark the spot except a cracker box or two for seats. General Pope talked very freely to the few officers around him and I recollect his complaining bitterly of what he termed 'the inaction of General Fitz-John Porter,' saying he had done nothing whilst the rest of the army was fighting, adding, personally addressing me, 'That is not the way for an officer to act, Gibbon.' I knew Porter's reputation as a soldier well and felt confident that he was not a man to stand by and do nothing when he ought to fight, but I knew little or nothing of the military situation and said nothing.

"The morning wore on and all seemed to be waiting on events. Reports were constantly coming from the field to General Pope and late in the [morning] I was surprised to hear him announce that the enemy was retreating. Everybody was now on the alert, and later some general officer rode up (I think either McDowell or Heintzelman) and before he could utter more than a word or two, General Pope interrupted him with, 'I know what you are going to say, the enemy is retreating.' Orders were at once issued for the pursuit."

STOP 4C   The Pursuit, 11:30 a.m.–12:00 p.m.

Directions   Remain in place.

What Happened   *Lee* and his subordinates, of course, had no intention of retreating from the battlefield that morning. This did not mean,
though, that he and his subordinates were resigned to remaining where they were. As the early morning passed with no
sign that the Federals were planning on doing anything significant, *Lee* assembled his subordinates at his headquarters
on Stuart's Hill. He informed them that if the Federals did
not attack that day, he wanted to make another attempt at
maneuver that evening. While *Longstreet's* command held Pope
in place, *Jackson* would take his divisions across Bull Run and
then move north and east around the Federal right in an
attempt to once again interpose his command between Pope
and Washington.

Shortly after the meeting of the Confederate high command
ended, *Jackson* and *Longstreet* finished making minor adjust-
ments in their lines. As they did so, the Confederate position
was made considerably more formidable by the posting of eighteen guns from the army's artillery reserve, commanded by
Col. *Stephen D. Lee*, on a commanding ridge near the Brawner
Farm.

Lee's plan became moot shortly after noon, when Pope issued
orders to his army for the pursuit of the supposedly fleeing
Confederate army. Porter's command, supported by two divisions from McDowell's corps, would advance west on the
Warrenton Turnpike toward Gainesville. McDowell's other division, Ricketts's, supported by Heintzelman's corps, would push
north to Sudley and then follow a road from there to Haymarket, where it connected with a road leading to Gainesville.

Despite his earlier brush with the Confederates, Ricketts
dutifully complied with the order to advance. Almost as soon
as his column reached Sudley Church, though, it came under
heavy fire from Confederate artillery that brought his march
to a screeching halt. When word of what was happening reached
McDowell, to whom Pope had formally delegated command
of the pursuit, he authorized Ricketts to break off his advance.

For his part, when Porter received the orders laying out the
plan for the pursuit and his role in it, he had already pushed
forward a strong skirmish line and a division, commanded by
Brig. Gen. Daniel Butterfield, from Dogan Ridge into Groveton
Woods. As they did so, they came under heavy fire from Confederate skirmishers, a clear sign that the Confederates still
had a strong force posted along the unfinished railroad, and
Col. *S. D. Lee's* guns near the Brawner Farm. Porter was making

preparations for an assault when Pope's pursuit order reached him. He immediately informed McDowell that in light of what he had encountered, moving to and along the Warrenton Turnpike at that point would not be a prudent move. First, the Confederates north of the turnpike would have to be dealt with, which he proposed to do by having Butterfield's command attack and clear the unfinished railroad, then take *S. D. Lee's* guns.

When Ricketts's and Porter's reports that the Confederates were not retreating reached headquarters, Pope quickly adjusted his plans. Porter, he decided, would make a massive assault against *Jackson's* line with the assistance of Hatch's division from McDowell's corps.

Further Exploration   If you did not stop here while doing the First Manassas tour, turn to page 26 for information on the Stone House.

Further Reading   Hennessy, *Return to Bull Run*, 309–34; Hennessy, *Second Manassas Map Study*, 226–73, 279–82.

STOP 5   Deep Cut

Directions   Exit the parking area for the Stone House and *turn right* onto
LEE HIGHWAY (U.S. 29). *Proceed* 1.3 miles on LEE HIGHWAY to
the intersection with FEATHERBED LANE. *Turn right* onto
FEATHERBED LANE and travel 0.5 mile to the Deep Cut parking area on the left side of the road. Exit your vehicle and walk
over to the NPS marker "Attack at Deep Cut" located next to
the parking area and face toward the stone Groveton Monument at the top of the hill in front of you.

Sudley Church. From a
photograph. BLCW 2:510.

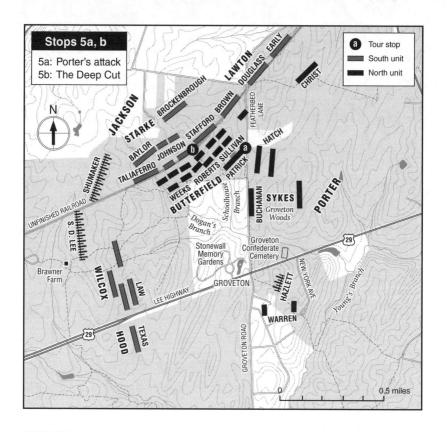

STOP 5A   Porter's Attack, 2:30–3:15 p.m.

Orientation   The Groveton Monument is about 350 yards from where you are standing. The unfinished railroad is about 50 yards beyond that. The woods located directly behind you on the other side of Featherbed Lane are known as Groveton Woods. The Brawner Farm is located to your left front about 1 mile from where you are standing.

What Happened   Porter was anything but optimistic regarding the prospects for a successful attack on *Jackson's* position when orders to make one arrived from Pope. Nonetheless he dutifully went to work organizing the three divisions at his disposal for the assault. The left and center of his force was composed of Butterfield's division, with Col. Henry Weeks's brigade on the left and Col. Charles Roberts's brigade to the right. On Roberts's right, Hatch's four brigades would go into action for the third day in a row, with Col. Timothy Sullivan's brigade spearheading the division's advance and Brig. Gen. Marsena Patrick's following. When Butterfield's and Hatch's men went forward, Brig. Gen. George Sykes's division would advance behind them into Groveton Woods, so it would be available to follow up any success that might be achieved.

At around 2:30 p.m. the advance of Butterfield's division rushed forward from Groveton Woods across the Groveton-Sudley Road to a ravine through which a tiny stream now known as Schoolhouse Branch sometimes ran and drove off Confederate skirmishers. About a half hour later Roberts's and Weeks's men emerged from the cover of the woods. As Col. *S. D. Lee's* eighteen guns opened fire at the Brawner Farm, Brig. Gen. *William E. Starke's* infantry division took up positions defending the unfinished railroad with Col. *A. G. Taliaferro's* brigade on the right, Col. *Bradley T. Johnson's* in the center, Col. *Leroy Stafford's* on the left, and Col. *William Baylor's* in reserve.

Sullivan's two lead regiments, the 30th and 24th New York, were able to cross the Groveton-Sudley Road to reach open ground in front of *Stafford's* position. As they did so *Stafford's* men opened a ferocious fire but were unable to prevent the New Yorkers from reaching the bank of the unfinished railroad and driving the Confederates to the other side of the fill. Maj. Andrew Barney of the 24th New York, in an incredible act of personal bravery, tried to lead his men forward on horseback but was quickly cut down by Confederate small arms fire as the New Yorkers clung to their position at the railroad.

Meanwhile Butterfield's men pushed forward across the Groveton-Sudley Road to Schoolhouse Branch. The ravine offered little protection from the overwhelming weight of artillery fire the Federals were subjected to. Thus Roberts and Weeks continued pushing their men forward. They then pivoted to the right to advance up the hill leading to the railroad. Within a few minutes Roberts's men had reached the top and were engaged in a fierce firefight with *Johnson's* and *Stafford's* men in the unfinished railroad.

Unlike Sullivan and Roberts, Weeks had waited until after his command had emerged from Groveton Woods to deploy all of it from column into line. This was always an extremely hazardous undertaking while under fire, and particularly so in this situation given the amount of ordnance *S. D. Lee's* guns were throwing at Weeks's men. Although able to successfully adjust his lines, the time it took Weeks to do this meant that only the 17th New York—the only one of his regiments that had been in line when it left the woods—was able to keep up with Roberts's and Sullivan's commands as they advanced. When they finally reached the top of the hill to come up on the left of the 17th New York, Weeks's men found themselves face-to-face with *Taliaferro's* and *Johnson's* brigades.

Analysis

Porter was right to be pessimistic about the prospects for success. After emerging from Groveton Woods, Butterfield's men had to advance about 600 yards across a wide open stretch of ground that offered clear fields of fire to the Confederates—above all, the Confederate artillery massed on high ground near the Brawner Farm. Then, while still in the open and under fire, Butterfield's men had to pivot to the right and climb a hill to reach *Starke's* position. Hatch's men had to cover only half the distance Butterfield's men did. However, until they pivoted to the right in conjunction with Butterfield, their right flank was exposed to Confederates defending the unfinished railroad.

Vignette

"The enemy were well posted on the hills in our front," one man in Weeks's brigade later recalled, "and, having selected their own position, they compelled our troops to be the attacking party. The order was now given to advance and charge upon the enemy. The brigade passed through the woods and over a rail fence, into an open field, in columns by division, and then deployed and formed line of battle en echelon. This movement they executed in splendid order, in face of the enemy and amidst the roar of artillery and the crashing of musketry which were directed upon them. . . . The men of the Eighty-Third dashed forward with a yell. The enemy's batteries vomited forth showers of grape and canister into their faces as they approached. But still they faltered not, nor did the lines waver. . . . In spite of the terrible opposition they met with, the Eighty-Third charged forward until the other regiments of the brigade halted and commenced firing. They then halted and commenced firing also. The understanding was that the division of troops on our right were to clear the railroad cut of rebel infantry, while our division was to advance and charge the batteries on the left of it; but their part of the programme the troops on our right failed to fulfill. The consequence was that, in addition to the artillery fire in their front, our men were now exposed to a galling flank fire from the rebel infantry in the railroad cut. They fought on, however, without any expectation of success, losing fearfully at every discharge of the enemy's guns."

STOP 5B

The Deep Cut, 3:15–4:00 p.m.

Directions

From the "Attack Deep Cut" sign, you can either remain in place or walk up to the Groveton Monument and unfinished railroad. (NOTE: This is the best, clearest route to take as of this writing. The NPS currently is working on plans to reorient the trails here in order to provide a bit more direct route from the parking area to the Groveton Monument.) To reach the monument, walk back to the parking area, then *turn right* and proceed in the direction of FEATHERBED LANE until you reach the "Deep Cut Loop Trail" sign. *Turn right* and walk for about 150 yards to a gravel path. *Turn right* here and proceed about 200 yards to where the trail forks just after crossing Schoolhouse Branch. (At the fork, you will see the N P S marker "On the Skirmish Line" and what is known as the "Cedar Pole Marker," stating, "The Wisconsin Company 1st Regiment of Berdan's Sharpshooters used many cartridges on this spot, August 30, 1862, losing 1 man killed and 8 wounded.") *Take the right fork* and proceed a little over 350 yards up the hill to a point just beyond the monument, where you are in front of the unfinished railroad.

What Happened In the fierce firefight between Porter's and *Starke's* men, *Johnson's* brigade was especially hard-pressed. When the battle began, *Johnson* had two of his four regiments posted along the unfinished railroad. On his left, the 42nd Virginia had to defend the deepest section in the unfinished railroad—which came to be known as the "Deep Cut"—while the 48th Virginia's position on his right ran through a woodlot and had no cuts and fills to protect it. When he saw Porter's men advancing, *Johnson* attempted to move his two reserve regiments forward to bolster his line, but they were decimated by Federal fire as they crossed the open field behind the unfinished railroad.

Making matters worse for *Johnson*, when Roberts's brigade and the 17th New York reached the front of the unfinished railroad, the 48th Virginia had angled forward in an attempt to engage the flank of the 17th New York. Thus when the rest of Weeks's command arrived, it was in a perfect position to crush the 48th Virginia. As the 48th Virginia collapsed, *Starke* ordered *Baylor's* Stonewall Brigade to fill the gap that had suddenly opened between *Taliaferro's* and *Johnson's* brigades. Like *Johnson's* reserves, *Baylor's* men had to cross an open field to reach the front line and suffered devastating casualties as they did. Seeing a color-bearer fall, *Baylor* personally rushed forward to grab the flag and cried out, "Boys, follow me!" Shortly thereafter he was killed by a hail of bullets and fell down wrapped in the flag. Col. *Andrew J. Grigsby* promptly stepped forward to assume command of the Stonewall Brigade and pushed it forward to eliminate the gap in *Starke's* line. He then sent an officer to *Jackson* to plead for reinforcements. *Jackson* told the officer, "Go back, give my compliments to them and tell the Stonewall Brigade to maintain her reputation. Go tell *Grigsby* to hold his position at all hazards and I will send *Pender's* Brigade to his assistance in ten minutes."

As Sullivan's, Roberts's, and Weeks's men battled the Confederates along the unfinished railroad, Porter moved a brigade from Sykes's division forward to the edge of Groveton

Woods. However, the weight of artillery fire the Confederates were able to pour into the field that separated them from their comrades at the unfinished railroad was so heavy that Porter decided against sending any of Sykes's command forward. Thus as *Pender's* command moved to the scene in response to *Jackson's* directions, the only reinforcements the beleaguered Federals would receive as they battled for the unfinished railroad would come from Hatch's command. However, the brigade following Sullivan suffered such heavy casualties in their attempt to move up on Sullivan's right that they were unable to even reach the unfinished railroad.

Nonetheless, for about a half hour Sullivan's, Roberts's, and Weeks's men put up a ferocious fight. At one point some of *Stafford's* men were compelled to throw rocks in their effort to fight off Sullivan's men. Fortunately for the Confederates, by the time this occurred, the Federal attack was pretty much exhausted. It was also about this time that reinforcements *Jackson* had ordered over from *A. P. Hill's* division began arriving on the scene. As they saw fresh enemy troops approaching, with no prospect of receiving reinforcements themselves, the Federals began retreating. As they did so, *S. D. Lee's* guns continued to fire into the open fields, inflicting further damage on Butterfield's and Hatch's commands as they fell back.

Any thought *Starke* had of following up his victory was quickly killed, though. Several of his men pushed forward from the unfinished railroad to pursue the retreating Federals, only to run into two battalions of U.S. Regulars from Sykes's division that Porter had posted at the edge of Groveton Woods along the Groveton-Sudley Road. It took only one volley from Sykes's men to convince the Confederates to pull back to the unfinished railroad, allowing the rest of Porter's men to fall back through the woods to the relative safety of Dogan Ridge.

Vignette

Recalled one man in the 24th New York: "For half a mile or more to the left of us a long line of men in blue was marching forward with the same object. Now the bullets began to fly about our ears, and men to pitch forwards or backwards, out of the line, to the earth. Artillery from unseen locations back of the enemy's infantry line opened upon us, and the shouts and yells from both sides were indescribably savage.

"It seemed like the popular idea of pandemonium made real, and indeed it is scarcely too much to say that we were really transformed for the time, from a lot of good-natured boys to the most blood-thirsty of demoniacs. Without my being in the least degree conscious of any such thing, the bottom of my haversack had been torn away by a fragment of shell, and a bullet had pierced my canteen, relieving me of the weight of all my provision and drink, and my hat had somehow been knocked off my head on my way from the woods to the railroad grade. . . . Many, very many, were lying on the ground behind us, dead, or yielding up their young lives with the blood that was oozing from their gaping wounds. Those of us who were on the embankment were too few to even attempt to drive out the troops on the other side of it, and accordingly lay as flat to the slope as we could, crawling occasionally to the top, and discharging our muskets, held horizontally over our heads, in the direction which seemed to afford a chance of hitting somebody on the other side of the grade. In the meantime a second line of troops attempted to come across the field from our side, and the din instantly became so infernal that I desisted from the feeble efforts I had been making against the enemy, in order to see what was happening in our rear.

"As I looked back, I saw our line making a grand rush in our direction, many of the men holding their arms before their faces, as though to keep off a storm. Bullets were pouring into them from the infantry beyond us, but worst of all, *Longstreet's* batteries, freshly posted on a rise of ground a mile or so to our left, were enfilading the approaching troops with solid shot, shell, and sections a foot long or more, of railroad iron, which tore up the earth frightfully, and was death to any living thing that they might touch on their passage. Our second line gave way before this terrific storm, and ran back to the cover of the woods, leaving us on the embankment to our fate. . . . Huge stones began to fall about us, and now and then one of them would happen to strike one or another of us with very unpleasant effect. By this time all my friends on the rebel work at my side were badly wounded, and I had received a few scratches and bruises for my own part. The enemy kept up the showers of stones, and we were returning the favors to such extent as we were able, and bullets intended for the rebels from our soldiers back in the woods were striking the ground about us, and at least one of them struck a comrade at my elbow, wounding him in the back, and fatally. . . .

"I took time to cut away Cotter's shirt, find that his hurt was one that I could not relieve, and replace the garment with my own, and also to place a bandage about Ayer's arm, before finally deciding to try running over the embankment in the hope of obtaining a cessation of hostilities at that point, in case of my getting over alive. I was fortunate enough to be permitted to jump down from the top into the rebel line before anybody got a successful shot at me, and made bold to ask the further favor of being allowed to bring my wounded friends over the work. This request was not granted, and I probably owe my life to the refusal. The stone-throwing ceased there, however, and I helped bandage up the wounded arms of a few of their soldiers who had been retired into the ditch at the foot of the grade. Shortly afterwards an officer seized me by the collar, drew me to my feet, and bade me look at the greatest soldier, he said, that ever lived. It was indeed Stonewall Jackson, who was riding down the line, a stalwart figure, in rusty uniform, his slouch hat in his hand, and accompanied, of course, by a retinue of mounted officers. He was greeted with hearty cheers, but his own aspect was rather pre-occupied, as though he were thinking of something out of the range of present vision."

Further Reading   Hennessy, *Return to Bull Run*, 335–60; Hennessy, *Second Manassas Battlefield Map Study*, 286–315.

Brigadier-General William E. Starke. From a tintype. BLCW 2:628.

STOP 6   New York Avenue

Directions   Exit the parking area and *turn right* onto FEATHERBED LANE. *Proceed* 0.5 mile from the Deep Cut parking area to the intersection with LEE HIGHWAY (U.S. 29). *Turn left* onto LEE HIGHWAY, drive 0.2 mile, then *turn right* onto NEW YORK AVENUE. *Proceed* 0.2 mile on NEW YORK AVENUE to the parking area. Exit your vehicle and walk over to the 5th New York (Duryee Zouaves) Monument (the one with the Maltese Cross on top of it). *Turn around* and face across the parking lot with the monument behind you.

Orientation   Note how the ground behind you slopes downward toward Young's Branch. On the other side of that stream the ground slopes upward to Chinn Ridge, the top of which is about 600 yards from where you are standing. Groveton Road is about 350 yards from you on the other side of the woods directly in front of you.

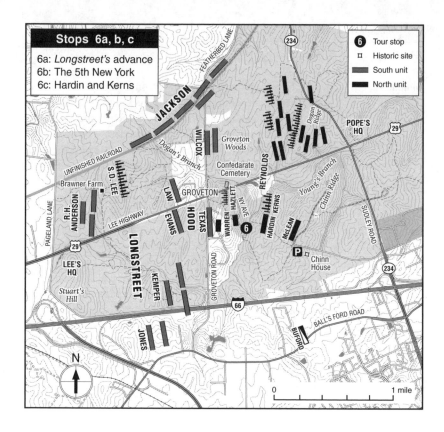

6 Tour stop
¤ Historic site
    South unit
    North unit

STOP 6A   *Longstreet's* Advance, 4:00 p.m.

What Happened   When evidence of the repulse of Porter's attack reached *Lee* and
                     Longstreet, both recognized that the time had come to throw
                     the latter's wing of the army into the battle. Even before he
                     received orders to do so, *Longstreet* directed his subordinates to
                     push their commands forward. Leading the attack would be
                     Hood's division. Neither *Longstreet*, *Lee*, nor *Hood* had a particu-
                     larly clear idea of what the Federals had south of the turnpike
                     between Groveton and Henry Hill. Nonetheless *Longstreet* made
                     the latter the objective of the attack, for he understood that if
                     his 25,000 men could quickly seize Henry Hill, that would place
                     Pope's line of retreat along the Warrenton Turnpike and the
                     entire Federal force north of the road in extreme peril.

                     At around 4:00 p.m. *Longstreet's* command began rolling for-
                     ward. *Hood* would advance with one brigade on either side of
                     the turnpike, supported by a brigade commanded by Brig. Gen.
                     Nathan Evans. The division in the center of *Longstreet's* advance,
                     Brig. Gen. *James Kemper's* division, would advance to Hood's
                     right, while Brig. Gen. *David R. Jones's* advanced on *Kemper's*
                     right. A division commanded by Maj. Gen. *Richard H. Anderson*
                     would advance behind the other three to support the advance.

Analysis

Fortunately for the Confederates, the situation *Longstreet* faced when he launched his attack was more favorable than it had been or would be at any other time in the battle. As Porter's command fell back through Groveton Woods, McDowell became concerned that its repulse had set the stage for *Jackson* to launch a counterattack that might overrun the Federal position on Dogan Ridge. Thus he directed Reynolds, commander of the only full Federal division then south of the turnpike, to move north to Dogan Ridge. This meant that fewer Federals were south of the Warrenton Turnpike than at any time that day. Nonetheless in order to reach Henry Hill, *Longstreet's* men would have to cover over 1.5 miles of rolling, broken terrain and had only a few hours of daylight left to do so.

Vignette

Longstreet later wrote of the atmosphere on the Confederate line when the repulse of Porter's assault was evident, "The heavy fumes of gunpowder hanging about our ranks, as stimulating as sparkling wine, charged the atmosphere with the light and splendor of battle. Time was culminating under a flowing tide. The noble horses took the spirit of the riders sitting lightly in their saddles. As orders were given, the staff . . . pressed their spurs, but the electric current overleaped their speedy strides, and twenty-five thousand braves moved in line as by a single impulse. My old horse, appreciating the importance of corps headquarters, envious of the spread of his comrades as they measured the green, yet anxious to maintain his role, moved up and down his limited space in lofty bounds, resolved to cover in the air the space allotted his more fortunate comrades on the plain. . . . As the plain along *Hood's* front was more favorable for the tread of soldiers, he was ordered, as the column of direction, to push for the plateau at the Henry House, in order to cut off retreat at the crossings by Young's Branch. . . . At the first sound of the charge, General *Lee* . . . asked me to push the battle, ordered *R. H. Anderson's* division up, and rode himself to join me."

STOP 6B

The 5th New York, 4:00–4:15 p.m.

Directions

Remain in place.

What Happened

As Reynolds began moving his division north in response to McDowell's orders, that left two Federal brigades holding positions south of the turnpike when *Longstreet* began his advance. The first was Col. Nathaniel McLean's brigade from Sigel's corps, which was posted on Chinn Ridge. The other was Col. Gouverneur K. Warren's small brigade from Porter's corps.

Warren's command consisted of only two regiments, the 5th and 10th New York, both of which were known for their distinctive Zouave uniforms.

Warren's men had the task of supporting the six guns of Lt. Charles Hazlett's Battery D, 5th U.S. Artillery, which were posted on the high ground overlooking the Groveton crossroads that had figured prominently in the battle between *Hood's* and Hatch's men the previous evening. Six companies from the 10th New York had been pushed forward about 400 yards to serve as a skirmish line, while the 5th New York occupied the ground west of a small stream known as Young's Branch, which separated Warren's command from McLean's on Chinn Ridge.

Shortly after they began their advance, *Hood* and his men encountered the skirmishers of the 10th New York, to whom it immediately became clear that they were in contact with an enemy force that was far too strong for them to handle. They barely got off a single volley before they began falling back, with *Hood's* men hot on their heels. As the 10th New York retreated, though, they sowed confusion in the ranks of Capt. Cleveland Winslow's 5th New York. Concerned lest they fire on their comrades, Winslow's men let Confederates approaching their position through the woods get close enough to their left flank to unleash a vicious fire into their ranks. Making matters worse, part of the 10th New York attempted to rally directly in front of Winslow's position, blocking the 5th New York's own field of fire.

Warren was able to clear them away, but by the time he did so *Hood's* men were less than 50 yards away, with one regiment bearing down and lapping around Winslow's left and two others moving forward to overwhelm the Federal center and right. Within ten minutes, the fire into his lines became so intense that Warren had no choice but to order his wrecked command to retreat. As the Federals tumbled down the slope to Young's Branch, the Confederates poured an unrelenting fire into their shattered ranks, cutting down many more of Warren's men.

Fortunately for Hazlett, the regiment that should have been attacking his position was delayed at the outset of *Hood's* advance, which enabled Hazlett to withdraw his guns safely to Dogan Ridge. This was cold comfort to Warren's men, especially the members of the 5th New York. Although they eventually managed to rally on Henry Hill, 120 of the approximately 500 men in its ranks had been killed. In the entire Civil War, no other infantry regiment would have more men killed in a single engagement.

Vignette

"The Zouaves, it seems," one of *Hood's* men later wrote, "were posted just under the crest of the hill, and a hundred feet from the edge of the timber, and fired the moment the heads of the Texans showed above the crest. Of course they aimed too high, and before they could reload the Texans poured such a well-directed and deadly volley into their closely formed ranks that half of them sank to the ground, and the balance wheeled and ran. Not waiting to reload, the Texans rushed after the fugitives, and, clubbing their muskets, continued the work of destruction until every enemy in sight was left prone upon the ground.... Looking up the hill, a strange and ghastly spectacle met our eyes. An acre of ground was literally covered with the dead, dying, and wounded of the Fifth New York Zouaves, the variegated colors of whose peculiar uniform gave the scene the appearance of a Texas hillside in spring, painted with wild flowers of every hue and color."

STOP 6C Hardin and Kerns, 4:15–4:30 p.m.

Directions *Turn left* and walk south for a little over 50 yards to the monument to the 10th New York (National Zouaves). You can either do the stand here or follow the "Further Exploration" directions at the end of this stop to the point where they indicate the approximate location of Hardin's and Kerns's positions.

What Happened It was not long after *Longstreet's* advance began when McDowell realized he had made a horrible mistake in pulling Reynolds's command north. He responded by grabbing Col. Martin Hardin's brigade and a battery commanded by Capt. Mark Kerns before they could cross to the north side of the turnpike and ordering them to take up a position on the western slope of Chinn Ridge. Hardin and Kerns deployed on a knoll about midway up the slope, with Kerns's guns on the right and Hardin's four Pennsylvania regiments to the left, deployed in two lines of two regiments each with about 30 yards separating them, just in time to watch the destruction of Warren's command.

As the Texas Brigade pushed across Young's Branch, Kerns's gunners unleashed a volley of canister. *Hood's* men immediately recoiled back down the slope to the cover of the creek bed. Then, on their own initiative, Lt. Col. *B. F. Carter's* 4th Texas on the left of the Texas Brigade and Col. *Jerome Robertson's* 5th Texas on the right resumed the advance. As the 18th Georgia and Hampton Legion in the center joined in the assault, Hardin and Kerns continued to fire into the Confederate ranks. This compelled *Robertson's* men to shift to the right, which enabled them to reach a position from which they could fire into Hardin's left flank. Hardin responded by ordering his second line forward, but the ferocity with which the Texans fired into his ranks was unbearable. Hardin soon fell, badly wounded, and within minutes his command was in full flight from the field.

This enabled *Hood's* men to focus their energies on Kerns. Fortunately for them, Kerns was unable to depress his guns far enough to fire down the slope, and as a consequence much of his fire went over the heads of *Hood's* men. With Hardin's brigade having collapsed and their own horses and men falling all about, it did not take long for Kerns's gunners to decide they had better leave the field. One man, though, refused to do so. Kerns continued to work his guns, single-handedly loading and firing them. Astonished by Kerns's extraordinary courage, shouts arose among the Texans to hold their fire as they approached his position. However, just as Kerns finished loading a gun with canister and was prepared to fire, they shot him down and overran his position.

Vignette   A member of the 4th Texas later recalled, "It was a singular coincidence that the Zouaves and the battery which suffered so heavily at the hands of the Texans at Second Manassas should have also fought us at Gaines' Mill the 27th of June previous, when the Zouaves lost about one-third of their number while the battery lost two of their guns, besides many of their men killed and wounded. The battery was composed of Pennsylvania soldiers and was commanded by Captain Mark Kerns, who although wounded early in the day at Gaines' Mill, stayed with his guns until the Federal line was swept from the field, and at Second Manassas, although nearly all his men had fallen, he loaded and fired his guns until he himself was struck down when we were only a few steps from him. When we reached the gun beside which he fell, with his life blood fast ebbing away, he said: 'I promised to drive you back, or die under my guns, and I have kept my word.'"

Further Exploration   This walk, about 1-mile round-trip, will take you down into the Young's Branch valley and up the slope of Chinn Ridge. It will give you a good sense of the terrain over which *Longstreet's* men advanced and the physical effort it took just to reach Chinn Ridge. Keep in mind, of course, that even before they reached Warren's position, the Confederates had already covered a respectable distance from the start point of their advance. This trail will also take you to the approximate point where Hardin and Kerns fought *Hood's* Texans.

From the 10th New York monument, *proceed south* for about 20 yards to the gravel path and *turn left*. After walking downhill for about 250 yards, you will see the trail fork just before it reaches Young's Branch. *Take the left trail* and, after crossing the bridge over the creek, proceed 20 yards to another fork and *turn left*. Follow the trail along the creek for about 250 yards. At this point, the trail turns right to ascend Chinn Ridge. *Continue* following it for another 250 yards or so to a plateau about midway up the slope. In the woods to your left was the approximate location of Hardin's and Kerns's position. From here, you can continue hiking for about another 500 yards to reach the parking area for Chinn Ridge. From there, you can turn to the next section of the guide, which covers the fighting on Chinn Ridge, and begin your study of this part of the battle. Alternatively you can retrace your steps back to your vehicle at the New York monuments and follow the directions provided to drive to Chinn Ridge.

Further Reading   Hennessy, *Return to Bull Run*, 362–78; Hennessy, *Second Manassas Map Study*, 318–19, 321–24, 326–29, 332–38; Patchan, *Second Manassas*, 18–28.

General John B. Hood, C.S.A. From a photograph. BLCW 4:275.

STOP 7   Chinn Ridge

Directions   Drive back to the intersection of NEW YORK AVENUE and LEE
                              HIGHWAY (U.S. 29). *Turn right* onto LEE HIGHWAY and drive 0.9
                              mile to the traffic light at the intersection with SUDLEY ROAD
                              (VA 234). *Turn right* onto SUDLEY ROAD and proceed 0.4 mile,
                              then *turn right* onto the one-way park road and drive 0.6 mile
                              to a T intersection. *Turn right* and proceed to the parking lot
                              at the top of the hill. Exit your vehicle, walk over to the end
                              of the parking area, and *turn right* to reach the paved path and
                              NPS marker "Fight at the Fence Line." You can do the stand
                              here or continue walking on the paved path for about 100
                              yards to the NPS marker "73rd Ohio Infantry." Either way, you
                              should then *turn left* and face toward the woods.

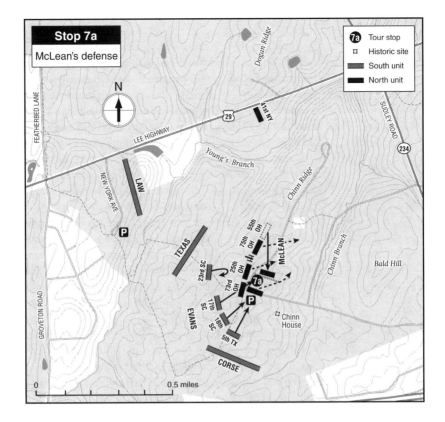

Stop 7a

McLean's defense

Tour stop
Historic site
South unit
North unit

N

0   0.5 miles

STOP 7A   McLean's Defense, 4:30–5:00 p.m.

Orientation   You are standing at the approximate point where Col. Nathan-
                     iel McLean's brigade was posted when the fight for Chinn
                     Ridge began. The New York monuments are on the other side
                     of the woods in front of you and about 1,000 yards from where
                     you are standing. To your right, Chinn Ridge runs to the north
                     and east for about 0.75 mile from where you are standing to
                     the Stone House intersection. If you look to your left rear, you
                     will see the foundation of the Chinn House ("Hazel Plain")
                     about 300 yards away on the other side of the fence line and
                     parking area.

What Happened   As the wreckage of Warren's and Hardin's commands fled the
                     field, they left the task of dealing with *Longstreet's* assault to
                     McLean's brigade and a battery commanded by Capt. Mark
                     Wiedrich. McLean had his four Ohio regiments deployed along
                     the crest of Chinn Ridge, with two on either side of Wiedrich's
                     guns. Except for some woods to their left and front, they had
                     a clear view of *Hood's* tired command as it moved into a dip in
                     the ground that separated the knoll where Kerns's and Har-
                     din's had fought from the crest of Chinn Ridge.

As they paused to catch their breath, *Hood* noted that despite the fact that the Texas Brigade had fought its way through two Union brigades, the rest of *Longstreet's* command had not yet come up on his right. Moreover *Hood* found his men were now in a perfect position for Union artillery on Dogan Ridge to fire into their left. Thus he ordered the 5th Texas, 18th Georgia, and Hampton's Legion to shift to the right to avail themselves of the cover provided by the woods. As he did so, McLean's men began firing at them, which led *Hood* to conclude they were too strong to be taken by just his command; he sent back orders to *Evans* to bring up his brigade.

As *Evans's* command began arriving on the scene, their commander immediately deployed them with an eye to attacking McLean's command directly over the open ground that separated the two. Then, however, *Evans's* men began taking fire from Union artillery on Dogan Ridge, which compelled them to slide to the right into the woods. McLean's men and Wiedrich's battery then began pouring a rain of fire into the woods.

The Confederates responded by sliding toward the buildings of the Chinn property. Ultimately the 18th and 17th South Carolina from *Evans's* command and the 5th Texas from *Hood's* found themselves in a position where they were facing McLean's left flank. As they then advanced toward the Chinn House, the two regiments to the left of Wiedrich's battery, the 25th and 73rd Ohio, attempted to shift their position so they could face the Confederates directly. However, the amount of fire *Hood's* and *Evans's* men were pouring into their ranks and the noise of the battle threw the entire effort into confusion. Within minutes McLean's entire left flank had disintegrated. Left unsupported, Wiedrich's gunners also fled. McLean responded by ordering his remaining two regiments to shift to the left. However, the 75th Ohio got tangled up with the retreating 25th and 73rd Ohio. Col. John Lee's 55th Ohio, though, managed to make the shift in relatively good order, which enabled them to stop the Confederate advance and reach a fence line located north of the Chinn House.

It was at this point that elements from Brig. Gen. *James Kemper's* division began to arrive on the field. Brig. Gen. *Eppa Hunton* quickly sized up the situation and ordered his two lead regiments to advance along the crest of Chinn Ridge. However, one of *Hunton's* regimental commanders refused to do so until he received written orders. With *Hunton's* advance stalled, it fell to Brig. Gen. *Montgomery Corse's* brigade to deal with the 55th Ohio and remnants from the rest of McLean's brigade that had rallied with it along the fence line. When *Corse's* command had advanced to less than 50 yards from the fence, the Ohioans blasted them with infantry fire. It took ten minutes for *Corse*, aided by elements from *Hood's* and *Evans's* commands, to finally drive the Ohioans from the fence line.

In his official report, McLean later recalled what occurred when he reached Chinn Ridge: "Much to my surprise General Reynolds put his troops in motion and marched entirely past and across my front to the right, to what point I am not informed. Finding that this movement had entirely exposed my left flank I immediately changed the position of my troops, and deployed in line of battle the Seventy-third and Twenty-fifth Ohio Regiments, fronting the west and to the left of the battery, and the Seventy-fifth and Fifty-fifth Ohio, then returned from its former position on the right of the battery, thus making my line of battle fronting the west, with the battery in the center and two regiments on each side. I could by this time see the enemy advancing on my front and a little to the right, driving before them a regiment of Zouaves.

"They came on rapidly, when some troops advanced to meet them from behind a hill on my right. These troops were also driven back in confusion, and as soon as they got out of the way I opened upon the enemy with the four pieces of artillery, throwing first shell, and as they approached nearer, canister. I also commenced a heavy fire with infantry, and in a short time the enemy retreated in great confusion. During this time my attention had been called to a body of troops advancing toward my position in the rear of my left flank, and supposing them to be enemies, I gave the order to turn two pieces of artillery upon them, but countermanded it upon the assurance of someone who professed to know the fact that they were our own troops, and I readily believed this, as their clothing was dark, and then rested easy, thinking re-enforcements were coming to take position on my left. . . .

"Soon after this a heavy force of the enemy, much superior to my own, marched out of the woods across the position formerly occupied by General Reynolds, in front of my left flank, and swept around, so as to come in heavy force both on the front and flank of my left wing. This force opened a heavy fire upon the Seventy-third Ohio, and the next moment the troops in my rear, supposed to be friends, also opened fire with musketry and artillery. Overpowered by such superiority in numbers, after a short time the Seventy-third and Twenty-fifth fell back over the crest of the hill, but were still exposed to the fire from both columns of the enemy. I immediately, when this attack was made, gave the order to change front, so as to repel it if possible, but the retreat of the battery at this moment interfered somewhat with the movements, as it passed through the Seventy-fifth in its retreat.

"The Fifty-fifth, on my right flank, at the command wheeled by battalion to the left and came up into line, fronting the enemy in fine order, and the other regiments speedily formed on his left, and delivered such a heavy and continuous fire that in a short time the enemy ceased to advance, and commenced to fall back. My men followed with cheers, driving the enemy back rapidly, and would have cleared them from the field but for the fact that the forces permitted to approach our rear had got into such a position as to rake us with grape, canister, and musketry, while we were attacked severely in front. Under all this, however, my brigade retained the hill until I myself gave the order, to fall back slowly. This order was given with great reluctance, and only when my attention was called to a heavy force of the enemy approaching to attack us on our then right flank but former front. I saw that it would but destroy my whole command to await that attack, and therefore gave the order under which we left the hill."

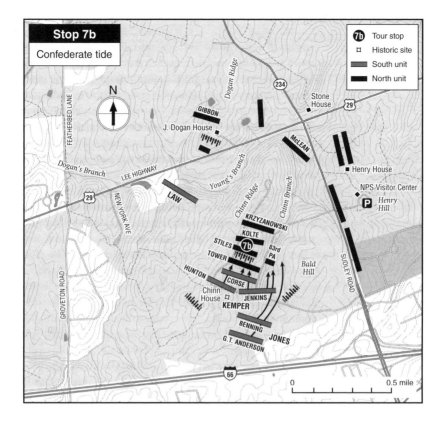

STOP 7B Confederate Tide, 5:00–6:00 p.m.

Directions Remain in place and *turn left* to face south, toward the parking lot, or, if you did the first stand at the "73rd Ohio Infantry" marker, you can resume walking on the paved path for about 400 yards to the NPS marker "Death of Fletcher Webster." *Turn right* here and walk over to the monuments visible about 75 yards away. At the monuments, *turn right* to face south.

What Happened Although ultimately driven from their position, McLean's Ohioans held up the Confederate advance long enough for McDowell to dispatch further reinforcements to Chinn Ridge. The first to arrive were Brig. Gen. Zealous Tower's and Col. John Stiles's brigades from Ricketts's division. Seeing McLean's line collapsing, Tower led his brigade of infantry and a four-gun battery commanded by Capt. George Leppien forward and deployed them just as the Confederate line resumed their advance. Tower's men put up a fierce fight, but the Confederate line extended beyond both of his flanks. As the left of his line began to give way down in Chinn Branch valley, which separated Chinn Ridge from Bald Hill, Tower was wounded, and shortly thereafter his entire line began falling back.

As Tower's brigade battled the Confederates, McDowell rode over to Stiles's command and ordered it forward. After sending the 83rd New York into the Chinn Branch valley, Stiles ordered the other three regiments forward along the ridge. As they reached the rear of Tower's collapsing position, Stiles's men halted and began fixing bayonets. When McDowell saw this, however, he directed Stiles to continue pushing forward. Unfortunately, McDowell's order did not reach the 13th Massachusetts on the left of Stiles's line. Consequently, as the 11th Pennsylvania and 12th Massachusetts pushed forward to reach Tower's men and helped them form a new firing line, they found that the Confederates had more than enough force to extend beyond both of their flanks.

This was in part a consequence of the arrival on the field of Brig. Gen. *Micah Jenkins's* brigade of *Kemper's* division and the fact that *Hunton* had finally gotten his brigade into the fight. When the right wing of *Jenkins's* command pushed into the Chinn Branch valley.

As this was going on in the valley below, the men of Tower's and Stiles's commands continued to battle *Corse's, Hunton's,* and *Jenkins's* brigades on the crest of Chinn Ridge. Despite suffering immense casualties, the Federals put up a fierce fight. Among the casualties was Col. Fletcher Webster, commander of the 12th Massachusetts and son of the famous Massachusetts statesman Daniel Webster, who was mortally wounded while riding along his lines. Already badly outnumbered by the Confederates on top of the ridge, Tower's and Stiles's position became completely untenable when Col. *Henry Benning's* fresh brigade from *Jones's* division began firing into their exposed left flank from Chinn Branch valley. Tower's and Stiles's regiments quickly collapsed, having in some cases lost nearly half their strength.

Their officers were able to rally enough of the men to form yet another new line about 200 yards from their previous one, where they resumed firing into the Confederates. At this point, Lt. Col. Ernest Holmstedt's 41st New York and the three regiments of Col. John Koltes's brigade arrived on Chinn Ridge, having been sent there by Sigel. Not content with fighting on the defensive and seeing Leppien's abandoned guns out in the field in front of them, Holmstedt's men rushed forward in an attempt to recapture the guns. But their efforts came to grief when their comrades, unable to distinguish friend from foe through the thick battle smoke, poured a heavy fire into their rear.

Kemper's men then shifted their line of advance so as to come upon Koltes's right, their efforts supported by fire from a battery commanded by Capt. *J. B. Richardson's* battery. Just before an artillery shell took his life, Koltes ordered his men to charge Richardson's battery. It was a futile effort and resulted in several of his men being surrounded and taken prisoner.

At this point, a second brigade Sigel had sent to Chinn Ridge arrived on the scene. While able to easily handle a direct attack the Confederates threw at them, the men of Col. Wladimir Krzyzanowski's brigade soon began receiving fire that indicated the enemy's line overlapped both of its flanks. Krzyzanowski then ordered his men and the remnants of Tower's, Stiles's, and Koltes's commands to fall back to the north and east, bringing the fight for Chinn Ridge to an end at around 6:00 p.m., with the Confederates in complete possession of the ridge.

Analysis

While the Federals put up a tough fight, there were far too few of them to hold out for long given the much larger Confederate force they faced on Chinn Ridge. Nonetheless, aided by the fatigue *Longstreet's* men suffered in the course of advancing over 1 mile over fairly rough terrain and overcoming Warren's and Hardin's commands, their efforts did arrest the momentum of the Confederate assault enough to give Pope and McDowell time to dispatch reinforcements to Chinn Ridge and Henry Hill. While insufficient to turn the tide of the battle, their efforts did make it possible for the Union high command to preserve the army's line of retreat back across Bull Run.

Further Reading

Hennessy, *Return to Bull Run*, 378–406; Hennessy, *Second Manassas Map Study*, 343–57, 361–72, 375–78, 381–83, 392–99; Patchan, *Second Manassas*, 28–80.

STOP 8   Henry Hill

Directions   Exit the parking area and *proceed straight* on the park road 0.7 mile to SUDLEY ROAD (VA 234). *Turn left* and drive 0.4 mile on SUDLEY ROAD to the entrance to the Visitor Center. *Turn right* and proceed to the parking area. Exit your vehicle and walk over to and around the Visitor Center. *Continue* walking for about 75 yards to a point next to the artillery caissons. *Stop here* and *turn left* to face toward SUDLEY ROAD, with the *Stonewall Jackson* monument directly behind you.

Confederate sharp-shooter.
BLCW 2:202.

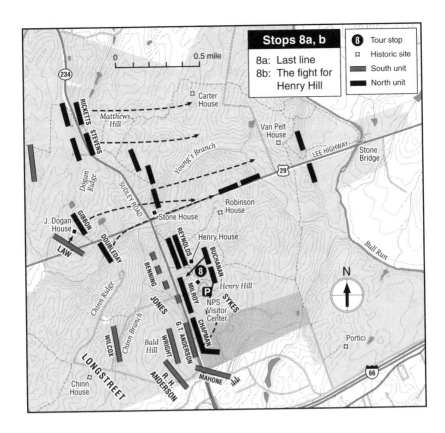

STOP 8A

Last Line, 4:30–6:00 p.m.

Orientation

You are standing on Henry Hill, the focal point of the First Battle of Manassas and site of the last significant fighting at Second Manassas. To your left front, Sudley Road exits a wood-lot and then runs across your front to the Stone House intersection, which is where you see the traffic lights on your right front. The Stone Bridge is a little over 1 mile behind you to your right rear. Portici is about 1 mile to your left rear.

What Happened

By the time the battle for Chinn Ridge ended at around 6:00 p.m., Pope had managed to patch together a strong line to defend Henry Hill. His efforts were facilitated by the fact that *Jackson's* command remained largely inactive throughout the afternoon, which allowed Pope to shift forces over from Dogan Ridge. The first Federal units to reach Henry Hill were two brigades from Reynolds's division, which shortly before 5:00 p.m. began taking up a position near the ruins of the Henry House overlooking the Sudley Road. Reynolds posted his men in two lines, with Brig. Gen. George Meade's brigade supporting Capt. Dunbar Ransom's battery in front and Brig. Gen. Truman Seymour's brigade just behind Meade.

Shortly thereafter Lt. Col. William Chapman's brigade from Brig. Gen. George Sykes's division of U.S. Regular troops from Porter's corps took up a position beyond Reynolds's left in the cut of the Sudley Road. To fill the gap between them, Pope's chief of staff directed Brig. Gen. Robert Milroy to move his brigade to Henry Hill. Upon arriving, Milroy posted his command in the road as directed. Posted higher up on Henry Hill to support Reynolds's, Milroy's, and Chapman's lines were two brigades commanded by Col. Robert Buchanan and Col. Sanders Piatt, as well as two batteries commanded by Capt. James Hall and Capt. J. Albert Monroe.

By the time Pope and McDowell finished the task of cobbling this line together, the only part of *Longstreet's* command on Chinn Ridge that still had sufficient energy to continue the attack was *Jones's* division. As the Federals withdrew from the ridge, *Jones* ordered his two brigades to continue pushing to the north and east toward the intersection of the Sudley Road and Warrenton Turnpike with Col. *Henry Benning's* brigade in the lead and Col. *George T. Anderson's* following him. As *Benning's* men reached a point within 200 yards from the intersection, possession of which would place them in the rear of the Federals still on Dogan Ridge, they marched across the front of Reynolds's command. Reynolds responded by ordering Meade's brigade to push forward toward the Sudley Road, while his artillery opened fire on the Confederates.

STOP 8B   The Fight for Henry Hill, 6:00–7:00 p.m.

Directions   Remain in place.

What Happened *Benning's* and *Anderson's* men were stunned by the appearance of a large Federal force on their flank and immediately began pivoting to the right to take on Reynolds's command. Protected by the cover provided by the worn roadbed, the Federal infantry unleashed a fierce storm of fire on the advancing Confederates. Meanwhile Federal artillery fired shot and canister at *Benning's* and *Anderson's* men. The Confederates, however, were able to force the left of Reynolds's division and Milroy's command back from the road, while Chapman's command found itself under assault by hornets whose nest had accidentally been opened and a battery commanded by Capt. *B. F. Eshelman* that managed to reach a position from which it could fire into Chapman's left flank. Then, as if this were not bad enough, at this point Maj. Gen. *Richard H. Anderson's* division began arriving on the scene and went into action to the right of *Jones's* command. *Anderson* ordered Brig. Gen. *Ambrose Wright's* brigade to assist *G. T. Anderson's* brigade and posted

Brig. Gen. *William Mahone's* division to *Wright's* right. *Mahone* then led his brigade across the Sudley Road beyond the southern flank of Chapman's line in the woods south of the Henry farm.

This compelled Chapman to pull back his left to confront them. Pressed in front by *Anderson's* and *Wright's* commands and on the flank by *Mahone's*, the soldiers of Chapman's command—and the rest of the Federal force trying to hold the Sudley Road line—soon found themselves in serious trouble. Fortunately as Chapman's men began falling back from their position, three regiments from Col. Robert Buchanan's brigade arrived on the scene. The Confederates failed to press their advantage with much vigor, as *R. H. Anderson* appeared unaware of the opportunity that was before him to roll up the Federal line from the south. Aided by the timely arrival of two other regiments from Buchanan's brigade, this enabled the Federals of Reynolds's and Milroy's commands to rally sufficiently to blunt *Benning's* and *G. T. Anderson's* efforts to push forward from the Sudley Road.

By then the Federals on Dogan Ridge had pulled back to a defensive position covering the approaches to the Stone Bridge. At around 6:00 p.m. *Jackson* had finally ordered part of his command forward, but its efforts and those of some cavalry to complicate the efforts of the Federals to extricate themselves from Dogan Ridge were frustrated by stubborn resistance by elements from Ricketts's, Hatch's, and Kearny's divisions.

Maj. Gen. John Pope, however, had had enough. By 6:30 p.m. his only thought was to get back across Bull Run and attempt to rally his command at Centreville. When Sigel tried to convince him to see if he could hold a position west of Bull Run, Pope bluntly replied that "he had not sent for him to receive suggestions but to give him orders, as his mind was made up what to do."

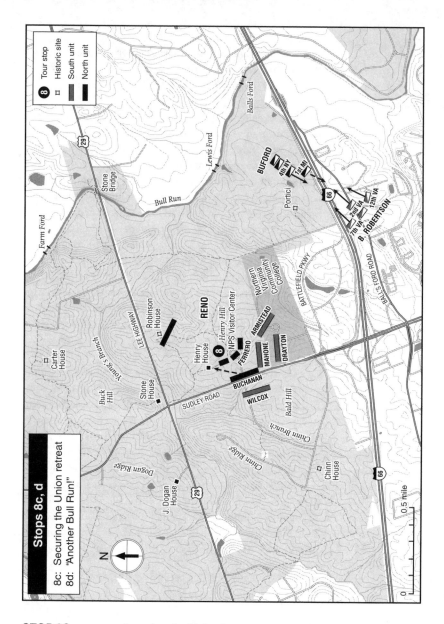

Stops 8c, d

8c: Securing the Union retreat
8d: "Another Bull Run!"

STOP 8C   Securing the Union Retreat, 6:00–7:00 p.m.

Directions   Remain in place.

What Happened   During the afternoon of August 30, Pope had ordered Brig.
                     Gen. John Buford to take his brigade of cavalry and the 4th
                     New York Cavalry to the south in order to cover the Union
                     left. As *Longstreet's* command attacked the Union positions
                     south of the Warrenton Turnpike, Buford felt compelled to
                     pull his cavalry back to the Lewis Farm near Lewis Ford on
                     Bull Run. At around 6:00 p.m., Buford received word that a

brigade of Confederate cavalry commanded by Brig. Gen. *Beverly Robertson* was approaching his position; he responded by deploying his command near the Lewis house (Portici) behind a low ridge. By then *Robertson* had learned that some Union cavalry was in front of him and, with no sense of their numbers or disposition, authorized Col. *Thomas T. Munford* to push forward his 2nd Virginia Cavalry to disperse them. As the Confederates approached, Buford ordered Col. Thornton Brodhead's 1st Michigan Cavalry to draw their sabers and charge.

Supported by the 4th New York Cavalry, Brodhead's men surprised *Munford's* Virginians, and within moments the two forces had slammed into each other and begun exchanging close-range fire and saber slashes. When the 4th New York pitched in, it was too much for *Munford's* men to handle, and their commander ordered a retreat. *Robertson* responded by ordering the rest of his command forward. Buford then managed to get the 1st Michigan and 4th New York back under order, but he neglected to bring forward his other two regiments. Thus when the 7th and 12th Virginia Cavalry joined the fight, they overpowered Buford's line. The Michiganders and New Yorkers quickly broke and began fleeing the scene, leaving Brodhead to be personally surrounded and mortally wounded by the Confederates as Buford's command fell back across Bull Run at Lewis Ford. *Robertson* then pushed two regiments across Bull Run but failed to accomplish anything more after doing so.

Meanwhile, back on Henry Hill, Reynolds had withdrawn his command shortly before 7:00 p.m. as Col. Edward Ferrero's brigade from Reno's command arrived on the scene and Buchanan's command made a slow, fighting retreat from the field. The Confederates made one last attempt to push up the slope of Henry Hill. After fighting a short but sharp series of skirmishes in the dark with Ferrero's command, the Confederates backed off, ending whatever hopes still remained that they might be able to secure Henry Hill and interdict the Federal line of retreat back to Centreville.

Vignette   One man who participated in the repulse of the final Confederate assaults on Henry Hill as part of Ferrero's brigade later recalled, "We moved into position on the crest of the hill, drowning the rebel yells with cheers for ten thousand men. The white-haired General Milroy, who stood alone on the crest as we came up, was frantic with joy as he welcomed us; and, as we dressed our lines, rode along our front, shouting like a crazy man. The rebels waited to re-form their disordered lines before essaying an attack, which gave General Reno time to get up a battery, and us an opportunity to observe the situation. We covered the crossing of the Centreville Pike over Young's Branch, and held a magnificent position for defense: the brigade was formed on a curved ridge, refusing the flanks a little; on the left was the 51st New York, . . . the 21st Massachusetts was in the centre, and the 51st Pennsylvania on the right. General Reno posted his battery of smooth-bores, double shotted with canister, on a line with the infantry, and in the short intervals between the regiments. In our front was an open space of a few hundred yards of gently sloping ground ending in a grove. Behind us a struggling mass of artillery and wagons were trying to cross the bridge over Young's Branch, blocking the road as far as we could see, and not a soldier that we saw or knew of besides ourselves stood in line of battle, or in reserve. . . .

"We had not long to wait: the sun had set, and it was beginning to grow dark, when we heard a confused hum, and the rush of many feet in our front; stand up was the order, and every man was on his feet; the open space in our front was now alive with the rebel masses, and General Reno gave the welcome order, 'Give them about ten rounds, boys. Fire!' A simultaneous volley rolled from infantry and artillery, and then it was every man for himself, and they made quick work: our cartridges were of such small calibre that no ramming was required, and the men had hardly got well warmed up before the firing was stopped. . . . For half an hour we were unmolested, and the quiet was unbroken except by the cries of the poor mutilated fellows who lay along our front, when a force of the enemy, who, concealed by the thick brush, had crawled along the banks of the creek on our left, struck the 51st New York on the flank with startling suddenness, and rolled them up with the loss of eighty-five men in a few seconds. The 21st made a rapid change of front to face the enemy in his new position, and added their fire to that of the indomitable 51st, who were now fighting most gallantly. Two pieces of the artillery were brought to the left, and the enemy was as fatally repulsed as before, and our line reestablished. Except feeling us in a harmless way with artillery, and reconnoitering us with a skirmish line, whom we gave good reason to remember that we were still there, the rebel attack was over. About nine o'clock General Reno passed along the line, and told us that we were to abandon our position, and that our lives depended upon the secrecy of the movement. . . . The poor wounded fellows who covered the ground behind us had borne their sufferings without complaint; but when the artillery and the 51st Pennsylvania had gone, and they knew that they were to be left to their fate, they besought us not to abandon them, or cursed us for doing so. With sad hearts that we were powerless to aid them, we left the horrid, hopeless field."

STOP 8D   "Another Bull Run!" 7:00 p.m., August 30–September 2, 1862

Directions   Remain in place.

What Happened   Unlike their predecessor the year before, the Federal army that withdrew to Centreville on August 30 had preserved most of its morale and organization. Moreover, on reaching Centreville it was greeted by the sight of the entire Sixth Corps, which had finally arrived that evening. In addition, it learned that the Army of the Potomac's Second Corps was on the march from Alexandria with orders to join Pope.

Although not fully aware of the degree to which Pope was being reinforced, Lee quickly dismissed the idea of following up his victory at Manassas by attacking Centreville directly. Instead he ordered Jackson to take his three divisions north to make another attempt to get in the Federal rear. As Pope debated with his subordinates and with Washington whether to stay at Centreville or fall back to Washington, Jackson and Stuart's cavalry moved north along the Gum Springs Road through a heavy rain to the Little River Turnpike, then turned east. Their objective was to reach the point just west of Fairfax Court House near Jermantown where the Little River Turnpike intersected Pope's main line of retreat along the Warrenton Turnpike.

However, by the time Jackson's command reached Ox Hill, a few miles west of Jermantown, on September 1, forces commanded by Hooker that Pope had ordered to secure his line of retreat were posted just west of Jermantown on high ground astride the Little River Turnpike that overlooked Difficult Run. Shortly after learning that Hooker's line effectively blocked the road to Jermantown, Jackson's command was attacked from the south by elements from two Union divisions. As a torrential rain fell, Jackson's men were able to repulse the Union attacks in what became known as the Battle of Ox Hill (Chantilly) and, in the process, mortally wounded Maj. Gen. Philip Kearny and Brig. Gen. Isaac Stevens. (To study this engagement in more detail, turn to the Chantilly Excursion.)

Nonetheless whatever hopes Lee had that he might get another chance to successfully strike at Pope's army before it reached the defenses of Washington were effectively dead. As Pope's men retreated toward the Washington defenses on September 2, they learned they would now be commanded by McClellan. Meanwhile Lee and his subordinates began setting their sights north, to the crossings of the Potomac River and Maryland.

Analysis   In all, Pope's command suffered 16,054 casualties, of which 1,724 were killed, 8,372 wounded, and 5,958 missing. Total

Confederate losses were much smaller, mainly due a large disparity in the number missing. Of the 9,197 casualties *Lee's* army suffered during the campaign, 1,481 were killed and 7,627 wounded, with only 89 missing. Nonetheless while the Federal army was in far better shape than had been the case after the previous year's battle at Manassas and Union military authorities could take some comfort in the relative attrition rates, there was no doubt in anyone's mind that by any other measure by which the outcome of military operations can be assessed, the Second Manassas Campaign had produced a spectacular Confederate victory.

Vignette   During the evening of August 30, Brig. Gen. John Gibbon had just posted his brigade near the Robinson House to help cover the retreat of the Federal army across Bull Run when he heard a fellow officer shout out, "Whose command is this?" Gibbon later recalled, "Turning to look, I recognized General Phil Kearny. I walked up to him and told him I was directed to act as a rear guard. He was a soldierly looking fellow as he sat, straight as an arrow, on a horse, his empty sleeve pinned to his breast. Turning towards me, he said in his curt way: 'You must wait for my command, sir.' 'Yes,' I replied, 'I will wait for all our troops to pass to the rear. Where is your command, General?' 'Off to the right, don't you hear my guns? You must wait for Reno, too.' 'Where is he?' 'On the left—you hear his guns? He is keeping up the fight and I am doing all I can to help.'

"Then in a short bitter tone he broke out with: 'I suppose you appreciate the condition of affairs here, sir?' I did not understand the remark and only looked inquiringly at him. He repeated: 'I suppose you appreciate the condition of affairs?' It's another Bull Run, sir, it's another Bull Run!' 'Oh!' I said, 'I hope not quite as bad as that, General.' 'Perhaps not. Reno is keeping up the fight. He is not stampeded. I am not stampeded. You are not stampeded. That is about all, sir, my God that's about all.' It is impossible to describe the extreme bitterness and vehemence with which he uttered these words as he rode away."

Further Exploration   To visit Portici, the scene of the cavalry engagement between Buford's and *Robertson's* men (and where Confederate Brig. Gen. *Joseph Johnston* established his command post during the First Battle of Manassas), *turn left* on exiting the Visitor Center onto SUDLEY ROAD (VA 234) and proceed 0.4 mile to the traffic light. *Turn left* onto BATTLEVIEW PARKWAY and drive 0.8 mile to the entrance on Portici on the left. *Turn here* and proceed to the parking area at the end of the road. Exit your vehicle and follow the trail for about 250 yards to the NPS markers "Confederate Headquarters" and "Cavalry Clash."

Further Reading　Hennessy, *Return to Bull Run*, 408–37; Hennessy, *Second Manassas Map Study*, 349, 358–59, 373, 378, 384, 387–88, 391, 403, 406–51; Patchan, *Second Manassas*, 83–107.

A tempting breastwork.
BLCW 2:196.

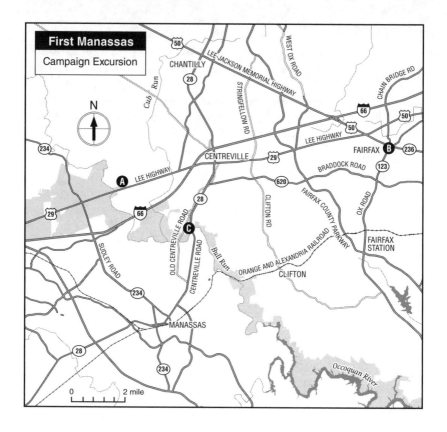

FIRST MANASSAS CAMPAIGN EXCURSION

Directions

Exit the parking area for the Henry Hill Visitor Center. *Turn right* onto SUDLEY ROAD (VA 234) and proceed 0.4 mile to the intersection with LEE HIGHWAY (U.S. 29). *Turn right* at the intersection onto LEE HIGHWAY. *Proceed* 1.4 miles to the parking area for Stone Bridge on the left side of the road. Exit your vehicle and *follow the trail* at the end of the parking lot for 100 yards to the overlook by the NPS marker "Stone Bridge: Strategic Crossing," *or continue* for about another 100 yards on the trail across the bridge, then *turn right* and follow the path for about 25 yards. *Stop here* and face east toward the bridge and Bull Run, which flows from left to right in front of you.

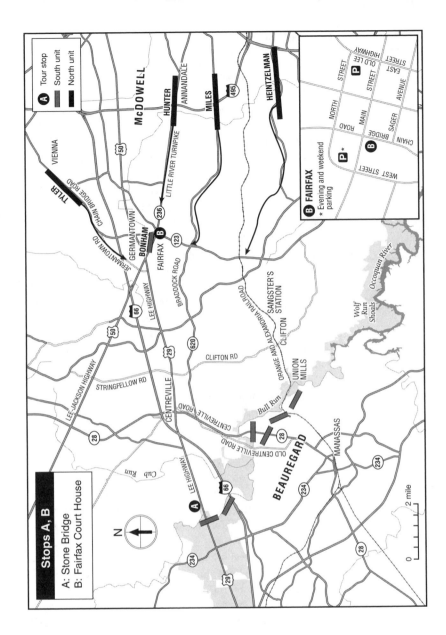

Stops A, B

A: Stone Bridge
B: Fairfax Court House

STOP A Stone Bridge

Orientation The Stone Bridge is the point where the historic Warrenton and Alexandria Turnpike (modern U.S. 29, Lee Highway) crossed Bull Run. The turnpike's intersection with the Sudley Road is a little over 1 mile west of where you are standing. The point where U.S. 29 crosses Cub Run is about 2 miles east of you, while Centreville is about 4. Sudley Ford is about 2 miles upstream, while Union Mills is about 8 miles downstream.

The Confederate Position along Bull Run,
April 23–July 15, 1861

What Happened

Confederate forces began assembling around Manassas Junction less than a week after the Virginia Convention voted to take the commonwealth out of the Union. The first commander was *Philip St. George Cocke*, who assumed command there on April 23. One month later, as a result of the transfer of Virginia troops to Confederate service, *Cocke* was superseded in command by Brig. Gen. *Milledge Bonham* of South Carolina. *Bonham* arrived to find that *Cocke* had pushed outposts all the way forward to the Potomac River. When Federal troops crossed the river on May 24, one day after Virginia voters ratified the convention's decision for secession, to seize Arlington Heights and Alexandria, *Bonham* ordered his advance units to pull back to Fairfax Court House and pushed his men to strengthen their positions around Manassas Junction. On June 1 the Confederate outpost at Fairfax Court House repulsed a Federal raiding force in a small skirmish that saw the first Confederate officer killed in battle of the entire war.

Bonham's tenure in command would be short-lived. The same day as the skirmish at Fairfax, Brig. Gen. *Pierre G. T. Beauregard*, the man who had commanded the effort to capture Fort Sumter in April, was in Richmond receiving instructions to take command at Manassas. Upon his arrival, *Beauregard* went to work organizing his troops. He dispatched *Bonham* to the army's advanced position at Fairfax Court House to command the troops there and deployed his command as best he could behind Bull Run. Counting *Bonham's* force, by mid-July *Beauregard* had seven brigades in his approximately 22,000-man Army of the Potomac.

By July 17 the six Confederate brigades behind Bull Run held a line extending from a point near Union Mills where the Orange and Alexandria Railroad crossed the creek to the Stone Bridge, which carried the Warrenton Turnpike over the creek. *Beauregard* concentrated most of his command around Blackburn's Ford, where the direct road from Centreville to Manassas Junction crossed the creek. On the far right, Brig. Gen. *Richard Ewell's* brigade guarded the railroad crossing at Union Mills, while on the far left Col. *Nathan Evans's* brigade guarded the Stone Bridge. Just downstream from *Evans, Cocke's* brigade guarded Lewis and Ball's Fords. Next in line came Brig. Gen. *James Longstreet's* brigade at Blackburn's Ford, with Col. *Jubal Early's* brigade in close support. Just downstream from there, Col. *David R. Jones's* command covered McLean's Ford.

STOP B	Fairfax Court House

Directions

Exit the parking area and *turn left* onto U.S. 29 (LEE HIGHWAY). *Proceed* 9.8 miles, then *turn right* onto MAIN STREET (VA 236). At 1 mile the historic Fairfax Court House will appear on your right, at the corner of the intersection of MAIN STREET and CHAIN BRIDGE ROAD (VA 123). If visiting during the evening or on the weekend, you will find convenient parking on the left-hand (north) side of the road about a block before you reach the courthouse. If visiting during the week, you will have to hunt for an available spot along MAIN STREET or use a lot a bit farther away. This can be found by *continuing* on MAIN STREET one block past the courthouse, then *turning left* onto UNIVERSITY DRIVE, after which you will see it on the right. From your vehicle, walk over to the front yard (at the MAIN STREET–CHAIN BRIDGE ROAD intersection) of the courthouse, where you will see two cannon and a monument to Capt. John Quincy Marr, who became the first Confederate officer killed during the war, when he was fatally wounded in a skirmish at Fairfax Court House on June 1, 1861. Walk over to the monument and do the stop here.

The Federal Advance to Fairfax Court House, July 16–17, 1861

What Happened

When Brig. Gen. Irvin McDowell ordered his Federal army of about 35,000 men to begin their march out of Washington on July 16, 1861, his first objective was to capture *Bonham's* command at Fairfax Court House. Thus he drew up a plan whereby the various divisions of his army would advance on that place from three directions. He directed Col. David Hunter's division to advance on Fairfax Court House directly by first marching west along the Columbia Turnpike to Annandale on July 16, then marching from Annandale to Fairfax along the Little River Turnpike (modern 236). Meanwhile Brig. Gen. Daniel Tyler's division was ordered to march first to Vienna on the 16th, then turn south to try to reach a position just west of Fairfax Court House near a small hamlet known as Jermantown, from which he could interdict the Confederate line of retreat back to Bull Run. Col. Dixon Miles's division would march west just south of Hunter's command and take the Braddock Road to a point from which it could advance on Fairfax Court House from the south. Finally, Col. Samuel Heintzelman received orders to march along the Orange and Alexandria Railroad to cover Miles's southern flank and try to reach a position from where he might be able to cross the Occoquan River (which Bull Run flows into) at Wolf Run Shoals to turn the right flank of *Beauregard's* line.

While good on paper, in light of the fact that it would be impossible to conceal the march of over 30,000 troops out of Washington, it was unlikely that even veteran troops with a good understanding of the road network could have successfully executed McDowell's plan quickly enough to prevent *Bonham* from escaping Fairfax Court House. For McDowell's green troops, there was no chance. Word reached *Bonham* that the Federals were approaching, and during the early afternoon of July 17 he directed his men to begin evacuating Fairfax Court House—just as the head of Tyler's command was approaching Jermantown and before Hunter's lead brigade entered Fairfax Court House from the east.

When McDowell arrived on the scene, he found Tyler's and Hunter's men looting and burning buildings in Fairfax Court House and Jermantown. After putting a stop to this, McDowell called Tyler to headquarters and directed him to advance along the Warrenton Turnpike toward Centreville the next day. He then rode over to Sangster's Station on the Orange and Alexandria to meet with Heintzelman and see how the effort to turn the Confederate right was going. By the time he finished discussing the situation with Heintzelman and reconnoitering the ground, McDowell concluded that the region was too wooded and roads too poor to hope that Heintzelman could successfully turn the Confederate right. Consequently he directed Heintzelman to move to Centreville and unite his division with the rest of the Federal army there.

Vignette

Leading the march to Fairfax Court House along the Little River Turnpike from Annandale on July 17 was the brigade commanded by Col. Ambrose Burnside, one of whose men later recalled, "Fairfax Court House was rendered untenable by the disposition of General McDowell's force. Nothing more formidable was found than an abandoned open breastwork, which had evidently been held by a battery of light artillery, and which had served to guard the road against any reconnoitering party. Fairfax Court House was occupied about noon. . . . The first regiment to enter the town, after the skirmishers, was the Second [Rhode Island], and Sergeant [J. M.] Duffy was ordered to display the national flag from the top of one of the buildings in the outskirts of the village, as an indication to General Tyler's column, which was advancing upon another road, that the place was in our hands. The town stands upon high ground, and the outlook was wide. The secession flag, however, was still flying from the flag-staff on the court house itself. Sergeant [James] Taggart and Corporal [A.] McMahon of Company A determined to capture it. The corporal ascended to the cupola and had the satisfaction of detaching the symbol of rebellion. As it was thrown from the roof it was caught by Taggart, and by him was handed over to the proper authorities. The sight of the flag and of the abandoned stores of the enemy somewhat inflamed the men, and the defenceless state of the town, so lately evacuated, invited plunder. As the troops were permitted to roam at will, many excesses were committed and considerable damage was done in and about the place, much to the mortification of the better disciplined part of the command. General McDowell was especially indignant, and issued a stringent order, in condemnation of such practices."

Feeling the enemy.
From a war-time sketch.
BLCW 3:224.

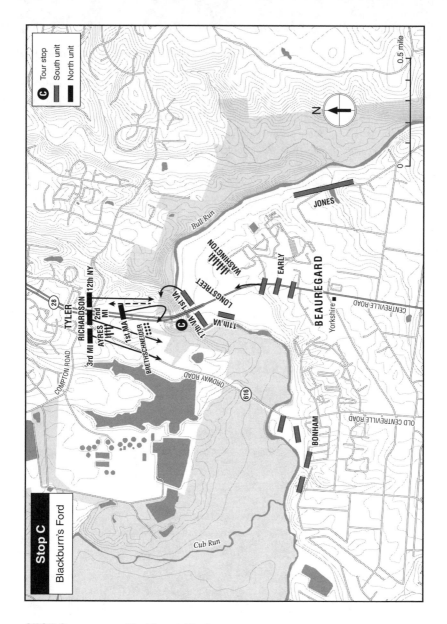

STOP C   Blackburn's Ford

Directions   Drive 1 mile west on MAIN STREET (VA 236) back to its intersection with LEE HIGHWAY (U.S. 29). *Turn left* onto LEE HIGHWAY and proceed 5.7 miles, then *turn left* onto OLD CENTREVILLE ROAD (VA 898). Drive 0.4 mile on OLD CENTREVILLE ROAD to the intersection with CENTREVILLE ROAD (VA 28). *Turn left* onto CENTREVILLE ROAD and proceed 2.3 miles. *Pull off* to access a side road on the right side of the road, whose location is indicated by a Civil War Trails sign. You will then immediately *turn left* to reach the parking area. As you enter the trail leading from the parking area, you will immediately see two Virginia Civil War Trails markers, "Blackburn's Ford: Guarding the Fords" and "Blackburn's Ford: Bullets 'Humming Like a Bee-hive.'" You can either walk over to the signs and do the stand there, or follow the trail down to the creek and do it there. Face toward Bull Run.

The Battle of Blackburn's Ford, July 18, 1861

What Happened   Despite clear orders from McDowell not to bring on an engagement with the Confederates, when Tyler's command reached Centreville during the morning of July 18 its commander could not restrain himself. By 10:00 a.m. he and the commander of his lead brigade, Col. Israel Richardson, had decided to push forward a force of about 150 men under the command of Capt. Robert Brethschneider toward Bull Run along the road connecting Centreville with Manassas Junction. Shortly before reaching the creek, the road divided, with one branch leading to Mitchell's Ford and the other leading to Blackburn's Ford. Guarding Mitchell's Ford was *Bonham's* command, which had assumed responsibility for its defense after falling back from Fairfax Court House. The Blackburn's Ford crossing was defended by *Longstreet's* brigade. *Bonham's* command was much larger than *Longstreet's*. It also had a more defensible position due to the fact that the Confederate side of the creek was fortified with earthworks and commanded the other side. At Blackburn's, though, the ground on the left bank was higher and provided good positions for engaging the Confederates on the west side.

As Tyler and Richardson struggled to get a good sense of the Confederate positions, Maj. John G. Barnard of McDowell's staff arrived on the scene and reminded them that the army commander did not want a battle that day. He also told them, though, that he did not think McDowell would object to their conducting a demonstration against the Confederate line.

Tyler eagerly seized upon this to order Brethschneider's men to continue moving forward toward Blackburn's Ford and called up two rifled guns to support them. When Capt. Romeyn Ayres's artillery reached the front, Tyler ordered them to open fire in the direction of the creek. The Confederates, however, wisely refused to reveal their positions and strength by returning fire. Ignoring the entreaties of Barnard not to do so, Tyler ordered Richardson to advance toward Bull Run.

As Richardson moved forward, skirmishers *Longstreet* had posted east of the creek rushed back to their comrades. The Confederates south of Bull Run immediately prepared for battle, and when three companies from the 1st Massachusetts commanded by Lt. Col. George Wells came within range, the Confederates opened fire. The Federals responded by charging toward the creek but were unable to reach it due to the volume of fire that ripped through their ranks. Wells's men recoiled back to the ridge overlooking the creek and returned fire. As they did so, Tyler decided to push Ayres's guns farther forward and agreed to Richardson's proposal that he advance his entire brigade and see if a charge across the creek might be a suitable course of action.

When Ayres's guns completed their move forward and fired a round of canister across the creek, the Confederates responded with such a volume of fire that Tyler later declared, "It appeared to me that there were 5,000 muskets fired at once." This convinced Tyler he had accomplished all that he could and it was time to break off the fight. However, by this point Richardson's men had become too heavily engaged to pull back. As Ayres's gunners began to quiver under the weight of the fire being directed at them, Col. Ezra Walrath decided the best way to secure their position was to push his 12th New York command forward into the woods on the left side of the road. Upon reaching the woods, Walrath's men advanced almost to Bull Run before *Longstreet's* men brought them to a halt. A sharp engagement between Walrath's New Yorkers and the Confederates lasted for about twenty minutes. It ended when one of Walrath's subordinates ordered his men to retreat, and within minutes the rest of the regiment followed suit. Walrath and Richardson tried to rally them but to avail.

As Walrath's men pulled back, some of *Longstreet's* men decided to push across Bull Run in pursuit. In doing so they put themselves in an excellent position to attack the flank of the three regiments from Richardson's command on the other side of the road. Although unable to drive them from the field, this development convinced Tyler to ignore Richardson's request to continue the fight. As the Federals withdrew, a few intrepid Confederates made a brief stab at a pursuit but broke it off when *Longstreet* ordered his infantry back across the creek. The two sides then exchanged artillery fire until around 4:00 p.m., when Tyler's guns pulled back toward Centreville. When McDowell arrived on the scene shortly thereafter, his anger toward Tyler was evident to all who came in contact with him. His command had suffered 83 casualties in the fight at Blackburn's Ford, compared to 68 on the Confederate side, and done nothing to advance the prospects for Federal success at Bull Run.

Vignette   As the first fight in which he and his comrades participated, the fight at Blackburn's Ford made a profound impression on

Alexander Hunter of the 17th Virginia, who later recalled, "With a sudden, frightful distinctness two guns went off less than twenty yards from us. . . . Instantly every man was on his feet, gun in hand. 'Fall in, men; fall in! Right dress!' came in quick succession from the colonel, and in a few seconds the line was formed and dressed. Now burst on our untried ears a rattling, stunning volley of musketry. Beginning down the stream some hundreds of yards and rolling toward us, the iron hail approached and hustled in our midst. The volley caused an icy shiver amongst us. The screaming hiss of the Minie-ball was frightful enough of itself to make the heart stand still, but the thud of the stroke against the body of some comrade, the sight of falling men, wounded and killed, was more terrible than any words can describe; it froze the blood in our veins.

"How we wanted to run! Many a man of us could have discounted the fabled winged Mercury in a fair-field race. . . . Every time a bullet whizzed near a man he would wince. Some would half drop down, and some very nervous fellow would give a howl as if he was actually struck. . . . But others stood their ground, firing back at an unseen foe, never flinching; others again, who had at first retreated, shamed by such brave example, rallied and advanced, until the flower of the Seventeenth stood game in their tracks. . . .

"Loading and firing sent the blood rushing through the veins. Instead of retiring, many of the men began to advance; and no longer firing wildly at the sun, and pulling trigger at the sky, they became cool and composed and discharged their muskets at the flash of the enemy's guns. It was earnest work; the bulldog instinct of humanity all aroused. No longer were needed the officers' commands. The whole line reformed itself, and standing stubbornly on the fringe of the woods delivered rattling volleys across the stream. . . . On the left of the ford there was a large tree. It was about ten yards from the water's edge, a great big sycamore, whose trunk was fully five feet in diameter, and whose spreading branches rose some fifty feet in the air. The flying bullets and hurrying shells had played the mischief with its top boughs, and the ground was covered with leaves and twigs cut off by the leaden and iron shower. On the safe side of the broad, knotty trunk some of the most timid had taken refuge, one behind the other. They had cast away their guns and they hugged each file leader close, forming a string of about forty men. The shells had frightened them, evidently preventing their departure to the rear. It was the screaming, shrieking, bursting shrapnel shot that kept them glued together.

"A shell from the enemy's battery on the left would hiss by them, and the whole string would gravitate toward the right, so as to get the sturdy trunk between them and the shot. All at once another battery on the right opened up on our lines, the balls sailing through the empty space, then the men, almost delirious with terror, would hang close and swing around on the opposite side, but only for a second. Here would come a shell from the left, and away would go the line like a pendulum, back through the half arc of the circle, and hardly a moment for breathing time before a half hundred weight of iron would rush by the tree with a demoniac yell, and the long, agonized queue described another parabolic curve. And so the band of brothers were kept shifting to and fro; the fortunate ones next to the tree having nothing to do comparatively, while those who composed the end of the string were kept on the swing all the time. . . .

"I was sitting on a log when two of the foe, beardless youths, came up to me and said they were lost and did not know what to do. I told them that I would show them the way, and we walked back to the ford, and they were very much surprised when they saw our men in solid line of battle, across the stream. I carried them about a half mile to the rear and they told me that they were from Boston, and that they were glad after all that they were prisoners; that the war would only last a few months and they wanted to see the inner life of the Rebels so that they would have lots to tell their folks at home. So that's how I captured two prisoners. I am free to confess that had they ordered me to follow them when in the woods, I certainly would have obeyed.

"Around the camp-fire that night rather big yarns were told, and most tremendous bragging done. Some went so far as to show notches on the stocks of their rifles for every man they had killed. Others narrated narrow escapes and displayed, by way of illustration, the hole torn in cap or jacket, the only damage done; but more were silent, willing, it is supposed, to let some future record speak their praises. . . . Many of us were beginning to think the war was over, fancying the little affair at Blackburn's Ford, wherein the enemy had lost a hundred men, had demonstrated the uselessness of any attempt to subjugate the South, and that with enlightened minds they had marched back to Washington, soon to sue for peace on the basis of the Southern Confederacy."

Further Reading   Hennessy, *The First Battle of Manassas*, 2–25; Rafuse, *A Single Grand Victory*, 72–99; Davis, *Battle at Bull Run*, 90–131; Gottfried, *The Maps of First Bull Run*, 4–21.

To return to Henry Hill Visitor Center: Return to your vehicle and *turn right* onto CENTREVILLE ROAD (VA 28). *Proceed* 3.5 miles, then *turn right* onto SUDLEY ROAD (VA Business 234). Drive 5.1 miles to the entrance to Henry Hill Visitor Center on the right.

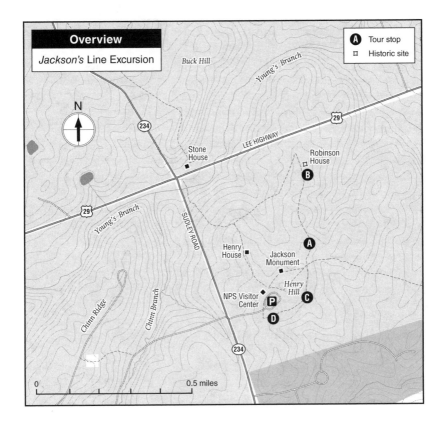

JACKSON'S LINE EXCURSION

Directions   From the *Jackson* monument, *follow* the mowed path for about 125 yards to the Confederate gun line, then *turn left* and proceed about 100 yards along the gun line to a point between the N PS markers "Historic Farm Road Trace" and "Various sections of Virginia Artillery." *Turn left* here and face toward the Henry House and Bull Run Monument.

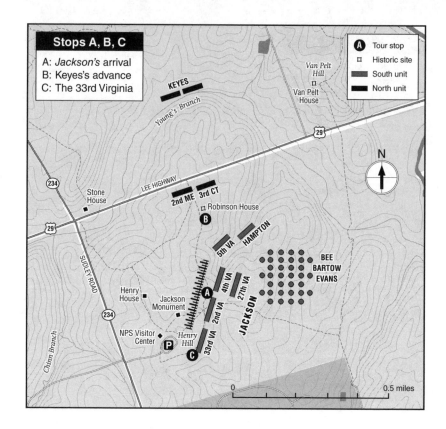

STOP A

Jackson's Arrival

Orientation

As the sign indicates, you are standing where in 1861 a farm road connecting Portici (site of Confederate headquarters for much of the battle) and the Sudley Road crossed Henry Hill. It was this road that *Jackson* used to reach the southeastern edge of the Henry Hill plateau, where you are now standing.

What Happened

Shortly before noon the five regiments of Brig. Gen. *Thomas J. Jackson's* brigade arrived on Henry Hill. *Jackson's* command had reached Manassas Junction from the Shenandoah Valley on July 19 and began the morning of July 21 by taking up positions from which it could reinforce the Confederate units around Blackburn's Ford. Shortly thereafter, *Jackson* received orders to move upstream toward the Stone Bridge, but upon learning of the fighting on Matthews Hill reoriented his march to follow a small farm road through the woods that led to Henry Hill. *Jackson* arrived as the forces that had fought at Matthews Hill were falling back and, when informed by Brig. Gen. *Barnard Bee* what had happened, replied, "Sir, we will give them the bayonet."

Jackson then deployed his five regiments under the shelter of the woods at the edge of the plateau. He posted the 4th and

27th Virginia in direct support of the artillery, with the 5th Virginia extending the Confederate right to near the Robinson House. To the left of the 4th and 27th Virginia, he deployed the 2nd Virginia and, at the far end of his line, the 33rd Virginia.

Vignette

Capt. *John Imboden* later wrote of events after he and his battery had been forced from their position overlooking the Stone House intersection, "We crossed the summit at the edge of the pines, midway behind the Henry and Robinson houses, and there met *'Stonewall' Jackson* at the head of his brigade, marching by the flank at a double-quick. . . . When I met *Jackson* I felt very angry at what I then regarded as bad treatment from General *Bee*, in leaving us so long exposed to capture, and I expressed myself with some profanity, which I could see was displeasing to *Jackson*. He remarked, 'I'll support your battery. Unlimber right here.' We did so, when a perfect lull in the conflict ensued for 20 or 30 minutes—at least in that part of the field. . . . When my retiring battery met *Jackson*, and he assumed command of us, I reported that I had remaining only three rounds of ammunition for a single gun, and suggested that the caissons be sent to the rear for a supply. He said, 'No, not now-wait till other guns get here, and then you can withdraw your battery, as it has been so torn to pieces, and let your men rest.'

"During the lull in front, my men lay about, exhausted from want of water and food, and black with powder, smoke, and dust. Lieutenant [*Thomas L.*] *Harman* and I had amused ourselves training one of the guns on a heavy column of the enemy . . . 1,200 to 1,500 yards away. While we were thus engaged, General *Jackson* rode up and said that three or four batteries were approaching rapidly, and that we might soon retire. I asked permission to fire the three rounds of shrapnel left to us, and he said, 'Go ahead.' I picked up a charge (the fuse was cut and ready) and rammed it home myself, remarking to *Harman*, 'Tom, put in the primer and pull her off.' I forgot to step back far enough from the muzzle, and, as I wanted to see the shell strike, I squatted to be under the smoke, and gave the word 'Fire.' Heavens! what a report. Finding myself full twenty feet away, I thought the gun had burst. But it was only the pent-up gas, that, escaping sideways as the shot cleared the muzzle, had struck my side and head with great violence. I recovered in time to see the shell explode in the enemy's ranks. The blood gushed out of my left ear, and from that day to this it has been totally deaf. The men fired the other two rounds, and limbered up and moved away. . . . The contest that ensued was terrific. *Jackson* ordered me to go from battery to battery and see that the guns were properly aimed and the fuses cut the right length. This was the work of but a few minutes. On returning to the left of the line of guns, I stopped to ask General *Jackson's* permission to rejoin my battery. The fight was just then hot enough to make him feel well. His eyes fairly blazed. He had a way of throwing up his left hand with the open palm toward the person he was addressing. And as he told me to go, he made this gesture. The air was full of flying missiles, and as he spoke he jerked down his hand, and I saw that blood was streaming from it. I exclaimed, 'General, you are wounded.' He replied, as he drew a handkerchief from his breast-pocket, and began to bind it up, 'Only a scratch-a mere scratch,' and galloped away along his line."

STOP B   Keyes's Advance

Directions   *Turn right* and continue walking along the trail for about 450 yards to the foundation of the Robinson House. Stand facing the location of the house and LEE HIGHWAY.

Orientation   To your front and left, clearly visible on the other side of the road, is Matthews Hill. To your front and right on the other side of Lee Highway the cleared high ground is known as Van Pelt Hill, which is where *Evans* had his headquarters when the battle began early on July 21, 1861. In the low ground behind you is where Confederate troops that had been routed on Matthews Hill rallied behind the protection of *Jackson's* line.

What Happened   At around 12:30 p.m. *Jackson's* line received its first test. At midmorning two brigades from Tyler's division crossed Bull Run about 600 yards upstream from the Stone Bridge. One of Tyler's brigades then marched west and linked up with the rest of McDowell's command north of the Stone House intersection. The other brigade, Col. Erasmus Keyes's, however, received orders from Tyler to halt several hundred yards to the east. Tyler then, without notifying McDowell, directed Keyes to deploy his four regiments and lead two of them south in the direction of the Warrenton Turnpike. Keyes's men quickly brushed aside a small Confederate cavalry force, crossed Young's Branch, and then pushed up the slope of Henry Hill toward the Robinson House. As they surged across the Warrenton Turnpike, howling, in the words of one participant, "as if two thousand demons had been suddenly let loose from Pandemonium," Keyes's two regiments advanced on the position held by Col. *Kenton Harper's* 5th Virginia, as well as elements from Col. *Wade Hampton's* Legion and the forces that had earlier fought on Matthews Hill. Taken by surprise and initially concerned that the force advancing toward them might be friendly, the Confederates briefly held their fire. By the time they recognized the advancing forces were Federals, they fired a few volleys but were eventually compelled to fall back.

Fortunately for *Jackson, Harper's* Virginians and the other Confederates on that section of the line were able to rally in the woods. Supported by fire from Capt. *H. Grey Latham's* Lynchburg Artillery, they poured a fierce fire into the Federal ranks. Keyes's men held their ground for a few moments—long enough for one of the thirsty men to attempt to drink out of a puddle in which the Robinsons' pigs had been wallowing—but with no support anywhere nearby, Tyler and Keyes had no choice but to break off the attack and fall back across the turnpike and back down the hill.

Analysis

Tyler and Keyes had unwittingly brought their forces onto the field at Manassas in a magnificent position to significantly alter the entire course of the battle in favor of the Union. Had they maintained the momentum of their advance, they might have rolled up *Jackson's* right flank and possibly destroyed whatever hope the Confederates had of holding their position on Henry Hill. Unfortunately at no time does it seem Tyler or Keyes comprehended that such an opportunity might be before them. Thus they committed only two regiments to the fight, which proved insufficient to accomplish anything decisive. Moreover their attack was made in isolation. Neither man made an attempt to contact McDowell to find out what the situation was on the rest of the field or what the commanding general's intentions were at that point in the battle, inform him of what they were doing, or attempt to coordinate their actions with the rest of the Union army. This was no doubt attributable largely to fatigue and inexperience on the part of Tyler and Keyes. The fact that Tyler resented being subordinate to the much younger McDowell and their relationship had been further soured by headquarters' manifest displeasure with Tyler's defying orders to initiate the fight at Blackburn's Ford on July 18 undoubtedly played a part as well. It would not be the last time in the Civil War that the bravery and enthusiasm of Billy Yank would go for naught, and an opportunity lost for a Federal army, due to problems in the high command.

STOP C   The 33rd Virginia

Directions   Turn around and *retrace your steps* for 500 yards to the NPS
                        marker "Like a Stone Wall." *Continue* walking along the gun
                        line, following the NPS trail for another 50 yards to a point
                        near the NPS marker "Washington (Louisiana) Artillery Bat-
                        talion," where it forks. *Continue straight* (if you turn right, you
                        will be returning to the *Jackson* monument and Visitor Center)
                        for about 175 yards to the NPS marker "Charge on Griffin's
                        Guns." *Turn right* here and face toward the Visitor Center.

What Happened   Col. *Arthur C. Cummings's* 33rd Virginia, which held the left of
                        Jackson's line and played an important role in the fight for
                        Henry Hill, was positioned in this area upon their arrival on
                        the field. *Jackson* demonstrated a keen eye for terrain in select-
                        ing the position for his infantry line. Here and elsewhere
                        along this side of the Henry Hill plateau, the men of *Jackson's*
                        brigade enjoyed the cover of the woods and a reverse slope
                        position behind a rise of ground that sheltered them from
                        enemy observation and artillery fire. It was from this posi-
                        tion that they would make a charge on a Union artillery posi-
                        tion that would turn the tide of the battle on Henry Hill.

Vignette   "After taking our position on the left of the brigade," *Randolph
                        Barton* of the 33rd Virginia later recalled, "we laid upon the
                        ground listening to the musketry and cannonading going on
                        to our right, or, rather, somewhat in front of our right, from
                        the Confederate fores, which was being vigorously responded
                        to by the Yankees. The 'Henry house' was in front of our bri-
                        gade, over the hill—the upper part of the house visible—and
                        the Robinson house was to the right of that a few hundred
                        yards. Occasional shells would explode over our regiment,
                        and the solemn wonderment written on the faces of the men
                        as they would crane their heads around to look out for fall-
                        ing branches was almost amusing. I was near the left flank
                        of the regiment, a few steps in rear, where, upon the forma-
                        tion of the regiment in line of battle, I belonged. Doubtless I
                        wished I was home, but I had to stick. I remember an elderly
                        man riding leisurely by towards the left, in rear of us, appar-
                        ently giving orders. . . . It was, in fact, Colonel [*William*] Smith,
                        a game old fellow, who, I suppose, was looking over the ground
                        for a position for his regiment, the 49th Virginia, as it subse-
                        quently took position on our left, and finally united in one
                        of the charges upon [Capt. Charles] Griffin's Battery.
                            "Colonel *Cummings* and Lieutenant Colonel [*E. G.*] *Lee* were
                        in front of our regiment, perhaps a hundred yards, stooping
                        down, and occasionally standing to get a view over the crest

of the hill that rose gently before us for a little over a hundred yards. The musketry kept up on our right, and then Colonels *Cummings* and *Lee* were seen to rise and, bending down, to come back with somewhat quickened steps to the regiment. I remember, as Colonel *Cummings* drew near, he called out: 'Boys, they are coming, now wait until they get close before you fire.'

"Almost immediately several pieces of artillery, their horses in front, made their appearance on the hill in front of us, curving as if going into battery, and at the same time I descried the spear-point and upper portion of a United States flag, as it rose in the hands of its bearer over the hill; then I saw the bearer, and the heads of the men composing the line of battle to the right and left of him. At the sight several of our men rose from the ranks, leveled their muskets at the line, and, although I called out, 'Do not fire yet,' it was of no use; they fired and then the shrill cry of Colonel *Cummings* was heard, 'Charge!' and away the regiment went, firing as they ran, into the ranks of the enemy, and particularly at the battery towards which our line rapidly approached."

STOP D   *Stuart's* Charge

Directions   From here, note how the mowed trail forks. *Take the left trail* (not the one that takes you directly to the Visitor Center). *Proceed* west for about 125 yards to the two cannon, then *continue* for another 100 yards beyond that to a rise from where you will have a clear view down to the Sudley Road. *Stop here* and face west toward the Sudley Road.

What Happened   As Capt. James B. Ricketts and Griffin led their guns up to Henry Hill, Maj. William Barry and McDowell went to work rounding up infantry support. Soon four units, Col. Willis Gorman's 1st Minnesota, Col. A. M. Wood's 14th Brooklyn, Maj. J. G. Reynolds's battalion of U.S. Marines, and Col. W. C. Farnham's 11th New York, were moving forward. Farnham's unit was perhaps the best known in the entire Union army in 1861. They were known popularly as the Fire Zouaves due to the distinctively colorful uniforms the men had worn when they were first organized and the fact that many of its members had been New York City fireman. (By the time of the battle, though, only their fireman-red shirts remained a particularly distinctive part of their uniform. The 14th Brooklyn, which had also adopted elements of the Zouave uniform, did fight at Manassas clad in red pants and kepis.) The 11th New York's first commander had been Col. Elmer Ellsworth. In addition to being a close friend of President Lincoln, in May Ellsworth had become the first Union officer killed in the

Civil War when, after pulling a secessionist flag down from the roof of a house in Alexandria, he was shot dead by its owner.

Upon reaching Henry Hill, Gorman's and Farnham's commands, accompanied by division commander Col. Samuel Heintzelman, moved up from the Sudley Road to a position to the right of Ricketts's position. There they encountered the men of the 33rd Virginia. Heintzelman, unable to determine to which side they belonged, directed his men to hold their fire long enough to enable the Confederates to send a series of effectively aimed volleys into Gorman's and Farnham's ranks. Not only were the two regiments compelled to fall back, but *Cummings's* volleys also had the range to reach Ricketts's guns. The intense fire they showered on Ricketts's position and the sight of men falling shattered the nerves of the battalion of recently recruited U.S. Marines directly supporting Ricketts's guns. As the Marines fled the field, Ricketts cried out in vain, "For God's sake boys, save my battery!"

Any chance that the Federals who managed to fall back to the Sudley Road might return to the fight and provide further help to Ricketts was soon eliminated, for after reaching the road they found themselves dealing with a new problem. To secure the flanks of his line on Henry Hill, *Jackson* had asked Col. *James E. B. Stuart* to provide cavalry to cover them. *Stuart* did so and at this point in the battle had about 150 men under his personal command under the cover of woods south of the Henry house. Seeing the Federal infantry endeavoring to rally in the Sudley Road, *Stuart* sensed an opportunity and ordered his men to charge down the road.

Stuart's men rushed forward so fast that it was not until they were about 50 yards away that the Federals realized what was happening. Although able to quickly form a line and get off a single volley, the weight and power of the Confederate charge was too much for them to handle and they were soon fleeing to the woods west of Sudley Road. With *Jackson's* flank secured, *Stuart* pulled back to his previous position.

Vignette

One of *Stuart's* staff officers later provided a vivid description of the charge along the Sudley Road. "Colonel *Stuart* and myself," he wrote, "were riding at the head of the column as the grand panorama opened before us, and there right in front, about seventy yards distant, and in strong relief against the smoke beyond, stretched a brilliant line of scarlet.... With a fringe of bayonets swaying above them as they moved, their appearance was indeed magnificent.... Waving his sabre, Stuart ordered a charge, but instantly pulled up and called a halt and turning to me said, 'Blackford, are those our men or the enemy?' I said I could not tell, but I had heard that Beauregard had a regiment of Zouaves from New Orleans. . . . Just then, however, all doubt was removed by the appearance of their colors, emerging from the road—the Stars and Stripes. . . . The instant the flag appeared, Stuart ordered the charge, and at them we went like an arrow from a bow. . . .

"Half the distance was passed before they saw the avalanche coming upon them, but then they came to a 'front face'—a long line of bright muskets was leveled—a sheet of red flame gleamed, and we could see no more. . . . The smoke which wrapped them from our sight also hid us from them, and thinking perhaps that we had been swept away by the volley, they, instead of coming to a 'charge bayonet,' lowered their pieces to load, and in this position we struck them. The tremendous impetus of horses at full speed broke through and scattered their line like chaff before the wind. As the scarlet line appeared through the smoke, when within a couple of horse's lengths of them, I leaned down, with my carbine cocked, thumb on hammer and forefinger on trigger, and fixed my eye on a tall fellow I saw would be the one my course would place in the right position for the carbine, while the man next to him, in front of the horse, I would have to leave to Comet. I then plunged the spurs into Comet's flanks and he evidently thought I wanted him to jump over this strange looking wall I was riding him at, for he rose to make the leap; but he was too close and going to fast to rise higher than the breast of the man, and he struck him full on the chest, rolling him over and over under hoofs and knocking him about ten feet backwards. . . . As Comet rose to make the leap, I leaned down from the saddle, rammed the muzzle of the carbine into the stomach of my man and pulled the trigger. I could not help feeling a little sorry for the fellow as he lifted his handsome face to mine while he tried to get his bayonet up to meet me; but he was too slow, for the carbine blew a hole as big as my arm clear through him."

Further Reading   Hennessy, *The First Battle of Manassas*, 68–108; Rafuse, *A Single Grand Victory*, 148–82; Gottfried, *The Maps of First Bull Run*, 41–47.

To return to the main tour: *Retrace* your steps back to the two cannon. Stand between them and face in the direction they are pointing. The *Jackson* monument will be to your left front. This marks the point that this excursion rejoins the main Henry Hill tour. Turn to page 35 and substop 4D ("Griffin's Ordeal") and pick up the narrative there.

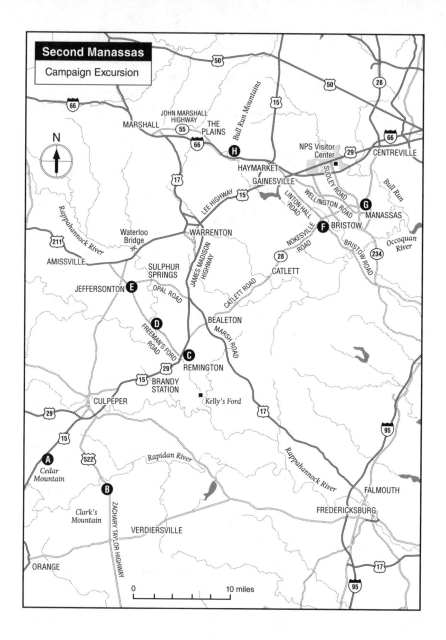

SECOND MANASSAS CAMPAIGN EXCURSION

This excursion will take you to sites that figured prominently in the operations of August 1862 that in a few short weeks carried the war from the banks of the Rapidan River to the banks of Bull Run. It will give you a good sense of the amount of ground these operations covered and the command decisions and events that shaped them. Because it involves travel over a number of back roads, it is recommended that you read this section, as well as the Road to Second Manassas chapter that appears along with the core tour, before you head out on this excursion in order to develop a fair understanding of what this will involve in terms of time and effort and to get a general understanding of what happened before you visit the specific sites.

Directions   Exit the parking lot of the Henry Hill Visitor Center and *turn right* onto SUDLEY ROAD (VA 234). *Proceed* 0.4 mile to the traffic light and *turn left* onto LEE HIGHWAY (U.S. 29). Travel 15 miles to where LEE HIGHWAY becomes the EASTERN BYPASS. *En route* it has become U.S. 29/U.S. 15; at the EASTERN BYPASS it also picks up U.S. 17. *Proceed* 3 miles until EASTERN BYPASS (U.S. 29/15/17) becomes JAMES MADISON HIGHWAY. *Continue* on JAMES MADISON HIGHWAY for 23 miles until you reach the point where U.S. 29 and U.S. 15 split south of Culpeper. U.S. 29 becomes JAMES MONROE HIGHWAY, while U.S. 15 continues as JAMES MADISON HIGHWAY. *Take the exit* to JAMES MADISON HIGHWAY (U.S. 15), and at the top of the ramp *turn left* toward Orange, then proceed 4.3 miles to GENERAL WINDER ROAD (VA 657). *Turn right* onto GENERAL WINDER ROAD and drive 0.1 mile. You will see a small parking area on the right side of the road where WINDER ROAD makes a sharp bend to the left. *Pull over here* and park your vehicle. Walk over to the historical marker "Cedar Mountain: Jackson Draws His Sword." *Stop here* and face north and east down the historic trace of the Culpeper Road bordered by the fence line.

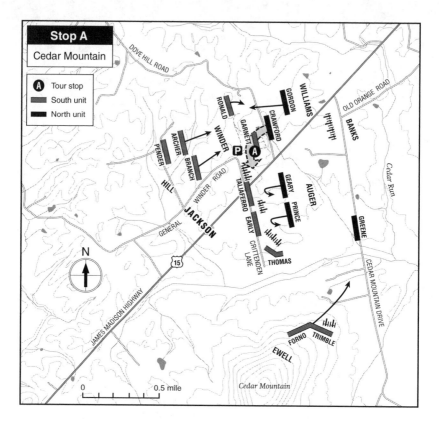

Stop A

Cedar Mountain

- **A** Tour stop
- South unit
- North unit

0   0.5 mile

Cedar Mountain

STOP A   Cedar Mountain

Jackson Challenges Pope, July 13–August 9, 1862

Orientation

In 1862 the section of General Winder Road you just drove on was known as Crittenden's Lane and extended south and east (to your right) from where you parked your vehicle to a point on the other side of modern James Madison Highway (Route 15). Culpeper is about 6 miles in front of you. Route 15 crosses the Rapidan River at Madison Mills, which is a little over 9 miles behind you. The fence line marks the location of the Orange-Culpeper Turnpike in 1862, as does General Winder Road behind you. The turnpike in 1862 connected with Crittenden Lane here at what was known as "the Gate."

What Happened

On July 13 Gen. *Robert E. Lee* directed Maj. Gen. *Thomas J. Jackson* to take two divisions to Louisa Court House. He did so in response to reports that Federal forces belonging to Maj. Gen. John Pope's Army of Virginia had reached Culpeper Court House on the Orange and Alexandria Railroad, which placed them only a few days' march from its junction with the Virginia Central Railroad at Gordonsville. Six days later *Jackson* reached Gordonsville, having decided to continue on to that town instead of halting his command at Louisa Court House. After about a week of anxiously sifting through intelligence reports regarding the movements and intentions of Pope's forces, *Lee* responded to a message from *Jackson* complaining that he lacked sufficient forces to deal with Pope by ordering Maj. Gen. *Ambrose P. Hill's* division to Gordonsville.

Thus, on August 7, one day after Pope issued orders to his command to concentrate at Culpeper Court House, *Jackson* ordered his three divisions to push across the Rapidan River and move toward Culpeper. When reports that *Jackson* had crossed the Rapidan arrived, Pope authorized Maj. Gen. Nathaniel Banks to move his corps forward to confront the Confederates without waiting for the other two corps of the Army of Virginia to reach Culpeper. Shortly before noon on August 9, Banks's cavalry made contact with the vanguard of *Jackson's* command, the brigade from Maj. Gen. *Richard Ewell's* division commanded by Col. *Jubal Early*, about 8 miles from Culpeper. Banks deployed artillery and cavalry on a ridge overlooking Cedar Run, which immediately began firing on *Early's* command. *Early* then formed his infantry into a line to the right of the Culpeper-Orange Turnpike. When the rest of *Ewell's* division came up, they extended the line to the right with six guns posted on the cleared forward slope of Cedar Mountain. When Brig. Gen. *Charles S. Winder's* division arrived, it went into position to the left of the turnpike. For his part, Banks deployed his command overlooking Cedar Run with Brig. Gen. Christopher Auger's division on the left side of the turnpike and Brig. Gen. Alpheus Williams's division on the right.

The Battle of Cedar Mountain, August 9, 1862

Directions

Remain in place or walk over from the markers to the entrance to the Cedar Mountain Battlefield Trail; from there *proceed* to the second marker, "The Battle of Cedar Mountain: The Awkward Position of the 21st Virginia." (It is about a 175-yard walk.) *Stop here* at the two trees next to the trace of the historic road to Culpeper. To your right rear you can see Cedar Mountain. In the distance beyond that, high ground with a tower on top of it will be visible on a clear day. That is Clark's Mountain on the other side of the Rapidan River. If you look to your left, you will see the trail takes you to a sign about 50 yards away. It indicates the approximate site where *Jackson* personally intervened in the fighting to rally his men, but it is recommended that you do the stand here in order to take advantage of the better sight lines and sense of terrain that this spot offers.

What Happened

As the two sides deployed and exchanged artillery fire for two hours in ninety-degree heat, *Jackson* developed a plan whereby *Early* would push forward along the road to Culpeper, while *Ewell* advanced two brigades against the Union left. For his part, *Winder* was to extend the line in order to operate against Banks's right. Before *Jackson* could execute his plan, though, Banks pushed forward infantry commanded by Auger against *Early's* position. From high ground behind *Ewell's* line *Jackson* responded to Auger's advance by sending orders back to *Hill* to move his division up from the rear. Then a courier rode up to inform him that *Winder* had been mortally wounded by Union artillery.

After briefly bowing his head in prayer, *Jackson* rode over to *Winder's* command just as the Federals launched a major assault on the Confederate left, command of which had passed to Brig. Gen. *William Taliaferro.* The Federal advance was spearheaded by Brig. Gen. Samuel Crawford's brigade of Williams's division, which slammed into *Taliaferro's* command as Brig. Gen. George Gordon's brigade moved into some woods to advance on Williams's right. The Confederate left quickly disintegrated under the weight of Williams's attack. Seeing what was going on, *Jackson* dug his spurs into his horse and raced into the wreckage of his command. He reached for his saber but found it so rusted that he could not withdraw it from the scabbard. Thus he removed both saber and scabbard and began waving them and a Confederate battle flag as he called on the men to rally.

Thanks in part to *Jackson's* personal leadership, the Confederates were able to restore their line. After rallying his men, *Jackson* rode to the rear and was greeted by the welcome sight of *Hill's* command arriving on the field. *Jackson* immediately ordered it to join the battle, and *Hill* promptly sent Col. *Edward Thomas's* brigade to the right to support *Early* and Brig. Gen. *Lawrence O'Bryan Branch's* brigade to the left to help the Confederate position there. After *Jackson* personally saluted their arrival, *Branch's* line pushed forward to secure the Confederate left and drive the Federals back. His line bolstered by the arrival of reinforcements, *Ewell* ordered Col. *Henry Forno's* and Brig. Gen. *Isaac Trimble's* brigades to advance against the Union left.

Badly outnumbered and with both ends of his line in trouble, Banks had no choice but to order his command to abandon the field. To cover Williams's and Auger's men as they pulled back at around 7:00 p.m., Banks pushed two squadrons of cavalry forward. Their advance, however, was greeted by such intense fire from the Confederates that over half their ranks fell. *Jackson* then sent his infantry forward in pursuit, but after they had covered about 1.5 miles, intelligence reached *Jackson* that Pope had moved forward elements of Maj. Gen. Franz Sigel's corps to assist Banks. Realizing this was probably more than his tired and fought-out commands could handle, he pulled his infantry back to the Cedar Mountain battlefield.

Both sides suffered significant casualties at Cedar Mountain. The Federals lost 320 killed, 1,466 wounded, and 617 captured or missing out of the approximately 8,000 who participated in the battle. As a consequence of the terrible beating it took at Cedar Mountain, Pope would keep Banks's command far away from any action in the subsequent Second Manassas Campaign. For its part, *Jackson's* command of 22,000 had suffered 314 killed and 1,062 wounded, and 42 captured or missing. *Jackson* held his position at Cedar Mountain until August 12, when, in response to reports that Pope had finished concentrating his entire command at Culpeper Court House, he ordered his men back across the Rapidan.

Analysis

Jackson's efforts at Cedar Mountain had produced a Confederate victory—albeit one that was much more hard-won than *Jackson's* advantage in numbers and previous record of success against Banks would have led one to expect. (Indeed before the battle *Jackson* confidently remarked to a staff officer, "Banks is in our front and he is generally willing to fight . . . and he generally gets whipped.") Banks demonstrated commendable aggressiveness and managed to strike a blow against the Confederate left that, for a brief moment, had *Jackson's* command teetering on the brink of defeat. Only through *Jackson's* personal interjection into the fight, hard fighting on the part of his men, and the timely arrival of reinforcements were the Confederates able to fight off the Federals and achieve a tactical victory. More important than the actual events of August 9 was the profound effect the fight at Cedar Mountain had on the Union high command. Pope had taken command in Virginia promising to conduct offensive operations with a degree of vigor that, in Washington's eyes, had to that point been missing from the Union war effort in Virginia. After Cedar Mountain, both Pope and Washington abandoned any thought of undertaking significant offensive operations until reinforcements from the Peninsula reached Pope's army. By going over to the defensive, Pope and Washington placed the operational initiative squarely in the hands of the Confederate high command. The course of the next few weeks would demonstrate just how dangerous this could be for the Union war effort.

Vignette

Staff officer Capt. *Charles Blackford* later wrote of his experience at Cedar Mountain, "After what seemed to me a long time firing on my front and to the left of the road became very sharp and was nearing me rapidly, showing that our men were either being driven or were falling back. . . . In an instant a regiment or two burst through into the spot where I was standing, all out of order and mixed up with a great number of yankees. I could not understand it; I could not tell whether our men had captured the yankees or the yankees had broken through our line. In an instant, however, I was put at rest, for *Jackson*, with one or two of his staff, came dashing across the road from our right in great haste and excitement. As he got amongst the disordered troops he drew his sword, then reached over and took his battleflag from my man, *Bob Isbel*, who was carrying it, and dropping his reins, waved it over his head and at the same time cried out in a loud voice, "Rally men! Remember Winder! Where's my Stonewall Brigade? Forward, men. Forward!'

"As he did so he dashed to the front, and our men followed with a yell and drove everything before them. It was a wonderful scene—one which men do not often see. *Jackson* usually is an indifferent and slouchy looking man but then, with the 'Light of Battle' shedding its radiance over him his whole person was changed. His action as graceful as *Lee's* and his face was lit with the inspiration of heroism. The men would have followed him into the jaws of death itself; nothing could have stopped them and nothing did. Even the old sorrel horse seemed endowed with the style and form of an Arabian.

"Just as this scene was being enacted a very handsome and hatless yankee officer . . . laid his hand on my knee as I sat on my horse and said with great emotion, 'What officer is that, Captain?' And when I told him, fully appreciating the magnetism of the occasion, he seemed carried away with admiration. With a touch of nature that makes the whole world kin he waved his broken sword around his head and shouted, 'Hurrah for General *Jackson*! Follow your General, Boys!' I leaned over, almost with tears in my eyes and said, 'You are too good a fellow for me to make prisoner; take that path to the left and you can escape.' He saluted me with his broken sword and disappeared in an instant. I hope he escaped."

This was not the only instance in which officers from the two armies interacted with mutual respect during the summer of 1862. Shortly after Cedar Mountain, Confederate cavalry officer Maj. Gen. *James E. B. Stuart* reunited with Brig. Gen. Samuel Crawford, an old comrade from the prewar army, during a truce and bet him the Northern press would declare Cedar Mountain a Union victory. The prize was a hat, which Crawford dutifully sent over the lines after *Stuart's* prediction was proven accurate. It would be captured by Federal raiders a few weeks later, after which *Stuart*, who found himself subjected to taunts from the men over his loss, vowed to "make the Yankees pay for that hat." When *Stuart's* men in turn seized Pope's dress uniform coat during the raid on Catlett's Station, *Stuart* sent a message through the lines to Pope: "You have my hat and plume. I have your best coat. I have the honor to propose a cartel for the fair exchange of the prisoners." Pope never responded, and his coat was placed on display in Richmond.

Further Exploration If you wish to study the fighting at Cedar Mountain in more depth, the Friends of Cedar Mountain Battlefield and the Civil War Trust have established a 0.5-mile loop trail where a series of wayside markers interpret the events that took place. The trail begins at the break in the fence line to your front and left.

Lieutenant-General J. E. B. Stuart, C.S.A. From a photograph. BLCW 2:582.

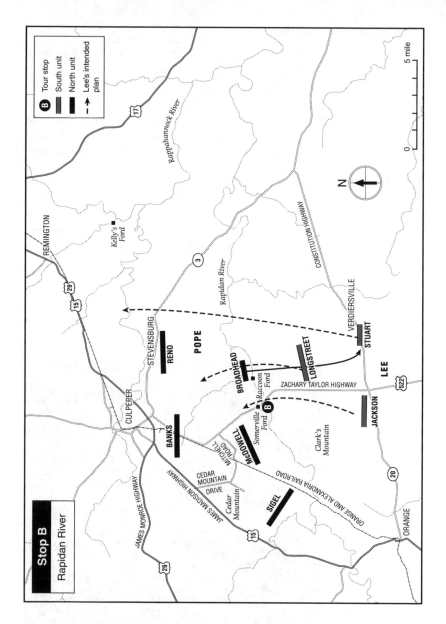

STOP B   Rapidan River

Directions   Exit the parking area and *drive back down* GENERAL WINDER ROAD to its intersection with JAMES MADISON HIGHWAY (U.S. 15). *Turn left* and proceed north for 0.8 mile to CEDAR MOUNTAIN DRIVE (VA 649). *Turn right* and proceed 1.9 miles to a fork. *Take the left fork* onto VA 652 (MITCHELL ROAD) and drive 1.3 miles to an intersection. (Immediately before reaching the intersection you will cross some railroad tracks.) *Proceed* through the intersection to stay on MITCHELL ROAD (which bears to the left directly after the intersection) and drive 2 miles to its terminus at ZACHARY

TAYLOR HIGHWAY (U.S. 522). *Turn right* onto ZACHARY TAYLOR HIGHWAY. At 2.7 miles you will cross the bridge over the Rapidan River. *Pull into* the small turnoff on the left that will appear just after you cross the bridge. Very carefully exit your vehicle and face north and west toward the river.

Lee's First Maneuver Foiled, August 15–19, 1862

Orientation

This bridge across the Rapidan River (which flows from left to right in front of you) is located at what in 1862 was known as Somerville Ford. You are standing at about 2 miles upstream from Raccoon Ford. Just upstream from Somerville Ford, Clark's Mountain, which provided an excellent observation point for the Confederates, overlooks the right bank of the Rapidan; its summit is about 3 miles to your left rear. Culpeper is about 8 miles from where you are standing. Fredericksburg is about 40 miles downstream (though a little under 30 as the crow flies). Verdiersville is about 7 miles to the southeast from where you are standing.

What Happened

Washington's directive to Pope to act on the defensive until Maj. Gen. George B. McClellan's army could reach him meant that when *Lee* arrived at Gordonsville on August 15, two days after ordering *Longstreet's* command to join *Jackson*, the initiative rested squarely with the Confederate commander. He immediately decided that upon completing the concentration of his command, he would advance to the crossings of the Rapidan in order to be in position to attack Pope on August 18. The plan was that *Jackson's* command would cross at Somerville Ford, while a little over 2 miles downstream *Longstreet's* wing of the army would cross at Raccoon Ford. After crossing the river, *Jackson* and *Longstreet* would advance north to attack the left of Pope's command at Culpeper Court House, while *Stuart's* cavalry cut the Federal retreat to the Rappahannock River. *Lee's* hopes that he could carry out his plan early on August 18, however, would be frustrated by delays in the arrival of Brig. Gen. *Fitzhugh Lee's* brigade of *Stuart's* command.

Although compelled to cede the initiative to the Confederates, Pope was anything but oblivious to his situation. He was fully aware that *Lee* might be planning an attempt to attack the Federal left and of the need to maintain contact with Fredericksburg, for troops from the Peninsula were under orders to land at Aquia Creek, proceed from there to Falmouth, a small village across the Rappahannock River from Fredericksburg, and then march north and west from there to their linkup with the Army of Virginia. Indeed by August 17 the first of those destined to arrive, Maj. Gen. Jesse Reno's two divisions of the Ninth Corps, was already with Pope's army and had taken up a position on the Federal left at Stevensburg. The rest of Pope's army was deployed south of Culpeper Court House with Sigel's corps on the right, McDowell's in the center, and Banks's in reserve. Despite Reno's arrival, Pope remained properly concerned about the threat of a Confederate thrust against his left. Thus on August 17 he directed Reno to push part of Brig. Gen. John Buford's cavalry brigade across the Rapidan at Raccoon Ford to see what was going on.

For the mission Buford selected two regiments and placed them under the command of Col. Thornton Brodhead. Remarkably Brodhead's men found Raccoon Ford undefended. *Longstreet* had assigned the task of guarding the ford to Brig. Gen. *Robert Toombs's* brigade. When *Longstreet* dispatched orders to *Toombs*, though, that officer was away from his command to meet with a political associate. Col. *Henry Benning*, however, took it upon himself to execute the order and posted two regiments at the ford as directed. When *Toombs* found out what *Benning* had done, he was not pleased that his subordinate had taken such an action without his knowledge and, in an act of foolish pique, ordered the two regiments back to camp.

Shortly after the Confederates departed, Brodhead's 1,000 cavalrymen appeared at the ford and splashed across. As darkness fell, Brodhead's men attempted to push south to the Orange Plank Road, but upon finding a considerable force of the enemy blocking the way, turned east and followed back roads for a while. Finally, well after nightfall, Brodhead's men managed to find a route that enabled them to reach the Plank Road and upon reaching it continued to push toward the small hamlet of Verdiersville, where *Stuart's* cavalry was in camp anticipating the arrival at any moment of *Fitz Lee's* brigade.

As they approached Verdiersville, Brodhead's men captured a courier *Stuart* had dispatched to find *Fitz Lee* and deliver him some papers laying out General *Lee's* plan for August 18. As the morning dawned, Stuart was at his headquarters at the Rhodes house and delighted to see a large dust cloud and hear the sound of horses approaching, presuming it was *Fitz Lee's* force. He then sent two staff officers west to greet its commander.

Almost as soon as the two officers started down the Plank Road, they were greeted not by *Fitz Lee* but by Brodhead's men charging toward them. They promptly turned around to alert *Stuart* to the danger. *Stuart* immediately mounted and rode off to safety, but not so far that he was unable to watch as the Federals reached the Rhodes house and spent a few minutes rummaging around the Confederate camp for spoils. After taking possession of *Stuart's* cloak and the hat he had recently won in a bet, the Federals began riding back in the direction from which they came.

("The tidings of our mishap and adventure had spread like lightning through the whole army, and excited a great sensation," one of *Stuart's* staff officers later recalled. "Wherever we passed an encampment on our way, the troops cheered us, and vociferously inquired of General *Stuart* what had become of his hat?")

Finding Confederates blocking the crossing at Raccoon Ford, Brodhead's command moved down the Rapidan and crossed at Germanna Ford, then proceeded to Culpeper Court House and delivered their prizes to Pope.

Included among the documents Brodhead's men had captured was an order from General *Lee* to *Stuart* that confirmed Pope's suspicions that the Confederates were preparing to turn his left. He immediately informed Washington that, in light of this information, he decided he had no choice but to order the Army of Virginia to pull back to the Rappahannock. General-in-Chief Henry Halleck fully endorsed his decision.

That night Pope's four corps began pulling back to the Rappahannock. Despite some difficulty negotiating the bottleneck at Culpeper Court House, the move was successfully completed on August 19. When information about the Federal withdrawal reached *Lee*, he summoned *Longstreet* (who had responded to the Raccoon Ford fiasco by placing *Toombs* under arrest), and together the two officers rode to the summit of Clark's Mountain. There they had a towering view of Culpeper County and watched in frustration as Pope's army rendered moot the grand plan to attack the Federal left by pulling his army out of reach.

Vignette

On July 14, Pope had issued a well-publicized order to his command boasting that he had "come to you from the West, where we have always seen the backs of our enemies" and haughtily proclaiming, "Let us study the probable lines of retreat of our opponents, and leave our own to take care of themselves. Let us look before us, and not behind." That Pope's actions a little over a month later were rather conspicuously in conflict with his words was not lost on his foe. *Longstreet* later wrote of his experience watching alongside *Lee* as the Federals slipped from their grasp on August 19, "From the summit [of Clark's Mountain] we had a fair view of many points. . . . Little clouds of dust arose which marked the tramp of soldiers, and these presently began to swell into dense columns along the rearward lines. Watching without comment till the clouds grew thinner and thinner as they approached the river and melted into the bright haze of the afternoon sun, General *Lee* finally put away his glasses, and with a deeply-drawn breath, expressive at once of disappointment and resignation, said, 'General, we little thought that the enemy would turn his back upon us this early in the campaign.'"

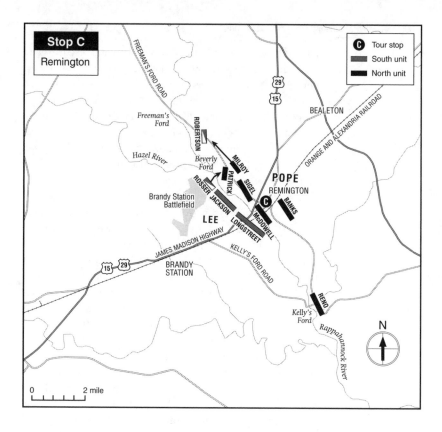

STOP C   Remington

Directions   *Turn right* onto ZACHARY TAYLOR HIGHWAY (U.S. 522) and drive
7.4 miles north to a T intersection. *Turn left* onto U.S. 522/VA
3. At 0.2 mile *exit right* onto JAMES MADISON HIGHWAY (U.S.
15/29). From the top of the ramp, *proceed north* on JAMES MAD-
ISON HIGHWAY for 10.6 miles, then *turn right* onto REMING-
TON ROAD (Business 15/29). Drive 0.7 mile on REMINGTON
ROAD (which becomes JAMES MADISON STREET after crossing the Rappahannock River; if you look to your right as you
cross the river, you will see the railroad bridge) to the parking area on the right side of the road next to the sign "Welcome to Remington, Va." (You will also see a Virginia Civil
War Trails wayside marker that discusses the November 1863
engagement in which the Federals overran a fortified Confederate position at Rappahannock Station.) *Pull in here* and,
upon exiting your vehicle, face south in the direction from
which you just came.

The Rappahannock Line, August 20–22, 1862

Orientation

At the time of the Civil War, the town of Remington was known as Rappahannock Station. If you look to your left, you should be able to see the tracks of the modern railroad. The railroad crossing of the Rappahannock River, which flows from your right to your left, is about 300 yards south of where you are standing and about 10 miles from Culpeper. Kelly's Ford is a little under 5 miles downstream from where you are standing. Fredericksburg is about 34 miles downstream from Remington, though only a little over 24 miles on a straight line. Beverly's Ford is about 2 miles upstream from the bridge at Remington, and Freeman's Ford is about 3 miles above Beverly's Ford. The crossing at Sulphur Springs is about 5 miles beyond that.

What Happened

Lee wasted little time lamenting Pope's escape from Culpeper Court House. Early on August 20 he ordered his command across the Rapidan with *Fitz Lee's* cavalry screening *Jackson's* advance on the left and Brig. Gen. *Beverly Robertson's* screening *Longstreet's* on the right. As the Confederate cavalry skirmished with the withdrawing Federals, Pope posted artillery along the north bank of the Rappahannock to cover the small bridgehead some of McDowell's men held covering the bridge at Rappahannock Station. Downstream, defending Kelly's Ford, was Reno's corps on the Federal left. Early on August 21 Sigel had his command in a position from where they could support McDowell's right, while Banks's command was held in reserve. Pickets stood watch at the various crossings upstream from Rappahannock Station.

Lee concluded that by posting his command this way Pope had placed himself close enough to Fredericksburg that any chance of maneuvering successfully against the Federal left had little prospect of success. The Federal positions along the river were too strong to be attacked directly as well. Thus *Lee* naturally began looking upstream to Beverly's Ford, in hopes he could find an opportunity to turn the Federal right. On August 21 he directed *Robertson* to move his cavalry upstream to Freeman's Ford and cross there. Afterward *Robertson* would move along the north bank of the Rappahannock and clear away any Federals who might be at Beverly's Ford. By doing so, he would enable *Jackson* and some cavalry to cross there and move into a position to crush Pope's right.

At around 8:00 a.m. Col. *Thomas Rosser's* cavalry, the vanguard of *Jackson's* force, reached Beverly's Ford and, easily brushing aside the small Federal force defending it, quickly pushed across. News of *Rosser's* crossing reached McDowell, who promptly ordered a brigade commanded by Brig. Gen. Marsena

Patrick, accompanied by a battery and some horsemen from the 5th New York Cavalry, to deal with the Confederates. When Patrick's force arrived on the scene to confront *Rosser*, the two sides began exchanging artillery fire. Upon learning what was going on, Sigel ordered Brig. Gen. Robert Milroy's brigade to go to Patrick's assistance. Milroy's approach was detected by *Robertson's* command, which had successfully crossed at Freeman's Ford, as was the fact that the Federals would soon be able to fall on *Rosser's* flank. *Stuart* responded by ordering his men to recross the river and informed *Lee* and *Jackson* that whatever hopes they had of turning the Federals via Beverly's Ford had been dashed.

Lee responded by looking farther up river. Early on August 22 he sent *Stuart's* cavalry to Freeman's Ford. However, when *Stuart* arrived, he found Milroy's brigade covering the ford, backed by a strong force of artillery. Concluding that nothing could be done there, *Lee* then made two major decisions. First, he approved a proposal *Stuart* had presented the previous evening to take his cavalry and attempt a raid against the Orange and Alexandria Railroad. Second, he ordered that *Jackson's* command, once it had reached Freeman's Ford around 10:00 a.m. and relieved *Stuart's* cavalry so it could begin its raid, would continue moving upstream in hopes that the next major crossing point at Sulphur Springs would be unguarded.

Trooper of the Virginia cavalry. BLCW 2:271.

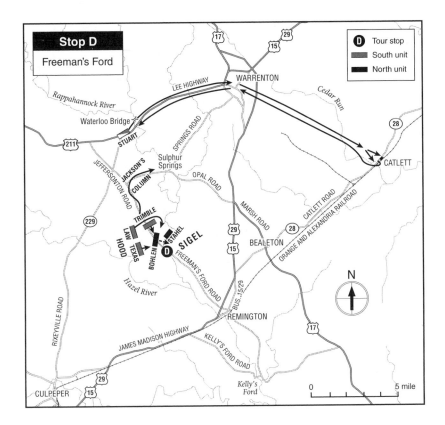

STOP D   Freeman's Ford

Directions

Exit the parking lot, *turning right* onto JAMES MADISON STREET (Business 15/29). After traveling 0.1 mile, *turn left* at the intersection with MAIN STREET. MAIN STREET becomes FREEMAN'S FORD ROAD as it exits Remington. After driving 0.4 mile you will come to the light at the intersection with JAMES MADISON HIGHWAY (U.S. 15/29). *Pass through* the intersection to remain on FREEMAN'S FORD ROAD. Drive 4.7 miles to a small pull-off on the left side of the road just after you cross a bridge over the Rappahannock River. *Pull over here* and park your vehicle. Stand and face north, with the river to your right. Traffic is not especially heavy here, but it travels fast, so be alert and very careful in your movements.

Orientation

The bridge crosses the Rappahannock at the location of the wartime Freeman's Ford. You are about 40 miles upstream from Fredericksburg (a little under 30 as the crow flies), 5 miles upstream from Remington, and 5 miles downstream from the Rappahannock crossing at Sulphur Springs. Warrenton is about 10 miles to the north and east from where you are standing. Catlett's Station is about 12 miles to the north and east.

The Rout of the Germans, August 22, 1862

What Happened

As *Jackson's* column moved upstream from Freeman's Ford toward Sulphur Springs, artillery on both sides of the Rappahannock kept up a steady fire. At Freeman's Ford, Milroy was joined during the afternoon by Sigel's corps. By around 3:00 p.m., Sigel could neither see nor hear anything to indicate Confederates were still guarding the ford. Consequently he directed Brig. Gen. Carl Schurz to push a regiment from his division across the river at Freeman's Ford to see what was going on. Within minutes Col. Alexander Schimmelfennig's 74th Pennsylvania from Brig. Gen. Henry Bohlen's brigade had plunged into the river and was moving up the high ground on the opposite bank. Upon reaching the top, Schimmelfennig's men made a stab at an unguarded Confederate wagon train and managed to gather some prisoners. Emboldened, Schimmelfennig sent a message back, urging the rest of Bohlen's command to move across the river. Personally accompanied by Schurz and Bohlen, the other two regiments of the brigade rushed across and linked up with Schimmelfennig, who anticipated gathering an even greater bounty by attacking *Jackson's* entire wagon train.

Schurz's move, however, came as little surprise to the Confederates. As he moved his command toward Sulphur Springs, *Jackson* directed that the brigade commanded by Brig. Gen. *Isaac Trimble* trail behind far enough to be able to respond in case the Federals decided to make a stab at the rear of the Confederate column. *Trimble* had smartly concealed his command in the woods. Thus it came as a considerable surprise to Bohlen when his skirmishers encountered stiff resistance almost as soon as they began to advance.

At this point *Trimble* unleashed a vicious attack on the Federal right flank. Within a few minutes Bohlen's right began falling apart. It was also at this point that *Longstreet's* lead brigade, commanded by Brig. Gen. *John B. Hood*, arrived on the scene and immediately threw itself into the battle on *Trimble's* right. With both his flanks collapsing, Bohlen had no choice but to fall back toward the river. He fell, mortally wounded, as he and Schurz tried in vain to restore order to their shattered commands. The Federals plunged into the river and, as they struggled to get back to the north bank, *Trimble's* and *Hood's* men rushed forward to high ground overlooking the river, from which they unleashed a merciless storm of musket fire into the Federals' panicked ranks. They were deterred from pursuing across the river by the presence of Milroy's command, which had just been joined by a battery commanded by Capt. Hubert Dilger and Brig. Gen. Robert Schenck's division.

Stuart's Raid, August 22–23, 1862

What Happened   As the Federals were coming to grief at Freeman's Ford, *Stuart's* cavalry force of about 1,500 men had safely crossed the Rappahannock well upstream and was approaching Warrenton. Upon reaching Warrenton, *Stuart's* men received an enthusiastic welcome from the town's residents, who eagerly informed them that a ride of less than 10 miles would bring them to Catlett's Station on the Orange and Alexandria Railroad. Near the station a bridge carried the railroad over Cedar Run, the destruction of which would greatly complicate Pope's logistical situation. *Stuart* thanked the residents for the information and at around 5:00 p.m. led his men out of Warrenton toward Catlett's Station.

When *Stuart's* men and horses reached the vicinity of Catlett's Station at around 7:30 p.m., they were thoroughly soaked, thanks to a steady rain that had only just stopped falling. *Stuart* proceeded to send one of his officers forward to reconnoiter, who found the Federals at Catlett's Station were completely unprepared to deal with an attack. In addition, he informed *Stuart*, among the large number of Federal wagons at Catlett's Station was the one carrying Pope's headquarters baggage.

Stuart responded by ordering *Rosser's* command to deal with the fewer than twenty Federals who had the misfortune of being on picket duty that night. Once this had been accomplished, *Rosser's* men and Col. *Rooney Lee's* 9th Virginia Cavalry were given the task of dealing with the Federals encamped around Catlett's Station. While they did this, Col. *W. C. Wickham's* 4th Virginia Cavalry would burn the Cedar Run bridge.

Unfortunately for the Confederates, the break in the weather proved to be brief. As *Stuart's* men executed their commander's plan, they found themselves battling heavy rains once again. The rain frustrated the efforts of *Wickham's* men to burn the bridge over Cedar Run. This, however, was the only sour note for the Confederates that night, for *Rooney Lee's* and *Rosser's* men easily overran the plucky, but small force of Pennsylvania Bucktails (so-called for their distinctive headgear) guarding Catlett's Station. They then proceeded to thoroughly plunder the station. They seized hundreds of prisoners, as well as hundreds of horses and mules, a payroll chest, and Pope's dress uniform coat. The most important thing they seized, though, was a batch of papers from Pope's headquarters wagons. By 3:00 a.m. *Stuart* had decided his men had accomplished enough, and the Confederate troopers began retracing their steps to Warrenton.

"Crossing at Waterloo Bridge with two thousand cavalry," one man later recalled. "General *Stuart* reached Warrenton early in the afternoon and was received by the inhabitants with great demonstrations of joy, as he and his staff at the head of his splendid cavalry rode down the street. . . . Upon hearing that we were going to attack Catlett's Station that night, a very pretty young girl, a Miss Lucas, clapped her hands with delight and exclaimed, 'Oh! General *Stuart*, if you will only capture Captain ——— (I do not remember his name) of Pope's quartermaster department he will win his bet with me, and then if you will bring him by here I will pay him. Won't that be funny for anything?' Our curiosity was excited and she proceeded to explain.

"During the occupation of the place, her family had taken, as a boarder and protector, a quartermaster who proved himself a gentlemanly fellow and was very kind to them. In their discussions about the war, she had maintained that Pope would be beaten as soon as he met General *Lee*, and he, that they would succeed in going into Richmond. The result was a playful bet, offered by him and accepted by the lady, of a bottle of wine that he would be in Richmond in thirty days. So now, if he went there even as a prisoner, she would lose the wine. We all laughed heartily and, turning to me, *Stuart* said, 'Take his name, *Blackford*, and look out for him'—which I did.

"Reaching the vicinity of Catlett's Station a little before dark, *Stuart* halted the command and sent me out to reconnoitre the position. Throwing an oilcloth over my uniform, I rode all around the outskirts of their encampment, and found a vast assemblage of wagons and a city of tents, laid out in regular order and occupied by the luxuriously equipped quartermasters and commissaries, and countless hangers-on and stragglers of the army, but no appearance of any large organized body of troops; and with the exception of a small camp guard at the crossroads, a few hundred yards from the camp, they had no pickets whatever posted. . . .

"I went in with the leading regiment, and the consternation among the quartermasters and commissaries as we charged down the main street, scattering out pistol balls promiscuously right and left among them, made the men laugh until they could scarcely keep their saddles. Supper tables were kicked over and tents broken down in the rush to get out, the tents catching them sometimes in their fall like fish in a net, within whose folds we could trace the struggling outlines of the frantic men within. . . . At the first alarm the Bucktails sprang to arms and awaited us in the wide doorways and on the platform of the depot. Receiving one withering volley, our men dashed among them with their sabres, leaping their horses upon the low platform and crashing right into the freight room. In less time than it has taken to tell the tale, all was over, and no further resistance was afforded to our work of destruction so far as the enemy was concerned. . . .

"All was going as well as we could wish, when a violent clap of thunder and a furious wind announced the coming of a storm; then came a deluge of rain; it seemed to come not in drops but in streams, as if it were pouring from buckets. . . . Every fire was extinguished and we were left in utter darkness. . . . As daylight approached we withdrew and after marching a few miles halted for breakfast. I now thought of our pretty friend's quartermaster, and without much hope that we had actually caught him, I thought I would see. After referring to his name, which I had taken down, I sought out the prisoners, who were assembled under guard in a field and looked very disconsolate. Riding up to them I asked if Capt. —— Q.M.D. was in the party. A much surprised and genteel looking young man came forward, who after hearing the story laughed very heartily, in which he was joined by his comrades with keen relish. It seemed to restore them all to good spirits, and they resumed the march talking all the way about the won wager.

"General *Stuart* was delighted when I told him we had Miss Lucas' quartermaster, and told me to ride on to Warrenton and let her know so she could be ready with the bottle of wine as we passed. Stuart halted the prisoners in front of the house and the Captain stepped forward to receive the bottle of wine from the pretty hands of the lovely girl, amid the enthusiastic cheers of his comrades."

Raid upon Union baggage train by Stuart's cavalry. From a war-time sketch. BLCW 2:501.

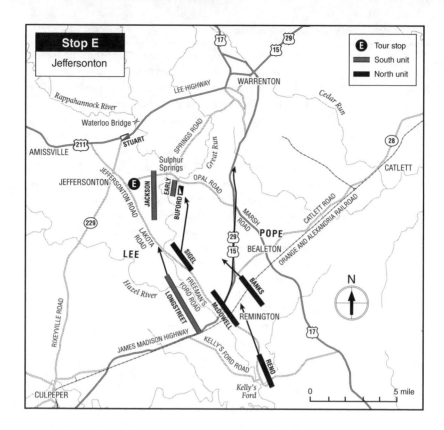

Stop E
Jeffersonton

Tour stop
South unit
North unit

WARRENTON

LEE HIGHWAY

Rappahannock River

Waterloo Bridge

AMISSVILLE

STUART

Sulphur Springs

JEFFERSONTON E

EARLY

JACKSON

BUFORD

OPAL ROAD

JEFFERSONTON ROAD

LAKOTA ROAD

SIGEL

LEE

Hazel River

FREEMAN'S FORD ROAD

LONGSTREET

McDOWELL

JAMES MADISON HIGHWAY

KELLY'S FORD ROAD

RIXEYVILLE ROAD

CULPEPER

Kelly's Ford

CATLETT

Cedar Run

Great Run

SPRINGS ROAD

MARSH ROAD

POPE

BEALETON

BANKS

REMINGTON

RENO

CATLETT ROAD

ORANGE AND ALEXANDRIA RAILROAD

N

0   5 mile

STOP E — Jeffersonton

Directions

Resume driving on FREEMAN'S FORD ROAD, which after crossing the river becomes LAKOTA ROAD. After driving 2.2 miles, you will reach an intersection. *Turn right* onto JEFFERSONTON ROAD (VA 621) and proceed 0.8 mile to a T intersection. *Turn left* to stay on JEFFERSONTON ROAD. After driving 1.5 miles, you will see Jeffersonton Baptist Church on the right. *Pull in here* and park your vehicle in front of the church in the spot marked for visitor parking. Exit your vehicle and walk up to the front steps of the church.

Early in Peril, August 22–23, 1862

What Happened

While *Stuart's* men romped about behind the Federal lines during the night of August 22–23, a far different drama was playing out along the Rappahannock. Shortly before 4:00 p.m. on August 22, *Ewell's* division at the head of *Jackson's* column had reached Sulphur Springs and found it relatively unguarded. Despite the rain that was falling, *Jackson* quickly ordered *Ewell* to push Brig. Gen. *Alexander Lawton's* and Brig. Gen. *Jubal Early's* brigades across the river. When Ewell expressed concern about the possibility of the rain swelling the river to a point where his men might find themselves trapped on the other side, *Jackson* replied dismissively, "Oh, it won't get up—& if it does, I'll take care of that." Thus at around 5:00 p.m. a Georgia regiment from *Lawton's* command and two batteries forded the river at the springs, while *Early* spent the night pushing his entire brigade across at a dam about 1 mile downstream from Lawton.

Almost as soon as the last of *Early's* men had crossed, what was a steady drizzle turned into a torrential downpour. The Rappahannock rose by at least six feet, and when the sun rose on August 23 it was clear that *Early's* and *Lawton's* men were in a very perilous situation. *Early* responded by immediately posting his command on a wooded ridge overlooking Great Run, with his right on the Rappahannock and his left in the vicinity of the road connecting Sulphur Springs with Rappahannock Station.

Pope had learned of the Confederate crossing at Sulphur Springs the previous evening. With the approval of General Halleck in Washington, he responded by ordering his men to cross undefended Kelly's Ford and attack the Confederate right and rear in conjunction with the Federals still holding the bridgehead at Rappahannock Station. However, when heavy rains swelled the river, Pope dropped this plan early on August 23 in favor of a strike at the Confederates trapped on the north bank of the river near Sulphur Springs. He ordered Sigel to immediately march his command toward Sulphur Springs to attack the Confederates and Banks and Reno to move up their commands to support Sigel, while McDowell received directions to move via Warrenton to Sigel's assistance.

As Pope was smartly moving to take advantage of the situation, *Jackson* directed his engineers to get to work repairing the bridge at Sulphur Springs. *Jackson* then spent several anxious hours astride his horse at one of the bridge abutments watching his men work. Meanwhile *Early* shifted his position in order to link up with *Lawton's* regiment and post his left on the Rappahannock. As this was going on, General *Lee* directed *Longstreet* to eliminate the Federal bridgehead held by elements of McDowell's command at Rappahannock Station. After a two-hour artillery bombardment, *Longstreet* ordered an attack by elements from *G. T. Anderson's* and *Evans's* brigades. Their advance was greeted by a storm of Federal artillery fire from across the river that enabled the last Federals in the bridgehead to cross the river to safety. The abandonment of the bridgehead was not a consequence of *Longstreet's* attack, though. Rather the Federals did so in order to move to Warrenton in line with Pope's orders to McDowell to assist Sigel. The Federal rear guard then completed the task of destroying the bridge, which was accomplished around noon.

Unfortunately Sigel did not march his men with the degree of urgency the situation demanded on August 23. Not until the afternoon did his lead infantry brigade, Milroy's, reach Great Run to link up with the cavalry force commanded by Buford that had fallen back in response to fire from *Early's* skirmishers. Milroy then brought up a battery to fire at the Confederates and cover the advance of his skirmishers toward Great Run. *Early's* men responded with stiff artillery and musket fire that drove back Milroy's skirmishers. Milroy then decided to await the arrival of reinforcements before doing anything more. As the sun set, Sigel arrived and ordered an attack against *Early's* left by a force of three regiments of infantry, but these accomplished nothing except to provoke two pieces of Confederate artillery into firing canister into them and dissuade Sigel from doing anything more that day.

At about the time this took place, *Jackson's* engineers completed their work on the bridge. *Jackson's* first response, though, was not to withdraw *Early* but to send more forces to the north side of the river. *Early* was appalled and persuaded *Ewell* during the night that the only proper course of action in light of the fact that the Federals were in force in their front was to recross the river. *Jackson* acquiesced by dawn on August 24 the last of *Early's* command was back on the south bank of the Rappahannock.

A Bold Plan, August 24, 1862

What Happened   When he learned from Sigel that *Jackson's* command had escaped, Pope directed Sigel to extend his line 4 miles upstream to Waterloo Bridge. Despite frustration at having missed an opportunity to inflict a significant blow on the Confederates, Pope was more than satisfied with his situation on August 24. He had the three corps of his Army of Virginia well in hand, plus the two divisions of Reno's command, with which he had thwarted every attempt by the Confederates to break the stalemate along the Rapidan and Rappahannock.

In addition Pope knew that the balance of strength was rapidly tilting in his favor. One division from Maj. Gen. Samuel Heintzelman's corps from the Army of the Potomac had reached Warrenton Junction, while the other one was scheduled to arrive via rail the next day. Moreover the two divisions of Maj. Gen. Fitz John Porter's corps were then moving up the Rappahannock from the direction of Fredericksburg and would soon link up with Pope's force, while the last two corps from the Army of the Potomac were expected to arrive within a few days. The campaign was Pope's to lose; he need only hold his ground, keep his command well in hand, and continue thwarting *Lee's* maneuvers until the time came when McClellan's units arrived to make the force under his command too much for the Confederates to handle.

Of course, the factors that made Pope so satisfied with his situation on August 24 served to arouse great anxiety for *Lee* and his subordinates. From the documents *Stuart* had seized during his raid on Catlett's Station, *Lee* learned just how far along the Federal effort to combine McClellan's and Pope's armies was. He needed to do something dramatic. Every day that passed would see the Federal army get stronger and stronger. However, there was no way a direct assault could succeed, and Pope had ably countered every attempt to maneuver against the Federal right, so making yet another attempt to do so held out little promise of success. Moreover, in the process of moving upstream, *Lee* had been compelled to leave the Rappahannock crossings at Freeman's Ford, Beverly's Ford, Rappahannock Station, and Kelly's Ford for all intents and purposes unguarded and thus his right and rear dangerously vulnerable.

Left with few other options available to him for breaking what had become an unacceptable stalemate along the Rappahannock, *Lee* decided on a bold move. During the afternoon of August 24 he summoned his subordinates to Jeffersonton to present it to them. Leaving just *Longstreet's* wing of the army to guard the Rappahannock, *Jackson* would replicate *Stuart's* exploit of a few days earlier—but on a far grander scale. He would take his three divisions on a long march around the Federal right, then push east to the Orange and Alexandria Railroad to cut Pope's line of supplies. This, it was surmised, would compel Pope to abandon his strong position along the Rappahannock and fall back toward Washington. In doing so Pope might present *Jackson* and *Longstreet's* command, which would leave the Rappahannock line thirty-six hours after *Jackson's*, an opportunity after they reunited to strike a decisive blow.

After consulting with his chief engineer, Capt. *J. Keith Boswell* (who also happened to be a native of the region through which his command would march) to select a route to Manassas Junction, *Jackson* decided his command would first move west along the south bank of the Rappahannock to Amissville. From there it would cross the river at Hinson's Mill Ford, push through Orleans to Salem on the Manassas Gap Railroad, then follow the railroad east through Thoroughfare Gap in the Bull Run Mountains to its junction with the Orange and Alexandria at Manassas Junction.

Analysis   After the war *Lee* remarked to an associate that "everything was risky in our war. He knew oftentimes that he was playing a very bold game, but it was the only *possible* one." Although

Lee made this comment during a conversation about Gettysburg, it is also suggestive of his thinking on August 24, 1862. The boldness of the plan he and his high command settled on that day was indisputable. As long as the Confederate army was divided, Pope would have an opportunity to fight it piecemeal. Yet at the time Lee faced a menu of decidedly bad choices. Sitting tight and accepting stalemate was not an acceptable course of action, for both sides understood that every moment that passed brought more time for McClellan's and Pope's armies to unite. Moreover, over the course of the past week, Pope had, in the words of historian Joseph L. Harsh, "proven a surprisingly adept foe," backing up his big talk with effective generalship. By carefully and methodically managing his forces, he had thwarted every attempt Lee had made to break the stalemate along the Rapidan and Rappahannock Rivers. The potential hazards of attempting to cross the river close to a foe that was clearly alert to the dangers and opportunities that might arise from a Confederate crossing had been vividly illustrated by the episode involving Early's force. On top of this, by August 24 the Confederate army had moved so far up river that its right and rear were now potentially vulnerable to a Federal thrust across the river downstream. And so Lee found himself in a situation where could not remain where he was; nor could he retrace his steps without surrendering whatever hopes he had of defeating Pope's command before too much of McClellan's army had joined it. In sum, the plan Lee and his subordinates developed was born of the fact that they had few if any options that offered a better possibility for breaking the unacceptable stalemate along the Rappahannock and creating the opportunity to achieve decisive results against Pope before all of McClellan's command reached him.

Vignette

"Jackson's Headquarters were near Jefferson on the 24th," a staff officer later recalled. "The Rappahannock could not be crossed at Sulphur Springs and a new move must be made. A council of war was held at the General's Headquarters that afternoon. It was a curious scene. A table was placed almost in the middle of a field, with not even a tree within hearing. General Lee sat at the table on which was spread a map. General Longstreet sat on his right, General Stuart on his left, and General Jackson stood opposite him; these four and no more. A group of staff officers were lounging on the grass of an adjacent knoll. The consultation was a brief one. As it closed I was called by General Jackson and I heard the only sentence of that consultation that I ever heard reported. It was uttered by the secretive Jackson, and it was—'I will be moving within the hour.'"

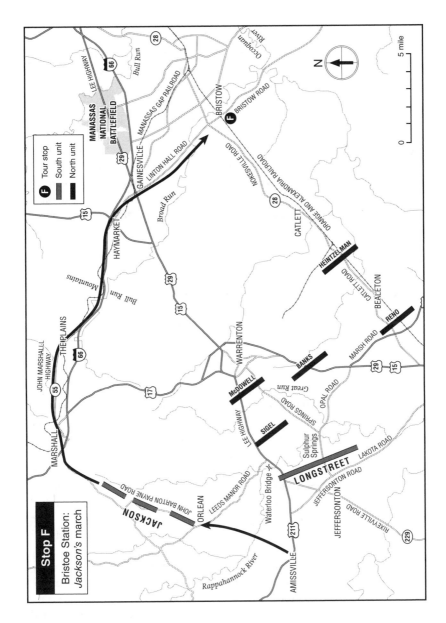

STOP F Bristoe Station

Directions Upon exiting the church parking lot, *turn right* onto SPRINGS ROAD (VA 802) and drive 2.7 miles. Just after crossing the Rappahannock River, you will come to a fork. *Turn right* at the fork onto OPAL ROAD and proceed 4.4 miles to its intersection with JAMES MADISON HIGHWAY (U.S. 29/15). (At 0.8 mile after turning onto OPAL ROAD, you will cross Great Run, behind which *Early* posted his isolated command on August 22–24.) *Proceed* through the intersection onto MARSH ROAD (U.S. 17) and drive 3.1 miles to the intersection with CATLETT ROAD (VA 28).

Turn left onto CATLETT ROAD (VA 28) and proceed 16.2 miles. *En route* CATLETT ROAD (VA 28) turns into NOKESVILLE ROAD. At 8 miles after turning onto CATLETT ROAD, you will cross Cedar Run, where the efforts of *Stuart's* men to burn the railroad bridge during their August 22–23 raid were thwarted by rain. Shortly thereafter you will pass Catlett's Station, the target of *Stuart's* raid. At 14.6 miles, you cross Kettle Run.

Turn right onto BRISTOW ROAD (VA 619). After driving 0.8 mile, you will cross over some railroad tracks. Immediately after doing so, you will see a parking area on the right. *Pull in here*, exit your vehicle, and face in the direction from which you just came (toward the tracks).

Jackson's March, August 24–26, 1862

What Happened   *Jackson's* command began its march shortly before dawn on August 25. At the head was Captain *Boswell*, whom *Jackson* had assigned the task of guiding the march. *Ewell's* command was the first to cross the Rappahannock and reached Salem (modern Marshall) as the sun set. Following *Ewell* on what would be a 25-mile march that day was *Hill's* division, while *William Taliaferro's* brought up the rear. Although reports of a large Confederate force moving to the north and west reached Pope, he dismissed their significance and kept his attention focused on the situation along the Rappahannock and the progress of McClellan's forces as they moved toward him.

Thus when *Jackson's* men resumed their march early on August 26 with *Ewell's* command once again in front, no Federals obstructed their march through Thoroughfare Gap in the Bull Run Mountains to Gainesville on the Warrenton Turnpike. Upon reaching Gainesville at around 4:00 p.m., *Stuart* and two brigades of cavalry *Lee* had dispatched to aid his command reached *Jackson*. Meanwhile *Longstreet* fired his artillery across the Rappahannock in a successful effort to distract Pope and his subordinates.

Instead of following the railroad directly to Manassas Junction from Gainesville, *Jackson* decided to take a side road that reached the Orange and Alexandria at Bristoe Station. With Col. *Thomas T. Munford's* 2nd Virginia Cavalry in the lead, *Jackson* pushed his column forward for two hours in the direction of Bristoe Station. *Munford's* command was not spotted until it was less than 100 yards from the station, which was guarded by only a few units of Federal infantry and cavalry. *Munford* immediately ordered a charge and in short order scattered the Federal defenders.

Ewell's lead brigade had just reached Bristoe Station when a train approached from the southwest, but the Confederates were unable to block the tracks to prevent it from pushing through to Manassas Junction. They were better prepared for the next train and managed to derail it, then knocked out its warning lights just before a third train approached the station and, unaware of the danger, crashed into it. Shortly thereafter a fourth train approached, but its quick-thinking engineer managed to reverse his gears and get his train moving back toward Warrenton Junction fast enough to elude a member of *Ewell's* staff who attempted to chase him down.

Shortly thereafter word reached *Jackson* that Manassas Junction was weakly defended and that the Federals had built up a huge depot of supplies there. *Jackson* quickly decided to accept Brig. Gen. *Isaac Trimble's* suggestion that a night attack be made on Manassas Junction. *Trimble* selected the 21st North Carolina and 21st Georgia for the operation. *Jackson* expressed concern that two regiments might not be enough to take Manassas Junction, but *Trimble* persuaded him to set aside his reservations. "I beg your pardon, General," said *Trimble*, "but give me my two Twenty-ones and I'll charge and capture hell itself!"

Accompanied by *Stuart's* cavalry, *Trimble* quickly covered the 4 miles between Bristoe and Manassas Junction. The commander of the Federal force at the depot, Capt. Samuel Craig, received a vague warning from the engineer of the first train that had eluded *Jackson's* men at Bristoe, but with only a few hundred men and eight pieces of artillery at his disposal he had no hope of fighting off *Stuart's* and *Trimble's* men. Five minutes after *Trimble* ordered his men to charge, they had overwhelmed the defenders of Manassas Junction, captured six guns and over three hundred Federals, and suffered only two killed and two wounded for their effort.

Vignette As the head of his column approached Salem on August 26, one of *Jackson's* staff officers recalled, "After a march of twenty-five miles . . . many of them had no rations, and subsisted upon the green corn gathered along the route; yet their indomitable enthusiasm and devotion knew no flagging. As the weary column approached the end of the day's march, they found *Jackson*, who had ridden forward, dismounted, and standing upon a great stone by the road-side. His sun-burned cap was lifted from his brow, and he was gazing toward the west, where the splendid August sun was about to kiss the distant crest of the Blue Ridge, which stretched far away, bathed in azure and gold; and his blue eye, beaming with martial pride, returned the rays of the evening with almost equal brightness. His men burst forth into their accustomed cheers, forgetting all their fatigue at his inspiring presence; but, deprecating the tribute by a gesture, he sent an officer to request that there should be no cheering, inasmuch as it might betray their presence to the enemy. They at once repressed their applause, and passed the word down the column to their comrades: 'No cheering, boys; the General requests it.' But as they passed him, their eyes and gestures, eloquent with suppressed affection, silently declared what their lips were forbidden to utter. *Jackson* turned to his staff, his face beaming with delight, and said: 'Who could not conquer, with such troops as these?'"

Lieutenant-General Richard S. Ewell, c.s.a. From a photograph. BLCW 1:251.

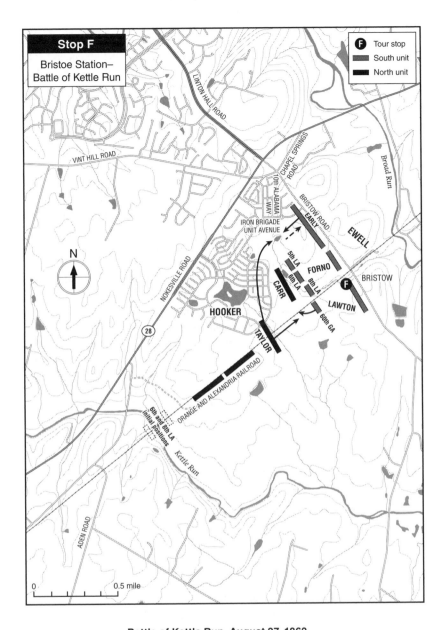

Battle of Kettle Run, August 27, 1862

What Happened   As *Trimble* and *Stuart* secured possession of Manassas Junction, *Jackson* kept the rest of his command at Bristoe Station during the night of August 26–27. But as soon as morning came, he put the rest of *Hill's* and *Taliaferro's* divisions on the march to Manassas Junction. To *Ewell's* command went the thankless task of remaining at Bristoe Station to keep an eye out to the south and west for Pope's army.

Word that Confederates were on the railroad between him and Washington reached Pope at his headquarters around 8:00

p.m. on August 26. (It was sent by the telegraph operator at Manassas, who took advantage of Confederate negligence during their first hour at Bristoe Station to cut the telegraph wire.) As more information arrived through the night indicating that it was a sizable force, Pope began to sense he had been given a magnificent opportunity to crush part of *Lee's* army and promptly moved to seize it. By dawn he had dispatched orders to his various commands to turn around and move north and east in three wings. One wing, composed of McDowell's and Sigel's corps operating under the former's overall direction, would take the Warrenton Turnpike and march toward the point where it intersected the Manassas Gap Railroad at Gainesville. Meanwhile Heintzelman would march Maj. Gen. Philip Kearny's division of his Third Corps, Army of the Potomac, which had just arrived from Alexandria, and Reno's IX Corps to the small hamlet of Greenwich. The rest of the army would follow the Orange and Alexandria Railroad, with Brig. Gen. Joseph Hooker's division of Heintzelman's corps in the lead, followed by Porter's Fifth Corps, Army of the Potomac, which had just linked up with Pope's command after a frustrating march from Falmouth, and Banks's corps.

To gather information regarding what might be in front of him, Hooker placed a New York regiment on a train and sent it forward ahead of his command toward Bristoe. By midmorning the New Yorkers had approached close enough to *Ewell's* command to send back a warning that the Confederates were "in very heavy force." Their presence also alerted *Ewell* to the fact that the Federals were active farther down the road and he needed to prepare for their arrival. He responded by directing Brig. Gen. *Alexander Lawton* to deploy his brigade south of the railroad in a position facing west and Col. *Henry Forno* to do the same on its north side. After posting his command, *Forno* ordered two Louisiana regiments to Kettle Run to serve as an advance guard as *Early's* brigade took up a position on the Confederate right, from where it could support *Forno* and keep an eye out in the direction of Greenwich.

Despite the warning from the New Yorkers, Hooker dutifully pushed his division forward along the railroad. As the Federals approached Kettle Run, *Forno's* two regiments were compelled to give ground and fall back across the creek; they then burned the bridge over it and took up a position next to a Georgia regiment *Lawton* had pushed forward about 300 yards in front of the main Confederate line.

As Hooker's men approached and began crossing Kettle Run, *Ewell* ordered his artillery to open fire. Hooker, however, was unfazed. He ordered Col. Joseph Carr to advance three regiments from his brigade directly along the railroad and personally led Carr's other two regiments off to the left in an attempt to find the Confederate flank. Carr's three regiments promptly obeyed, but after pushing through a strip of woods out onto an open field, they began receiving fire from *Ewell's* advanced line, which was posted in woods on the opposite side of the field. Carr's advance immediately halted and took up a position in a swale from which they kept up the fight. *Ewell* ordered forward another of *Forno's* regiments, while *Lawton's* Georgians on the Confederate left swung forward to the railroad embankment to fire into Carr's flank.

At this point Col. Nelson Taylor's brigade moved forward to join the battle. Taylor ordered three of his regiments to move to the left of Carr's men and assist him in his fight with *Forno*. Taylor's other two regiments moved up to support Carr's right by taking up a position from which they could engage *Lawton's* men. As it became evident to *Ewell* that his men were hard-pressed, a staff officer reached him at around 4:00 p.m. with instructions from *Jackson* to get a sense of the size of the enemy force, not get too heavily engaged with it, and fall back if necessary to avoid doing so. *Ewell* promptly directed his men to disengage and fall back through Bristoe Station and across Broad Run.

Hooker and his subordinates were under no such restrictions from their commander. Nonetheless when *Forno's* and *Lawton's* men began withdrawing, Hooker and his subordinates were largely content to let them go and merely occupy the positions their foes had held before leaving the field. With *Early's* brigade covering the withdrawal, at around 6:00 p.m. *Ewell's* men pulled back across Broad Run in almost perfect order, then set fire to the railroad bridge. In all, *Ewell's* command had lost only 124 men in the Battle of Kettle Run, while Hooker's losses came to over 300.

Analysis   Although he failed to anticipate or effectively analyze the evidence of *Jackson's* march as it was taking place, upon learning that the Confederates were at Manassas Junction, Pope smartly saw a potential opportunity in the situation and acted wisely to try to seize it. He developed a sound plan for moving on Manassas Junction, one that had promise of achieving decisive results, and moved his command with energy. That *Jackson* was able to have enough time to indulge his command at Manassas Junction and still be able to elude Pope's grasp was attributable to the first-rate job *Ewell* did holding off the vanguard of Pope's advance at Kettle Run. On August 27 *Ewell* effectively used the terrain and managed his command with the degree of skill that *Jackson* had come to expect from their service together in the Shenandoah Valley earlier in the year in what may well have been one of the better conducted rear-guard actions of the entire war. *Ewell's* incapacitation for several months due to the grisly leg wound he suffered the following evening near Groveton would be a blow of immeasurable consequence to the Confederate effort. Nonetheless so high was the regard for *Ewell's* ability that, on his return to duty in May 1863, he was immediately selected to succeed *Jackson* as commander of the Army of Northern Virginia's Second Corps.

Further Exploration Prince William County has established an extensive park where you can hike a series of trails to explore in more detail the ground where the 1862 Battle of Kettle Run was fought, as well as an October 1863 engagement at Bristoe Station. To reach this park, after exiting the parking area for the Bristoe Station, *turn left* onto BRISTOW ROAD, proceed 0.4 mile, and then *turn left* onto IRON BRIGADE UNIT AVENUE. *Proceed* 0.1 mile to the roundabout. *Take the third right* onto TENTH ALABAMA WAY and proceed to the parking area for Bristoe Station Battlefield Heritage Park. To return to the Second Manassas Excursion from the park: *Retrace your steps* to BRISTOW ROAD. *Turn left* onto BRISTOW ROAD and proceed 0.3 mile to the traffic light. *Turn right* onto NOKESVILLE ROAD (VA 28), then pick up and begin following the directions below at the appropriate point.

Confederate skirmish line.
BLCW 2:349.

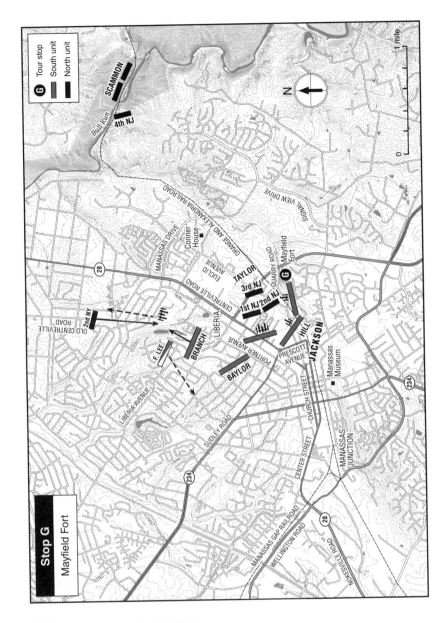

STOP G　　Mayfield Fort

Directions　　*Turn left* onto BRISTOW ROAD (VA 619). Drive 0.7 mile, then *turn right* onto CHAPEL SPRINGS ROAD. *Proceed* 0.3 mile to NOKES-VILLE ROAD (VA 28). Drive 4.2 miles on NOKESVILLE ROAD and *stay on* VA 28 (which becomes CENTER STREET when you enter the town of Manassas; at 2.9 miles you will cross the tracks of what in 1862 was the Manassas Gap Railroad) to a fork. *Continue driving straight* to remain on CENTER STREET. At 0.2 mile after the fork, just after CENTER STREET bends to the left to become PRESCOTT AVENUE, *turn right* onto QUARRY ROAD.

Proceed 0.3 mile on QUARRY ROAD to a fork, where you will *turn right* to stay on QUARRY ROAD. From the fork, continue on QUARRY ROAD for 0.3 mile, then *turn right* onto BATTERY HEIGHTS BOULEVARD. Immediately after doing so, you will see the parking area to Mayfield Fort on the left. Pull into the parking area and exit your vehicle. Walk over to the paved path leading to Mayfield Fort (you will see a Virginia Civil War Trails sign, "Mayfield Civil War Fort," at the entrance to the path). Hike 300 yards to the top of the hill, where you will come to a fork. *Turn right* and walk over to the cannon. Face north so that the cannon is pointing to your left front.

The Rout of Taylor's Command, August 27, 1862

What Happened   Upon reaching Manassas Junction early on August 27 with *Hill's* and *Taliaferro's* commands, *Jackson* directed Col. *William Baylor's* Stonewall Brigade and a battery commanded by Capt. *William T. Poague* to occupy a line of fortifications north and east of the junction to keep an eye out in that direction.

Almost as soon as they arrived, *Baylor* and *Poague* were greeted by the sight of *Fitz Lee's* cavalry engaged in a vigorous skirmish with a body of advancing Federal troops. These belonged to Col. Gustav Waagner's 2nd New York Heavy Artillery, a raw unit from the Washington defenses that had been hastily converted into infantry and ordered forward to reinforce Craig's garrison at Manassas Junction. Upon reaching Centreville late on the 26th, Waagner received word that Manassas had been attacked by some guerrillas and put his men on the march early the next morning. Shortly after crossing Bull Run at Mitchell's Ford, Waagner deployed his men into a skirmish line that, aided by fire from two pieces of artillery, managed to push *Fitz Lee's* cavalry back until the arrival of *Baylor's* and *Poague's* men put a halt to the Federal advance.

When the sound of firing reached *Jackson* at Manassas Junction, he responded by dispatching *Hill's* division to the scene. When *Hill* arrived, he posted 9,000 men and twenty-eight cannon in a 0.5-mile-long line with his right at "Mayfield Fort," which the Confederates had constructed during their occupation of Manassas the previous year. They then opened fire on Waagner's men and compelled them to fall back toward Bull Run.

Almost as soon as Waagner's men departed, trains carrying another Federal force out from the Washington defenses arrived nearby. These were the four regiments of Brig. Gen. George Taylor's brigade, which had been placed on trains during the night and ordered out to Manassas Junction. Shortly before reaching the Orange and Alexandria Railroad's bridge over

Bull Run, the train carrying Taylor's command was forced to halt when its engineer saw the tracks were obstructed. Taylor then disembarked his 1,200 men and, after detailing one of his regiments to guard the bridge, pushed the other three forward in the direction of Manassas Junction.

As they watched Taylor's men advance, *Jackson* ordered his men to hold their fire and allow the Federals to get close enough to the Confederate line that they could be subjected to a crossfire. Although some of his artillerists were unable to completely restrain themselves, sufficient fire discipline was maintained so that when *Jackson* finally gave the order to fire, it was too late for Taylor and his men to respond effectively. Finding to their intense dismay that they had stumbled into a very strong Confederate force that could fire into them from three sides, Taylor's men were subjected to a storm of artillery and infantry fire that tore their ranks apart.

Taylor vainly ordered his men to fix bayonets and charge, but there was nothing they could do. A merciful *Jackson* rode forward from his lines waving a white handkerchief to ask for their surrender, but he abandoned the effort when one of Taylor's men fired a round that barely missed the Confederate commander's head. Finally, less than fifteen minutes after the battle began, Taylor ordered his decimated command to retreat. *Jackson* immediately ordered his cavalry to pursue, and by the time the Federals managed to recross Bull Run, whatever organization Taylor had been able to maintain completely disintegrated as he fell, mortally wounded.

Taylor's men were finally able to rally on the opposite side of Bull Run behind the protection of the 11th and 12th Ohio of Col. Eliakim Scammon's brigade, which had just arrived on the scene from Alexandria. Of the 1,200 men in Taylor's command, 339 had fallen.

Analysis   The defeat of Taylor's command would have profound implications for the course of the campaign. Word of what had happened was immediately sent back to Alexandria, where Maj. Gen. George B. McClellan had just taken charge of the task of forwarding the corps from his Army of the Potomac to Pope. With the fate of Taylor's command in his mind, as well as a deep personal animus toward Pope, McClellan would exercise such excruciating caution in this work that no more reinforcements would reach Pope from Alexandria until after the Battle of Second Manassas had confirmed McClellan's belief that Pope's generalship could lead only to disaster for the Union cause.

The Sack of Manassas Junction, August 27, 1862

What Happened   As Taylor's men licked their wounds and *Ewell* kept a watch down the railroad in the opposite direction, *Hill's* and *Taliaferro's* men turned their attention to the veritable bounty of Federal stores that had come into their possession at Manassas Junction. *Jackson's* first impulse was to set up a process for distributing them to his commands, but the quantity of Federal supplies and the hunger of his men was so overwhelming that he quickly dropped the idea. While he made a point of seeing to it that whatever alcohol that was in the Federal warehouses and boxcars was destroyed, he otherwise left the task of plundering to the men. They proved fully up to the task.

Vignette   In his postwar memoir, *John Worsham* of the 21st Virginia recalled what happened shortly after arriving at Manassas Junction: "A scene around the storehouses was now witnessed, but cannot be described. Were you, when a boy, on some special occasion allowed to eat as much of everything you wanted? Were you ever a soldier, who had eaten nothing but roasting ears for two days? Well, if you have ever been either, you may probably have some conception of what followed. Only those who participated can ever appreciate it. Remember, that many of those men were hurried off on the march on the morning of the 25th with nothing to eat, that it was now the 27th, and we had marched in this time about sixty miles. . . . Now here are vast storehouses filled with everything to eat, and sutler's stores filled with all the delicacies, potted ham, lobster, tongue, candy, cakes, nuts, oranges, lemons, pickles, catsup, mustard, etc. It makes an old soldier's mouth water now, to think of the good things captured there. A guard was placed over everything in the early part of the day. . . . Gen. *Jackson's* idea was that he could care for the stores until Gen. *Lee* came up, and turn the remainder over to him, hence he placed the guard over them. The enemy began to make such demonstrations that he decided he could not hold the place, therefore the houses were thrown open, and every man was told to help himself.

"Our kettle of soup was left to take care of itself. Men who were starving a few hours before, and did not know when they would get another mouthful, were told to help themselves. Well, what do you think they did? Begin to eat. Oh, no. They discussed what they should eat, and what they should take with them, as orders were issued for us to take four days' rations with us. It was hard to decide what to take, some filled their haversacks with cakes, some with candy, others oranges, lemons, canned goods, etc. I know one who took nothing but French mustard, filled his haversack and was so greedy that he put one more bottle in his pocket. This was his four days' rations, and it turned out to be the best thing taken, because he traded it for meat and bread, and it lasted him until we reached Frederick City. All good times have an end, and, as night approached, preparations were made to burn everything that we could not carry; and not long after sunset the stores were set on fire."

Further Exploration   Construction on Mayfield Fort began in the spring of 1861, when Confederate forces first occupied Manassas Junction. In addition to the fort, the eleven-acre park contains the Hooe family cemetery and foundations of Mayfield, the name of the Hooe family farm in 1861, as well as wayside markers describing the history of the fort, the war's impact on local civilians, and the archaeological work that was done in the process of establishing the park.

Jackson's troops pillaging the Union depot of supplies at Manassas Junction. BLCW 2:532.

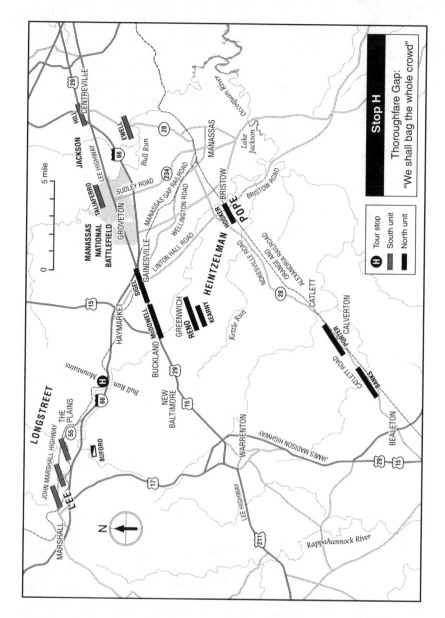

STOP H Thoroughfare Gap

Directions Exit the parking area by *turning right* onto BATTERY HEIGHTS
BOULEVARD, then *turn left* onto QUARRY ROAD. *Proceed* 0.5 mile
on QUARRY ROAD to its intersection with PRESCOTT AVENUE.
Turn right onto PRESCOTT AVENUE and drive 0.1 mile to its
intersection with CENTREVILLE ROAD (VA 28). *Turn left* onto
CENTREVILLE ROAD and drive 1.6 miles on VA 28 (*en route* VA
28 becomes CHURCH STREET, then CENTER STREET, and finally
NOKESVILLE ROAD) to its intersection with WELLINGTON ROAD.
Turn right onto WELLINGTON ROAD and proceed 7.3 miles to

LINTON HALL ROAD (VA 619). (At 3.6 miles you will cross Dawkins Branch, where Pope's effort to turn the Confederate right on August 29 was blocked.) *Turn right* onto LINTON HALL ROAD and drive 0.4 mile to its intersection with LEE HIGHWAY (U.S. 29). *Pass through* the intersection and reset your odometer. *Proceed* 4.6 miles on JOHN MARSHALL HIGHWAY (VA 55), passing through the town of Haymarket (JOHN MARSHALL HIGHWAY/VA 55 is known as WASHINGTON STREET as it passes through Haymarket), then *turn right* onto TURNER ROAD. Drive 0.1 mile on TURNER ROAD, then *turn left* onto BEVERLEY MILL DRIVE immediately after crossing INTERSTATE 66. Drive 0.7 mile on BEVERLEY MILL DRIVE to the parking area for the Bull Run Mountains Conservancy, which maintains public access to the battle site. You are required to fill out a waiver upon arrival if you wish to visit the battlefield, which you can do here.

Exit your vehicle and walk over to the trailhead kiosk just before the railroad crossing, where you will find important information to heed during your visit. Be especially on the lookout for rattlesnakes. *Proceed* from the kiosk through the gate and cross the railroad tracks. After crossing the tracks you will see a fork in the trail. *Take the main trail on the left* for about 150 yards to a fork. *Take the path on the left* where a wooden bridge carries you over some low ground and proceed for 300 yards on the trail to a point just beyond Chapman's (Beverley's) Mill on your left, where you see a large gash in the ridge on your right. *Stop here* and face west toward Thoroughfare Gap, with the mill to your left rear and the gash in the hill to your right.

Orientation

You are standing at the eastern end of the pass through the Bull Run Mountains known as Thoroughfare Gap. Quarry Ridge, where you are now standing, is about 500 yards east of the narrowest point in the gap. Haymarket is about 4 miles east of you; Gainesville is 2 miles beyond Haymarket; Marshall, known during the war as Salem, is about 9 miles west of you. Manassas Junction is about 13 miles to the south and east. The high ground on the south side of the gap (to your left) is known as Pond Mountain and runs south for about 4 miles to the gap in the Bull Run Mountains through which the wartime Warrenton Turnpike (modern Lee Highway/U.S. 29) passes at New Baltimore. The high ground north of the gap is known as Mother Leathercoat and runs north for about 6 miles to Hopewell Gap.

"We shall bag the whole crowd," August 27–28, 1862

What Happened   Despite the bloody nose Hooker's command received at Kettle Run on August 27, Pope was pleased with the situation he found upon his arrival at Bristoe Station that evening. The day ended with Sigel's corps at Gainesville and the rest of McDowell's wing right behind it in bivouac along the Warrenton Turnpike between Gainesville and Buckland Mills. Kearny's and Reno's commands had reached Greenwich, while Hooker's command was at Bristoe Station and Porter's corps had reached Warrenton Junction. Assuming *Jackson's* command was at Manassas, Pope issued a flurry of orders to his subordinates laying out his plans for the next day. Kearny received orders to "at the very earliest blush of dawn push forward with your command with all speed" to Bristoe Station. Once at Bristoe Station, Kearny's command would link up "at day—dawn, if possible," with Porter, who received orders to make a night march to Bristoe Station from Warrenton Junction. Meanwhile Reno would move directly on Manassas Junction from Greenwich. Pope instructed McDowell to have both of his corps at Gainesville by "daylight to-morrow morning" and moving toward Manassas Junction with his right on the Manassas Gap Railroad and left extending to the east. "*Jackson, Ewell,* and *A. P. Hill* are between Gainesville and Manassas Junction," Pope advised McDowell. "If you will march promptly and rapidly at the earlier dawn of day upon Manassas Junction we shall bag the whole crowd."

Although he had a well-conceived plan, Pope's hopes that he could "bag" *Jackson* on August 28 would go unfulfilled. *Jackson* was just as aware as Pope was of the potential peril his command was in and had no intention of sitting around Manassas Junction waiting to be "bagged." As his men gorged themselves on the Federal stores at Manassas Junction, *Jackson* decided to order his three divisions to make a night march north on the Sudley Road connecting Manassas Junction with the old First Manassas battlefield. For their destination he selected Groveton on the Warrenton Turnpike, which would place his command in close enough proximity to Thoroughfare Gap to link up with *Longstreet's* command, which he learned from couriers sent by *Lee* would be moving through the gap on the 28th.

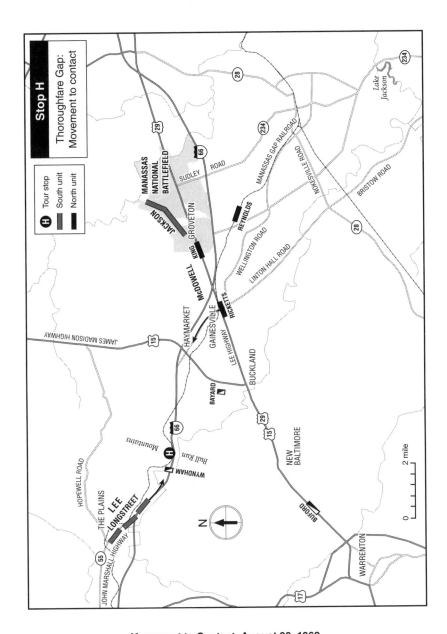

Movement to Contact, August 28, 1862

Directions   Remain in place.

What Happened   *Jackson* was not the only one who recognized the importance
of Thoroughfare Gap on August 28. As his two corps marched
east along the Warrenton Turnpike the previous day, McDowell had received reports from Brig. Gen. John Buford's cavalry
indicating a large Confederate force was on the move west of
the Bull Run Mountains This, McDowell recognized, could be
Longstreet's command marching to *Jackson's* assistance, and

that access to Thoroughfare Gap on the 28th, as the best and most direct route through the mountains, would be critical to *Longstreet's* efforts. After establishing his headquarters for the evening near Buckland Mills, McDowell wrestled with the question of how to address this problem. Finally, shortly before midnight, he decided he would have only two of the divisions in his column continue moving east to Gainesville and thence to Manassas Junction. The rest of his command, Sigel's entire corps plus a division commanded by Brig. Gen. John F. Reynolds, would move to Haymarket so they would be able to keep a watch on Thoroughfare Gap.

Unfortunately, shortly after McDowell made this decision, orders arrived from Pope for the next day's march on Manassas Junction. The urgency and optimism with which Pope laid out his plan for dealing with *Jackson* induced McDowell to drop his plan and instead direct Sigel and Reynolds, as well as the rest of his command, to immediately move on Manassas Junction in accordance with Pope's wishes. However, delays by Sigel in getting his men on the march during the night gave McDowell time to further ponder the problem of Thoroughfare Gap and modify his orders for August 28. Sigel was still to march to Gainesville, then turn right and advance on Manassas Junction with his right on the Manassas Gap Railroad. The divisions of Reynolds and Brig. Gen. Rufus King were to follow Sigel and then form on his left for the advance on Manassas Junction.

However, upon reaching Gainesville, McDowell decided the final division moving along the turnpike, Brig. Gen. James B. Ricketts's, would continue to follow the rest of his command only "if on arriving there no indication shall appear of the approach of the enemy from Thoroughfare Gap. . . . He will be constantly on the lookout for an attack from the direction of Thoroughfare Gap, and in case one is threatened, he will form his division to the left and march to resist it." McDowell also decided to send Col. Sir Percy Wyndham's 1st New Jersey Cavalry to the gap early on the 28th to keep a watch out for *Longstreet's* command.

As McDowell fretted over Thoroughfare Gap on August 27, *Lee* and *Longstreet* had marched four divisions (a fifth, Maj. Gen. *Richard Anderson's*, had been left behind on the Rappahannock in hopes of keeping the Federals distracted) from Orleans to White Plains (modern The Plains). Having received a series of positive reports from *Jackson* regarding the situation on the other side of the mountains, *Lee* and *Longstreet* did not exercise particular haste in beginning their march on August 28, and it was not until late in the morning that all of *Longstreet's* men were on the road. Shortly thereafter another message arrived from *Jackson* assuring *Lee* that his command was safe and that he had the situation well in hand, which did nothing to spur *Lee* and *Longstreet* to greater exertions. Thus it was not until around 2:00 p.m. that *Lee* and *Longstreet* finally reached Thoroughfare Gap after a 7-mile march and ordered forward Col. *George T. Anderson's* brigade from Brig. Gen. *David R. Jones's* division to secure possession of the gap.

As *Lee* and *Longstreet's* men were stirring from their bivouacs around White Plains, an anxious Wyndham arrived at Thoroughfare Gap with his cavalry and spent the morning cutting down trees and doing everything he and his men could think of to obstruct the road east of the gap. Shortly after 9:30 a.m. Wyndham sent word back to McDowell and Ricketts that he had made contact with advanced elements from *Longstreet's* command. Ricketts responded by promptly ordering his command to Haymarket.

Route step. BLCW 2:530.

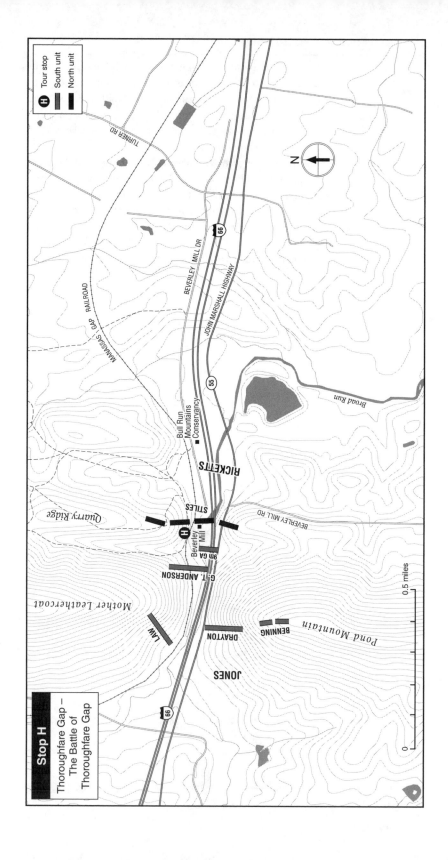

Stop H

Thoroughfare Gap –
The Battle of
Thoroughfare Gap

Tour stop
South unit
North unit

N

TURNER RD

66

BEVERLEY MILL DR

JOHN MARSHALL HIGHWAY

55

MANASSAS GAP RAILROAD

Bull Run
Mountains
Conservancy

Broad Run

RICKETTS

STILES

Quarry Ridge

Beverley
Mill

9th GA

G.T. ANDERSON

BEVERLEY MILL RD

Mother Leathercoat

LAW

DRAYTON

BENNING

JONES

Pond Mountain

66

0.5 miles

0

The Battle of Thoroughfare Gap, August 28, 1862

Directions   Remain in place.

What Happened   Upon arriving at Haymarket around 2:00 p.m., Ricketts directed
his men to discard their knapsacks and ordered skirmishers
forward toward Thoroughfare Gap. As he did so, Wyndham's
men informed Ricketts that *Longstreet's* command had just
driven his cavalry from the gap.

Ricketts immediately ordered his lead brigade, commanded
by Col. John Stiles, to march toward the gap to confront *Longstreet*. As Stiles's command approached the gap, their progress
was slowed by the obstructions Wyndham's men had placed
across the road earlier in the day. When Stiles's lead regiment,
Col. Richard Coulter's 11th Pennsylvania, finally managed to
reach a point about 0.75 mile from the gap, they deployed into
line. Shortly after resuming their advance, though, Coulter's
Pennsylvanians made contact with the 9th Georgia from *G. T.
Anderson's* brigade. Col. *Benjamin Beck* responded by deploying
his Georgians into line and then falling back to rejoin the rest
of *Anderson's* brigade at Thoroughfare Gap.

As *Beck's* Georgians fell back, Stiles moved up the rest of his
brigade and pushed forward toward the gap, with the 12th
Massachusetts on the left, the 13th Massachusetts in the center, and Coulter's men on the right. Supported by six pieces of
artillery, Stiles's Federals advanced until they reached the vicinity of Chapman's Mill, about 300 yards from the gap, and found
Anderson's command there, with the 9th Georgia in position
to the right of the Manassas Gap Railroad and four regiments
struggling to move up the rugged mountain slopes to positions to the left of *Beck*. Advanced elements from the 13th Massachusetts promptly occupied the mill, some climbing "up to
the second story windows to get better shots." Fire from *Anderson's* infantry, though, brought the Union advance toward the
gap to a halt shortly after it crossed Broad Run, while the Federal left began moving up the slopes of Pond Mountain. As
they approached the summit, they ran into two regiments
from Col. *Henry Benning's* brigade, which *Jones* had sent up Pond
Mountain in an attempt to turn the Federal left. Having reached
the summit first, *Benning's* men quickly sent the Massachusetts men tumbling back down the mountain.

Making matters worse for the Federals, *Lee* ordered Brig.
Gen. *Evander Law's* brigade from *Hood's* division to ascend Mother
Leathercoat to further extend the Confederate left. (*Lee* also
ordered Brig. Gen. *Cadmus Wilcox's* division to Hopewell Gap,
about 6 miles north of Thoroughfare Gap, hoping it might
maneuver around Ricketts's right, but it reached the gap too

late to have any effect on the battle.) It took some time, however, for *Law's* men to make their way up the steep mountain face, giving Ricketts time to order the 84th Pennsylvania forward to check the threat to his right. The Confederate effort on Mother Leathercoat was effectively halted by musket fire from the Pennsylvanians, and a bitter struggle along the quarry trench ensued between the two commands that would last for about an hour.

Nonetheless by the time the sun began to set, *Benning's* command was threatening to overwhelm the Federal left. Thus Ricketts, "considering our position untenable and all efforts to take the pass unavailing," decided he had accomplished all he could at Thoroughfare Gap and ordered his men to retreat toward Gainesville. At Haymarket, Ricketts encountered two cavalry brigades, commanded by Buford and Brig. Gen. George Bayard, respectively, which covered his withdrawal. That evening, understandably worried about his command's isolation and the obvious superiority of the forces in front of him, Ricketts decided to pull back all the way to Bristoe Station, clearing the way for *Lee* to reunite *Longstreet's* and *Jackson's* commands on August 29.

Analysis

While Ricketts's men put up a tough fight, they were far too few in number to hope to hold off *Longstreet's* command at Thoroughfare Gap. Pope's failure to take account of or appreciate the obvious importance of Thoroughfare Gap throughout the campaign or how the Confederates might use it is one of the most remarkable aspects of the entire Second Manassas Campaign. To anyone who could look at a map of northern Virginia in 1862, the gap's importance militarily would have been hard to miss. Yet Pope did nothing to prevent *Jackson* from using the gap to reach Manassas Junction on August 26. This could perhaps be forgivable, as it did not necessarily determine the outcome of the campaign. More important, though, from the time he learned of *Jackson's* raid—which should have made Thoroughfare Gap's importance unmistakable— Pope seems to have become so focused on his effort to "bag" *Jackson* that he became oblivious to the possibility that *Longstreet's* command might use the gap to reach *Jackson* and the battlefield. (It was only because of McDowell's exercising commendable initiative on August 28 that Ricketts's command was sent there.) It was one of the more astonishing failures of generalship in the entire war and, though not decisive in and of itself, would do much to determine the course and outcome of the Second Manassas Campaign.

The Battle of Second Manassas Begins, August 28, 1862

What Happened   As Ricketts's and *Longstreet's* commands moved toward their collision at Thoroughfare Gap, Kearny's division reached Manassas Junction around noon to find only the destruction *Jackson's* men had wrought the day before and some Confederate stragglers. From them Pope learned the Confederates had marched to Centreville just that morning. Pope then spent three hours gathering further evidence that confirmed their story that a large body of Confederate troops had marched to Centreville.

In fact at around 9:00 p.m. on August 27—about the same time Pope was sending orders to his commanders for the next day's movements—*Taliaferro's* division had left Manassas Junction and began marching north on the Sudley Road. Three hours later *Hill's* division departed, followed shortly before daybreak on August 28 by *Ewell's* division, which once again found itself responsible for serving as the rear guard for *Jackson's* force.

Taliaferro's command encountered no problems in its march and managed to reach the Sudley Road's intersection with the Warrenton Turnpike early on August 28. *Hill*, however, thanks to a confused guide *Jackson* had sent to assist him, put his command on the march in the direction of Centreville via Blackburn's Ford. *Hill* learned of his error a few hours after reaching Centreville and at dawn put his command on the march toward Groveton along the Warrenton Turnpike. For his part, the only guidance *Ewell* received was to follow *Hill*, and thus he naturally put his command on the march toward Centreville as well. *Ewell's* men were crossing Blackburn's Ford when a staff officer arrived from *Jackson* notifying their commander of the error and directing him to march his division cross-country to the Warrenton Turnpike and then turn west to join the rest of the Confederate force around Groveton.

Reports that *Jackson* had taken his command to Centreville came as a great relief to Pope, for they suggested that an opportunity to bag *Jackson's* command still existed. At 2:00 p.m. he sent a message to McDowell stating, "The enemy has retreated in the direction of Centreville. . . . Pursue in that direction." McDowell responded by redirecting the march of King's division. Instead of moving toward Manassas Junction, King learned, he was to move east along the Warrenton Turnpike toward Centreville.

A few hours later King's march along the Warrenton Turnpike brought him into contact with *Jackson's* command near Groveton. This produced a fierce but indecisive two-hour struggle during the evening of August 28 between King's and *Jackson's* men at the Brawner Farm. The Battle of Second Manassas had begun.

Further Exploration   *Turn around* and walk back about 40 yards to a point directly overlooking the large gutted structure just below you on the right, where you will also see a trail to your left. *Stop here* and *turn right* to face down toward Broad Run, the railroad, and the mill. The mill was originally built in 1742 by the Chapman family, and corn and wheat were ground here for soldiers serving in nearly every American war until it closed in 1951. It reached its current dimensions in 1858 and was destroyed by Confederate troops during the Civil War. By 1880 the mill was under the ownership of the Beverley family and once again operating. Fire gutted the interior in October 1998.

If you wish to see where some of Ricketts's and *Longstreet's* men fought higher up on Quarry Ridge, *turn left* and follow the main trail until you see a side trail on your left. *Turn onto the side trail* and follow it up the mountain for about 200 yards to where it crosses the trench. You will see a small wayside marker, "One Soldier's Story," nearby.

Further Reading   Krick, *Stonewall Jackson at Cedar Mountain*; Ropes, *The Army under Pope*, 16–74; Hennessy, *Return to Bull Run*, 22–167; Harsh, *Confederate Tide Rising*, 108–55; Cooling, *Counter-Thrust*, 32–106; Hennessy, *Second Manassas Battlefield Map Study*, 15–19, 23–29.

To return to the Manassas National Battlefield Park Visitor Center: Drive 0.7 mile on BEVERLEY MILL DRIVE back to TURNER ROAD. *Turn right* onto TURNER ROAD and proceed 0.1 mile to JOHN MARSHALL HIGHWAY (VA 55). *Turn left* onto JOHN MARSHALL HIGHWAY and proceed 4.9 miles through Haymarket to the intersection with LEE HIGHWAY (U.S. 29). *Turn left* onto LEE HIGHWAY (U.S. 29) and proceed 4.7 miles to the light for SUDLEY ROAD (VA 234). *Turn right* and drive 0.4 mile to the driveway to the Visitor Center on your left.

To reach the first stop for the Second Manassas Battle Tour: After returning to your vehicle, drive 0.7 mile on BEVERLEY MILL DRIVE back to TURNER ROAD. *Turn right* onto TURNER ROAD and proceed 0.1 mile to JOHN MARSHALL HIGHWAY (VA 55). *Turn left* onto JOHN MARSHALL HIGHWAY and proceed 4.9 miles through Haymarket to the intersection with LEE HIGHWAY (U.S. 29). *Turn left* onto LEE HIGHWAY (U.S. 29) and proceed 2.3 miles to the light at PAGELAND LANE. *Turn left* onto PAGELAND LANE, proceed 0.4 miles, then *turn right* to enter the driveway leading to the parking area for the Brawner Farm. Exit your vehicle at the parking area and follow the 300-yard paved path leading to the Brawner Farm Interpretive Center.

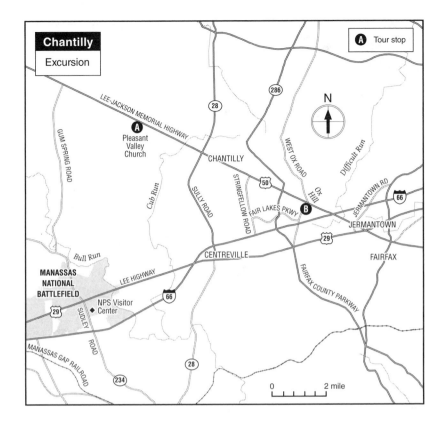

CHANTILLY EXCURSION

Directions

From the Visitor Center, *turn right* onto SUDLEY ROAD (VA 234). *Proceed* north on SUDLEY ROAD for 2.6 miles, then *turn right* onto GUM SPRING ROAD (VA 659). Drive 6.6 miles north on GUM SPRING ROAD to JOHN MOSBY HIGHWAY (U.S. 50). *Turn right* onto eastbound JOHN MOSBY HIGHWAY and drive 3.3 miles. On the right you will see the parking lot for Pleasant Valley United Methodist Church. *Pull in here* and park your vehicle near the "Campaign of Second Manassas" marker next to U.S. 50, walk over toward the marker, and *turn right* to face east.

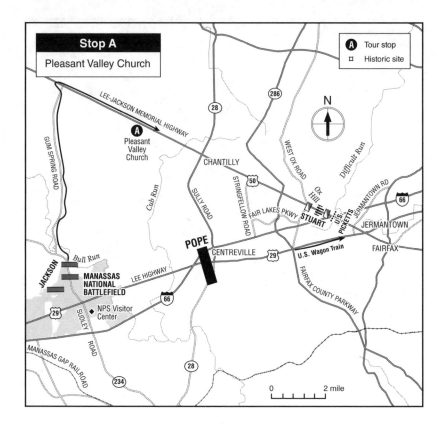

STOP A   Pleasant Valley Church

Jackson's **March**

Orientation   In 1862 John Mosby Highway (U.S. 50) was known as the Little River Turnpike. You are about 7 miles west of Ox Hill, 9 miles from Jermantown (which is the modern and correct historical spelling, though Civil War maps and reports spelled it "Germantown"), and 9.5 miles from where modern U.S. 50 intersects with modern Lee Highway/U.S. 29 (the historic Warrenton Turnpike). Fairfax Court House is 1 mile beyond that intersection. Centreville is about 6 miles to the south and east of where you are standing.

What Happened   As Maj. Gen. John Pope's command rallied at Centreville during the night of August 30–31, Gen. *Robert E. Lee* was not satisfied just to have won what he described to Richmond as "a signal victory" at Manassas. The fact that Pope's army retained much of its organizational cohesion and was able to avail itself of strong fortified positions made a direct attack on Centreville out of the question. In any case, *Lee* already had developed a plan on August 30 for maneuvering against the Federals. Despite the fact that it would demand more hard marching from his already exhausted men, he quickly resolved to implement it. He directed Maj. Gen. *James Longstreet* to menace Centreville with his wing of the army, while Maj. Gen. *Thomas J. Jackson's* three divisions, with their movements screened by Maj. Gen. *James E. B. Stuart's* cavalry, would once again attempt to maneuver around the Federal right and get in their rear. Once the last of *Jackson's* command had crossed Bull Run, *Longstreet* would end his demonstration against Pope's army and put the bulk of his command on the road behind *Jackson's*. Lee's ultimate objective was to reach Jermantown, located just west of Fairfax Court House, and the point where the Little River Turnpike connected with the Warrenton Turnpike. If they could do this, the Confederates would be squarely on Pope's line of communications back to Washington.

As a heavy rain fell over northern Virginia, Maj. Gen. *Ambrose P. Hill's* division led *Jackson's* column north across Bull Run shortly before noon. They then followed the Gum Springs Road north to the Little River Turnpike. Upon reaching the turnpike, *Jackson's* men turned east toward Fairfax Court House and continued marching until around 8:00 p.m., when *Jackson* halted the head of his 4-mile-long column near Pleasant Valley Church, having completed a 14-mile march.

Stuart's "Smash-ups"

What Happened

Moving well in front of *Jackson's* command on August 31, *Stuart's* two brigades of cavalry were able to capture two companies of Union cavalry while moving east down the Little River Turnpike. This encouraged Stuart to continue forward until around 7:00 p.m., when he reached the point where the turnpike crossed Difficult Run about 1 mile northwest of the small hamlet of Jermantown. Finding Federal pickets posted on the east bank of the stream, *Stuart* halted his command and ordered them to pull back toward Ox Hill where the Little River Turnpike and Ox Road intersected.

Before doing so, though, he brought up two guns and ordered them to fire on Federal wagon trains that had been spotted moving along the Warrenton Turnpike. "A few rounds," *Stuart* later wrote, "sufficed to throw everything into confusion, and such commotion, up-setting, collisions, and smash-ups were rarely ever seen." Satisfied with his work, at around 8:00 p.m. he finished pulling back his command and put it in camp 2 miles north of Ox Hill. Then, without bothering to send any word to *Jackson* of his activities, he led his staff farther north to Frying Pan to spend the night at the plantation home of an old friend.

Analysis

While *Stuart* was one of the South's finer cavalry commanders, there were a number of instances during the war when he acted in ways that did not serve the cause of Confederate independence particularly well. August 31 was one of them. Whatever hopes the Confederates might have had for achieving anything decisive through their movements of that day and the next were effectively dashed by *Stuart's* firing on the Federal wagons near Jermantown. This provided Pope, who was uncertain whether to continue holding his position at Centreville, unmistakable evidence that what he recognized to be a potential threat to his line of retreat had in fact materialized. Consequently he was able to dispatch forces east quickly enough to foil whatever hopes *Lee* and *Jackson* might have had that they could achieve more in northern Virginia in the fall of 1862.

A disorganized private. BLCW 2:556.

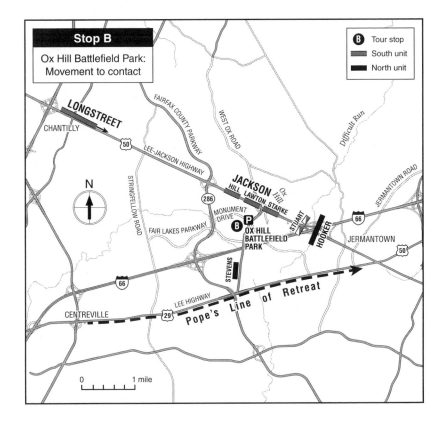

Stop B

Ox Hill Battlefield Park:
Movement to contact

B Tour stop

South unit

North unit

STOP B   Ox Hill Battlefield Park

Directions   Exit the parking area and *turn right* onto JOHN MOSBY HIGH-
WAY (U.S. 50). Drive 6.6 miles east to the ramp onto south-
bound WEST OX ROAD (VA 608). (*En route* U.S. 50 becomes LEE-
JACKSON MEMORIAL HIGHWAY.) *Proceed* 0.2 mile to the
intersection of WEST OX ROAD and MONUMENT DRIVE. *Go
straight* to remain on WEST OX ROAD. The entrance to Ox Hill
Battlefield Park will be on the right just after the traffic light
at MONUMENT DRIVE. *Pull into* the parking area and exit your
vehicle. Walk over to the information kiosk set up by the Fairfax County Park Authority. *Turn around* and face toward WEST
OX ROAD.

Orientation   Jermantown is about 2 miles east of where you are standing.
Fairfax Court House is 1.5 miles beyond that. The historic
Warrenton Turnpike (modern Lee Highway/U.S. 29) is a little
under 1.5 miles south of where you are.

Movement to Contact, September 1, 1862

What Happened   *Jackson* awoke his men and put them on the march down the
Little River Turnpike early on September 1. He reshuffled the

order of march so that Brig. Gen. *William Starke's* division was in the lead, with Brig. Gen. *Alexander Lawton's* marching behind Starke and *Hill's* division in the rear. Four miles from Pleasant Valley Church, *Jackson* linked up with *Stuart* at Chantilly plantation but received little in the way of useful information. *Jackson* then directed *Stuart* to ride back down the Little River Turnpike ahead of the infantry to take another look at what was between them and Jermantown. Upon reaching Ox Hill, *Stuart* halted his command; when *Jackson* arrived there around 4:00 p.m., *Stuart* reported that he had found no evidence of any significant body of enemy troops nearby.

How he missed the fact that Pope, alerted to the danger in his rear by *Stuart's* antics of the night before, was in the process of moving significant elements from two army corps to Germantown is a mystery. To command this force, at 1:00 p.m. Pope had sent Maj. Gen. Joseph Hooker to Jermantown with orders to defend the rest of the army's line of retreat back to Fairfax Court House. Pope also sent orders during the afternoon to Maj. Gen. Jesse Reno to take his two divisions to the point approximately 2.5 miles west of Jermantown where the Ox Road connected with the Warrenton Turnpike in case the Confederates tried to interdict the Federal line of retreat there. Because Reno was ill, the orders were delivered to division commander Brig. Gen. Isaac Stevens, who took responsibility for implementing them.

Meanwhile *Jackson* directed *Stuart* to push east along the turnpike toward Jermantown and Fairfax Court House. *Stuart's* men found a considerable body of Federal troops posted along Difficult Run and reported this to *Jackson*, who responded by deploying *Starke's* division for an advance against Hooker's position, but decided to await the arrival of *Longstreet's* command before making a major push east along the Little River Turnpike.

Almost as soon as *Jackson* deployed *Starke's* division, though, reports arrived from scouts who had been patrolling to the south that a considerable Federal force had been spotted moving north from the Warrenton Turnpike. This was Stevens's command, whose commander was personally leading them toward *Jackson's* position at Ox Hill.

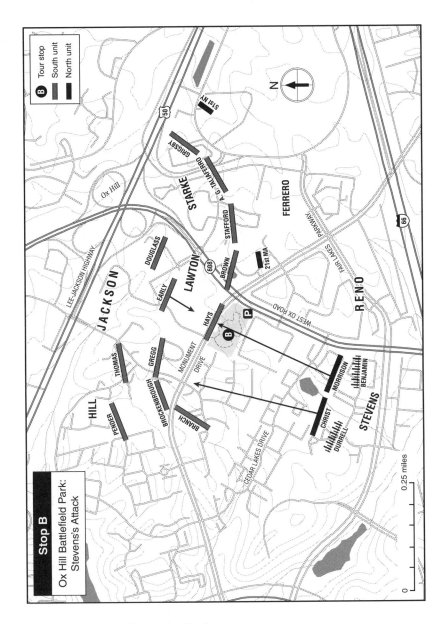

Stevens's Attack

Directions

Remain in place or *turn around* and, after passing through the
information area, *turn left* onto the paved path. *Proceed* about
125 yards to the wayside marker "The Attack and Death of
General Stevens." *Turn right* here and face north toward the
two stone monuments.

What Happened

Stevens had turned his command off the Warrenton Turnpike onto a small cart path through the woods just west of
the Ox Road. At around 4:00 p.m. he personally reached open

ground and spotted Confederate skirmishers scattered around a railroad cut (part of the same unfinished railroad line along which *Jackson* had posted his command a few days earlier) that ran perpendicular to the Ox Road. Immediately recognizing that these were elements from *Jackson's* command and unaware that Hooker's command had the defense of Germantown well in hand at that point, Stevens decided to attack *Jackson*. Shortly after receiving the order to advance, Stevens's men crossed the railroad cut and drove back the Confederate skirmishers. Upon reaching the vicinity of the Reid house, Stevens's skirmishers briefly halted to reform their lines. Behind them Stevens's main line deployed into line of battle shortly after crossing the unfinished railroad, then continued pushing north with Lt. Col. David Morrison's brigade on the right, Col. Benjamin Christ's in the center, and Col. Daniel Leasure's on the left. To support their advance, Stevens posted a battery on a ridge just south of the railroad cut near the Millan house.

By this point *Jackson* had deployed his entire command with *Starke's* command on the left between the Little River Turnpike and Ox Road. In the center, two brigades from *Lawton's* division posted on either side of Ox Road served as the link between *Starke's* right and the left of *Hill's* division, which was deployed behind a fence overlooking a large cornfield, with Brig. Gen. *Maxcy Gregg's* brigade posted next to Brig. Gen. *Harry Hays's* brigade of *Lawton's* division on the left, Brig. Gen. *Charles Field's* brigade (commanded by Col. *John Brockenbrough*) in the center, and Brig. Gen. *Lawrence O'Bryan Branch's* posted on the right of *Jackson's* line.

As Stevens finished preparations for his advance, an unwell Reno rode up to his position to discuss the situation. Although not enthusiastic about his subordinate's plan to engage the enemy, Reno approved it and rounded up another brigade and battery to assist. Finally, at around 4:30 p.m. Stevens dismounted from his horse and ordered his men to advance on *Jackson's* line as lightning lit up the sky and a heavy rain began to fall.

As soon as they came into range, *Jackson's* men demonstrated that two days of hard marching had not dulled their ability to fight by opening a blistering fire on Stevens's ranks. As his line staggered, Stevens rushed to the front, to the position of the 79th New York, which was also known as the Highland Regiment. Stevens grabbed the regimental colors and personally carried them forward. Following their general, the Highlanders and the rest of Morrison's brigade pushed forward toward the fence at the northern end of the cornfield and compelled *Hays's* brigade to fall back into a patch of woods behind the fence. After they knocked down the fence, Stevens and his men pushed into the woods to pursue the Confederates and exploit the penetration they had made in their line. Just as Stevens personally crossed the fence, though, a Confederate bullet struck him in the head, killing him instantly. As he fell, his enraged men rushed forward to engage elements from *Hays's* broken command in a wild melee of hand-to-hand combat in the woods.

As other members of *Hays's* brigade fled through the woods, they were relieved to encounter three fresh Virginia regiments from Brig. Gen. *Jubal Early's* brigade. As Stevens's men approached, the Virginians unleashed brutal volleys of musket fire that shattered Morrison's brigade and sent it reeling back through the woods.

Meanwhile on the Union left, Christ's brigade had pushed north through the cornfield toward the Confederate right and compelled two of *Hill's* brigades to fall back from the fence to the woods. From their new positions, though, Hill's men were able to fire into Christ's command from three sides and compel Christ to halt the Federal advance. As this was going on, a brigade that Reno had pushed across Ox Road to test the Confederate right accomplished little, and by 5:30 p.m. a lull had settled over the field as both sides reassessed the situation.

Vignette   In a biography of his father, whom he served as an aide at Ox Hill, Hazard Stevens later recalled, "The troops, under the withering hail of bullets, were now wavering. . . . Five color-bearers of the Highlanders had fallen in succession, and the colors again fell to the ground. At this crisis General Stevens pushed to the front, seized the falling colors from the hands of the wounded bearer, unheeding his cry, 'For God's sake, don't take the colors, General; they'll shoot you if you do!' and calling aloud upon his old regiment, 'Highlanders, my Highlanders, follow your general!' rushed forward with the uplifted flag. The regiment responded nobly. They rushed forward, reached the edge of the woods, hurled themselves with fury upon the fence and the rebel line behind it, and the enemy broke and fled in disorder. The 28th Massachusetts joined gallantly in the charge, and the other brigades as gallantly supported the first. . . . General Stevens fell dead in the moment of victory. A bullet entered at the temple and pierced his brain. He still firmly grasped the flagstaff, and the colors lay fallen upon his head and shoulders."

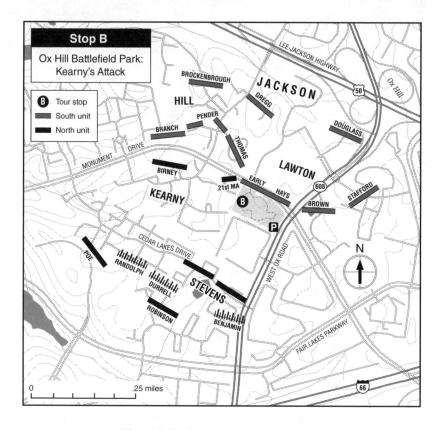

Kearny's Battle

Directions

Remain in place or *resume walking west* along the paved path for about 60 yards to the wayside marker "The Death of General Kearny," located just beyond a reconstructed fence line. Face west.

What Happened

Shortly after Stevens began his advance against *Jackson's* line, a staff officer he had sent back to the Warrenton Turnpike to find reinforcements ran into Maj. Gen. Philip Kearny, who immediately agreed to bring his division up, declaring, "By God, I will support Stevens anywhere!" Kearny immediately grabbed Brig. Gen. David Birney's brigade and personally led it north toward the sound of the fighting. Meanwhile, with Christ's command no longer a problem, *Jackson* directed *Hill* to push his lines forward into the cornfield. This eliminated a salient orienting the Confederate right behind the crooked fence at the northern end of the cornfield had created that shaped *Hill's* earlier efforts to fight off Christ. *Jackson* also began shifting forces from his left to his center and had largely completed this task by 5:45 p.m., when Birney's brigade arrived on the field.

On Kearny's orders, Birney immediately reported to Reno and received directions to move into the cornfield. As Birney deployed his command at the southern end of the cornfield after relieving Stevens's exhausted division, Kearny arrived and after a quick survey of the scene directed a staff officer to bring up Col. Orlando Poe's brigade so it could support Birney's command. Kearny then oversaw the posting of a battery south of the cornfield to support an attack by Birney against the Confederate right.

Shortly thereafter Birney's brigade began advancing north through the cornfield toward *Hill's* position. As soon as they came into view, *Hill's* men unleashed a hail of musket fire in their direction. Birney's men returned fire as they advanced and soon were close enough to the Confederate line that *Hill's* commands began to express concern about their ammunition. *Hill* dispatched a courier to *Jackson* requesting permission to withdraw from the line due to the fact that his ammunition was all wet. *Jackson* unsympathetically directed a staff officer, "Give my compliments to General *Hill*, and tell him that the Yankee ammunition is as wet as his; to stay where he is."

Meanwhile, as his men battled *Hill's*, Birney noticed to his great consternation that there were no Federals supporting his right and rode back to find Kearny. When he reached Kearny and reported his concerns, Kearny told Birney that he had ordered Poe's brigade forward. Seeing no sign of Poe's command, though, Kearny decided to personally ride over to Stevens's men and attempt to bring them back into the battle to cover Birney's right. Unable to get more from the battered and demoralized 79th New York than pledges to hold their ground, Kearny continued over to the east side of Ox Road, where he found the 21st Massachusetts in line and ordered them to move up to support Birney's right. However, Kearny failed to give the regiment's commander any sense of where he might find Birney's command.

When the Massachusetts men, understandably nervous about what they might encounter, moved toward and into the cornfield with more caution than Kearny believed the situation warranted, he rode over to inject more haste in their movements. When an officer informed him that they had just taken some prisoners whose presence suggested there was a considerable Confederate force nearby, Kearny scornfully dismissed the warning and spurred his horse forward into the corn to conduct a personal reconnaissance.

Kearny's horse promptly carried him over a ridge in the cornfield and to a clearing without incident. Then, however, Kearny heard the sound of troops moving to his right and front. Unable to determine who they belonged to, the general called out, "What troops are these?" "The 49th Georgia," was the immediate response. When Kearny yanked his horse around and desperately spurred it, one of the Georgians cried out, "That's a Yankee officer!" His comrades promptly opened fire, and within seconds Kearny fell from his horse, mortally wounded. At this point the Georgians' brigade commander, Col. *Edward Thomas*, ordered his men to push forward into the cornfield. They soon encountered the 21st Massachusetts, however, who put up a fierce fight that induced *Thomas* to return to its position north of the cornfield.

Birney soon assumed command of the division and sent staff officers to Poe and Brig. Gen. John Robinson with orders to bring up their brigades. By the time they arrived, shortly before 7:00 p.m., though, it was clear to Birney that it was too late to hope to accomplish anything more.

Meanwhile, on the other side of the lines, the lead elements of *Longstreet's* command had finally reached *Jackson*. Both sides had had enough. As Birney and Reno withdrew their soaked and exhausted commands south from the cornfield, *Jackson's* equally miserable men were more than content to let them go. By this time Pope had reached Fairfax Court House, and when the last Federals able to do so left the field at Ox Hill around 3:00 a.m., the security of the Union army's march back to the Washington defenses was beyond doubt. In all, *Jackson* had lost about 700 of the 15,000 men in his command, while of the 6,000 Federals on the field, about 500 had been killed or wounded.

Analysis

Whatever prospects there might have been for *Lee* and *Jackson* to cut Pope's line of retreat back to Washington and do further damage to the Federal army were dashed by the arrival of Hooker's force at Jermantown. Consequently, the Battle of Ox Hill was an engagement that had and achieved no real operational purpose. But this was not evident at the time to either Stevens or Kearny, and it is questionable whether it would have mattered even had they known this was the case. Both were naturally combative officers, as evidenced by the former's decision to initiate the fight and the latter's effort to keep it going even when it was clear that it could not achieve anything commensurate with the costs the battle entailed. When it was over, the Confederates could claim victory in that they had successfully fought off the Federal attacks, but this was insufficient to outweigh the fact that September 1 ended with the Federals having successfully preserved their road back to Washington.

Vignette

"As we moved forward through the dense dark wood," one member of the 21st Massachusetts recalled, "a tremendous thunder-storm burst upon us, and our line was badly broken up by fallen trees and other obstacles. . . . In a few minutes we came in sight of a body of troops in front of us, in dark uniform, and approached until portions of the regiment were within twenty yards of them, when we halted and began to dress our line, which was badly broken, some companies having been detached by long intervals from the rest by the obstacles met on the march.

"The heavy rain and darkness made it impossible for us to feel sure about these men in our front, and half a mile into the woods and entirely alone and unsupported we felt nervous and anxious. More than one man said, 'Those are rebels,' but from what we knew of the situation the chance seemed to be otherwise. A few scattered shots came in on our right, to which our answer was, 'Cease firing; we're friends.' Then, while most of our poor fellows were standing with their guns at the shoulder, one of the deadliest volleys ever fired rolled upon us from our right and front. In the sudden anguish and despair of the moment the whole regiment seemed to be lying bleeding on the ground, indeed, almost every man who had stood in the more open spaces of the wood did fall: yet there still was a 21st, and a 21st that could fight: some standing still in line, some from behind the trees, we opened fire on our brutal enemy; but in the drenching rain it being almost impossible to load a gun without wetting the powder, the guns on both sides soon became unserviceable, and, except a shot now and then, the firing ceased. . . .

"Birney's men were firing sharply in an advanced position on the left of Stevens's Division on the further side of a large corn-field, and about a quarter of a mile from the place where we came out of the woods, their line in the twilight being indicated only by the flashes of their muskets. General Kearney, in command of the field, in fierce haste was looking for our brigade to throw it in upon Birney's right; and . . . gave us a peremptory order to move into that position. We tried to steal a few minutes to get the wet charges out of our guns, but the general, in hot and angry impatience, would brook no delay, and under his sneers, threats, and curses, we again moved forward. The rain had now ceased, but the sky was still heavily overcast, and it was so dark that at a few yards' distance it was impossible to tell friend from foe, especially now that many of the rebels were wearing Union uniforms. We moved to the edge of the corn-field, with our right still close to the woods, and halted to advance a line of skirmishers, not proposing to be caught again, as we had been half an hour before, if we could help it. Our company G had just been deployed to our right and front, when an officer galloped up from the rear, and ordered a rapid advance to the indicated point, saying that General Kearney would turn a battery on us if we hesitated longer.

"We moved slowly forward, and almost immediately a dropping fire was opened upon us from the corn in our front, and our skirmishers coming in from the right reported that a body of the enemy was advancing from the woods upon our right flank. We came to a halt, and threw back our right company to cover that flank, at the same time opening a skirmishing fire to the front. General Kearney now rode up again in person, and, in if possible a more emphatic manner than before, stated that he did not believe that there were any rebels near us, and ordered us forward. We had the proof in two prisoners (an officer and private of the 49th Georgia regiment). Lieutenant [A. F.] Walcott, of our brigade staff, took these men to the general, saying: 'If you don't believe there are rebels in the corn, here are two prisoners from the 49th Georgia, just taken in our front.' Fiercely crying out, '—— you and your prisoners,' the general, entirely alone, spurred his horse through the sticky mud of the corn-field, past the left of the regiment. I watched him moving in the murky twilight, and when ten or twelve yards from our line saw his horse suddenly rear and turn, and half a dozen muskets flash around him. So died the intrepid and dashing soldier, General Philip Kearney.

"Kearney's death was quickly followed by a rush of rebels against our front and flank. For a few moments there was no firing, and the brave enemies, standing face to face, demanded the surrender of each other in language rather forcible than polite.... The rebels stood within a dozen feet of our men; the guns on both sides came down to a level ... and every gun that would go off along our line joined in. Though the enemy surged back a little as they received the deadly volley, it was but for a moment, and then came their return fire.... Then, as the rebels charged through our line in overpowering mass, men snatched the guns from each other's hands, and for the first, and so far as I know the last, time in our experience wounds in fight were given with the bayonet. All was now confusion, and it seemed as if the fight must go on till ended by death or surrender, with mortal enemies mingled together; but, strange to say, the fighting now ceased almost entirely; it was so dark that one could not tell whether the man next him was a friend or foe, and nobody was willing to say who or what he was; soon both parties, scarcely knowing how it happened, found themselves drawing apart again, and falling back towards their original position, leaving the corn-field neutral ground."

Further Exploration Instead of retracing your steps back to the parking area, *continue walking* along the paved trail to do the entire loop trail. At about 120 yards, you will come to the centerpiece of the park, the monuments to Kearny and Stevens. Dedicated in

October 1915, for many decades these and the small "Kearny stump" located a few yards farther along the path were the only reminders of the fierce battle that was fought here. As development exploded in this part of Fairfax County in the 1980s, a vigorous effort by preservationists resulted in the saving of the five-acre plot of land (the battle actually took place over about five hundred acres) that is now the Ox Hill Battlefield Park. A subsequent effort by the Fairfax County Park Authority to develop the site culminated in 2008 with completion of the current system of trails and wayside markers.

Further Reading Hennessy, *Return to Bull Run*, 441–51; Harsh, *Confederate Tide Rising*, 165–73; Hennessy, "Thunder at Chantilly," 47–60; Welker, *Tempest at Ox Hill*; Cooling, *Counter-Thrust*, 139–53.

To return to the Manassas National Battlefield Visitor Center: *Turn right* out of the parking area onto WEST OX ROAD (VA 608) and proceed 0.3 mile. *Turn right* at the second traffic light onto FAIR LAKES PARKWAY and drive 0.6 mile to FAIRFAX COUNTY PARKWAY (VA 286). *Turn left* onto FAIRFAX COUNTY PARKWAY and proceed 0.4 mile to the *ramp on the right* onto westbound INTERSTATE 66 (toward Front Royal). Drive 7.3 miles on INTERSTATE 66, then *take the exit* (Exit 47B) to northbound SUDLEY ROAD (VA 234). Once on SUDLEY ROAD, *proceed* 0.6 mile to the entrance on the right to the Manassas National Battlefield Visitor Center.

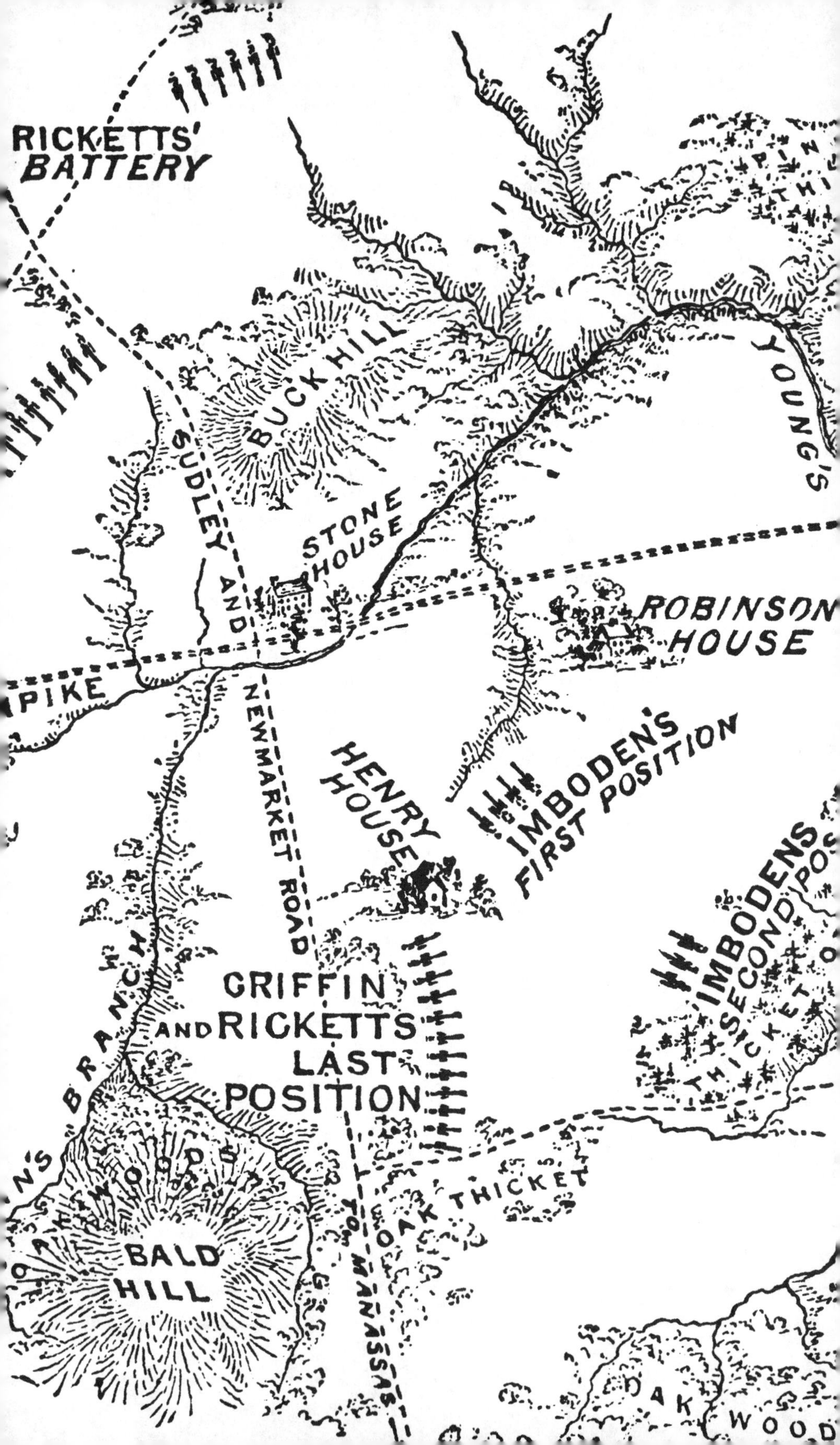

RICKETTS' *BATTERY*

BUCK HILL

SUDLEY AND

STONE HOUSE

YOUNG'S

PI NE THICK

PIKE

NEWMARKET ROAD

ROBINSON HOUSE

HENRY HOUSE

IMBODEN'S *FIRST POSITION*

IMBODEN'S *SECOND POS*

GRIFFIN and RICKETTS LAST POSITION

THICKET O

OAK THICKET

'S BRANCH

WOODS

TO MANASSAS

TO G

BALD HILL

OAK WOOD

Appendix A: Orders of Battle

Union Forces

First Battle of Manassas

Abbreviations:

BDE: brigade

BN: battalion

S.S.: sharpshooters

CO: company

A notation such as 1/12th indicates the first battalion of the twelfth regiment.

ARMY OF NORTHEASTERN VIRGINIA (McDowell)

1st Division (Tyler)

1ST BDE	2ND BDE
(Keyes)	(Schenck)
2nd ME	2nd NY
1st CT	1st OH
2nd CT	2nd OH
3rd CT	CO. E, 2nd U.S. Artillery

3RD BDE	4TH BDE
(Sherman)	(Richardson)
13th NY	1st MA
69th NY	12th NY
79th NY	2nd MI
2nd WI	3rd MI
CO. E, 3rd U.S. Artillery	CO. G, 1st U.S. Artillery
	CO. M, 2nd U.S. Artillery

2nd Division (Hunter, Porter)

1ST BDE	2ND BDE
(Porter)	(Burnside)
8th NY (Militia)	2nd NH
14th NY (Militia)	1st RI
27th NY	2nd RI
U.S. Infantry BN (8 COS.)	71st NY
U.S. Marine Corps BN	2nd RI Battery
U.S. Cavalry BN (7 Cos.)	
CO. D, 5th NY Artillery	

3rd Division (Heintzelman)

1ST BDE	2ND BDE	3RD BDE
(Franklin)	(Willcox, Ward)	(Howard)
5th MA	11th NY	3rd ME
11th MA	38th NY	4th ME
1st MN	1st MI	5th ME
4th PA	4th MI	2nd VT
CO. I, 1st U.S. Artillery	CO. D, 2nd U.S. Artillery	

5th Division (Miles)

1ST BDE	2ND BDE
(Blenker)	(Davies)
8th NY	16th NY
29th NY	18th NY
38th NY	31st NY
27th PA	32nd NY
CO. A, 2nd U.S. Artillery	CO. G, 2nd U.S. Artillery
8th NY Militia Battery	

Confederate Forces (Johnston)

ARMY OF THE POTOMAC (Beauregard)

1ST BDE	2ND BDE
(Bonham)	(Ewell)
11th NC	5th AL
2nd SC	6th AL
3rd SC	6th LA
7th SC	1st CO., Washington Artillery
8th SC	
8th LA	3RD BDE
Alexandria Light Artillery	(Jones)
1st CO., Richmond Howitzers	17th MS
30th VA Cavalry (Radford Rangers, Botetourt Dragoons, Hanover Light Dragoons, Fairfax Cavalry)	18th MS
	5th SC
	Appomattox Rangers
Munford's Squadron (Black Horse Troop, Chesterfield Light Dragoons, Franklin Rangers)	2nd CO., Washington Art.
	Jenifer's Cavalry BN

4TH BDE	5TH BDE
(Longstreet)	(Cocke)
5th NC	8th VA
1st VA	18th VA
11th VA	19th VA
17th VA	28th VA
24th VA	49th va Battalion
3rd CO., Washington Artillery	Loudoun Artillery
Amherst Mounted Rangers	Lynchburg Artillery
	Wise Troop

6TH BDE
(Early)
7th LA
13th MS
7th VA
4th Co., Washington Artillery

7TH BDE
(Evans)
1st LA BN
4th SC
Campbell Rangers
Clay Dragoons

RESERVE BDE
(Holmes)
1st AR
2nd TN
Purcell Artillery
Hampton's Legion
Camp Pickens's Battery

ARMY OF THE SHENANDOAH (Johnston)

1ST BDE
(Jackson)
2nd VA
4th VA
5th VA
27th VA
33rd VA
Rockbridge Artillery

2ND BDE
(Bartow)
7th GA
8th GA
Wise Artillery

3RD BDE
(Bee)
4th AL
2nd MS
11th MS
6th NC
Staunton Artillery

4TH BDE
(Smith, Elzey)
1st MD BN
3rd TN
10th VA
Culpeper Artillery

NOT BRIGADED
1st VA Cavalry
Thomas Artillery

Second Battle of Manassas

Union Forces

ARMY OF VIRGINIA (Pope)

HEADQUARTERS ESCORT: COS. A & C, 1st OH Cavalry;
5th NY Cavalry; 36th OH

I Army Corps (Sigel)

ESCORT: COS. I & K, 1st IN Cavalry

1st Division (Schenck, Stahel)

1ST BDE	2ND BDE
(Stahel, Buschbeck)	(McLean)
8th NY	25th OH
41st NY	55th OH
45th NY	73rd OH
27th PA	75th OH
2nd NY Light Artillery	Battery K, 1st OH Artillery

2nd Division (Steinwehr)

1ST BDE
(Koltes, Muhleck)
29th NY
68th NY
73rd PA

3rd Division (Schurz)

1ST BDE	2ND BDE
(Schimmelfennig)	(Krzyzanowski)
61st OH	54th NY
74th PA	58th NY
8th WV	75th PA
Battery F, PA Artillery	Battery L, 2nd NY Artillery

UNATTACHED	INDEPENDENT BRIGADE
Troop C, 3rd WV Cavalry	(Milroy)
Battery I, 1st OH Artillery	2nd WV
	3rd WV
CAVALRY BRIGADE	5th WV
(Beardsley)	82nd OH
1st CT BN; 1st MD;	Troops C, E, and L, 1st WV
4th NY; 9th NY;	Cavalry
6th OH	12th OH Battery

RESERVE ARTILLERY (Buell, Schirmer): Battery I, 1st NY Light;
13th NY; Battery C, WV Artillery

II Army Corps (Banks)

1st Division (Williams)

1ST BDE	3RD BDE
(Crawford)	(Gordon)
10th ME	2nd MA
46th PA	3rd WI
28th NY	27th IN
5th CT	

2nd Division (Greene)

1ST BDE	2ND BDE	3RD BDE
5th OH	111th PA	1st DC
7th OH	109th PA	78th NY
66th OH	3rd MD	60th NY
29th OH	102nd NY	Purnell Legion
28th PA	8th U.S. Infantry	3rd DE
	12th U.S. Infantry	

ARTILLERY: 4th & 6th Batteries, ME Light Artillery; Battery E, PA Light Artillery; 10th Battery, NY Light Artillery; Battery M, 1st NY Light Artillery; Battery F, 4th U.S. Artillery

III Army Corps (McDowell)

1st Division (King, Hatch)

1ST BDE	2ND BDE
(Hatch, Sullivan)	(Doubleday)
22nd NY	56th PA
24th NY	76th NY
30th NY	95th NY
84th NY	
2nd U.S. SS	

3RD BDE	4TH BDE
(Patrick)	(Gibbon)
21st NY	2nd WI
23rd NY	6th WI
35th NY	7th WI
80th NY (29th Militia)	19th IN

ARTILLERY: 1st NH; Battery D, 1st RI; Battery L, 1st NY; Battery B, 4th U.S.

2nd Division (Ricketts)

1ST BDE	2ND BDE
(Duryea)	(Tower, Christian)
97th NY	26th NY
104th NY	94th NY
105th NY	99th PA
107th PA	90th PA

3RD BDE	4TH BDE
(Stiles)	(Thoburn)
12th MA	7th IN
13th MA	84th PA
83rd MA (9th Militia)	110th PA
11th PA	1st WV

ARTILLERY: 2nd ME Light; 5th ME Light; Battery F, 1st PA; Battery C, PA

CAVALRY (Bayard): 1st ME; 2nd NY; 1st NJ; 1st PA; 1st RI

ARMY OF THE POTOMAC

III Army Corps (Heintzelman)
ESCORT: 5th NY Cavalry (3 COS.)

1st Division (Kearny)

1ST BDE	2ND BDE	3RD BDE
(Robinson)	(Birney)	(Poe)
20th IN	3rd ME	37th NY
30th OH	4th ME	99th PA
63rd PA	1st NY	2nd MI
105th PA	38th NY	3rd MI
	40th NY	5th MI
	101st NY	
	57th PA	

ARTILLERY: Battery E, 1st RI; Battery K, 1st U.S.

2nd Division (Hooker)

1ST BDE	2ND BDE	3RD BDE
(Grover)	(Taylor)	(Carr)
2nd NH	70th NY	2nd NY
1st MA	71st NY	5th NJ
11th MA	72nd NY	6th NJ
26th PA	73rd NY	7th NJ
	74th NY	8th NJ
ARTILLERY: 6th ME Battery		115th PA

V Army Corps (Porter)

1st Division (Morell)

1ST BDE	2ND BDE	3RD BDE
(Roberts)	(Griffin)	(Butterfield,
2nd ME	9th MA	Weeks, Rice)
18th MA	32nd MA	12th NY
22nd MA	14th NY	17th NY
13th NY	62nd PA	44th NY
25th NY	4th MI	83rd PA
1st MI		16th MI
		1st U.S. SS

ARTILLERY: 3rd MA; Battery C, 1st RI; Battery D, 5th U.S.

2nd Division (Sykes)

1ST BDE	2ND BDE	3RD BDE
(Buchanan)	(Chapman)	(Warren)
3rd U.S.	CO. G, 1st U.S.	5th NY
4th U.S.	2nd U.S.	10th NY
12th U.S. (1st BN)	6th U.S.	
14th U.S. (1st & 2nd BNS)	10th U.S.	
	11th U.S.	
	17th U.S.	

ARTILLERY (Weed): Batteries E & G, 1st U.S.; Battery I, 5th U.S.; Battery K, 5th U.S.

Reserve Division (temporarily attached) (Sturgis)

PIATT'S BDE
(Piatt)
63rd IN (4 COS.)
86th NY

IX Army Corps (Reno)

1st Division (Stevens)

1ST BDE	2ND BDE	3RD BDE
(Christ)	(Leasure, Leckey)	(Farnsworth)
50th PA	46th NY	28th MA
8th MI	100th PA	79th NY

ARTILLERY: Battery E, 2nd U.S.

2nd Division (Reno)

1ST BDE	2ND BDE
(Nagle)	(Ferraro)
6th NH	21st MA
48th PA	51st NY
	51st PA

ARTILLERY: Battery D, PA Light

Confederate Forces   **ARMY OF NORTHERN VIRGINIA** (Lee)

Longstreet's Wing

Anderson's Division (Anderson)

ARMISTEAD'S BDE	MAHONE'S BDE	WRIGHT'S BDE
(Armistead)	(Mahone, Weisiger)	(Wright)
9th VA	6th VA	44th AL
14th VA	12th VA	3rd GA
38th VA	16th VA	22nd GA
53rd VA	41st VA	48th GA
57th VA		
5th VA BN		

ARTILLERY: Norfolk Artillery; Goochland Artillery; Moorman's Battery

Jones's Division (D. R. Jones)

TOOMBS'S BDE	DRAYTON'S BDE	JONES'S BDE
(Benning, Toombs)	(Drayton)	(G. T. Anderson)
2nd GA	50th GA	1st GA
15th GA	51st GA	7th GA
17th GA	15th SC	8th GA
20th GA	Phillip's (GA) Legion	9th GA
2nd CO., Washington Art.		11th GA

Wilcox's Division (Wilcox)

WILCOX'S BDE	PRYOR'S BDE	FEATHERSTON'S BDE
(Wilcox)	(Pryor)	(Featherston)
8th AL	14th AL	12th MS
9th AL	2nd FL	16th MS
10th AL	5th FL	19th MS
11th AL	8th FL	2nd MS BN
	3rd VA	

ARTILLERY: Thomas Artillery; Dixie Artillery

Hood's Division (Hood)

HOOD'S BDE	LAW'S BDE
18th GA	(Law)
Hampton's Legion	4th AL
1st TX	2nd MS
4th TX	11th MS
5th TX	6th NC

ARTILLERY (Frobel): German Artillery; Palmetto Artillery; Rowan Artillery

EVANS'S INDEPENDENT BDE
(Evans, Stevens)
17th SC
18th SC
22nd SC
23rd SC
Holcombe Legion
Macbeth Artillery

Kemper's Division (Kemper)

KEMPER'S BDE	PICKETT'S BDE	JENKINS'S BDE
(Corse, Terry)	(Hunton)	(Jenkins, Walker)
1st VA	8th VA	1st SC
7th VA	18th VA	2nd SC
11th VA	19th VA	5th SC
17th VA	28th VA	6th SC
24th VA	56th VA	Palmetto SS
Loudoun Artillery	4th CO., Washington Artillery	Fauquier Artillery

ARTILLERY (S. D. Lee): 1st & 3rd CO., Washington Artillery; Lee's BN; Donaldsonville Artillery

Jackson's Wing

Jackson's Division (W. B. Taliaferro, Starke)

1ST BDE	2ND BDE
(Winder, Baylor, Grigsby)	(Johnson)
2nd VA	1st VA BN
4th VA	21st VA
5th VA	42nd VA
27th VA	48th VA
33rd VA	

3RD BDE	4TH BDE
(A. G. Taliaferro)	(Starke, Stafford)
47th AL	1st LA
48th AL	2nd LA
10th VA	9th LA
23rd VA	10th LA
37th VA	15th LA
	Coppen's Louisiana BN

ARTILLERY: Alleghany Artillery; Baltimore Artillery; Danville Artillery; Hampden Artillery; Lee Artillery; Rice's Battery; Rockbridge Artillery; Winchester Battery

Light Division (A. P. Hill)

BRANCH'S BDE	ARCHER'S BDE	PENDER'S BDE
(Branch)	(Archer)	(Pender)
7th NC	5th AL BN	16th NC
18th NC	19th GA	22nd NC
28th NC	1st TN (Provisional Army)	34th NC
33rd NC	7th TN	38th NC
37th NC	14th TN	

FIELD'S BDE	GREGG'S BDE	THOMAS'S BDE
(Field, Brockenbrough)	(Gregg)	(Thomas)
40th VA	1st SC	14th GA
47th VA	1st SC (Orr's Rifles)	35th GA
55th VA	12th SC	45th GA
22nd VA BN	13th SC	29th GA
	14th SC	

ARTILLERY: Fredericksburg Artillery; Crenshaw's Battery; Letcher Artillery; Middlesex Artillery; Branch Artillery; Pee Dee Artillery; Purcell Artillery

Third Division (Ewell, Lawton)

LAWTON'S BDE	TRIMBLE'S BDE
(Lawton, Douglass)	(Trimble, Brown)
13th GA	15th AL
26th GA	12th GA
31st GA	21st GA
38th GA	21st NC
60th GA	1st NC BN
61st GA	

HAYS'S BDE	EARLY'S BDE
(Forno, Strong)	(Early)
5th LA	13th VA
6th LA	25th VA
7th LA	31st VA
8th LA	44th VA
14th LA	49th VA
	52nd VA
	58th VA

ARTILLERY: Staunton Artillery; Chesapeake Artillery; LA Guard Artillery; 1st MD Battery; Johnson's Battery; Courtney Artillery

Cavalry Division (Stuart)

ROBERTSON'S BDE	LEE'S BDE
(Robertson)	(F. Lee)
2nd VA	1st VA
6th VA	3rd VA
7th VA	4th VA
12th VA	5th VA
17th VA BN	9th VA

ARTILLERY: Stuart Horse Artillery

A straggler on the line of
march. BLCW 2:515.

Appendix B: Organization, Weapons, and Tactics

You will get much more from your battlefield tour if you take a few minutes to become familiar with the following information and then refer to it as necessary.

The Organization of Civil War Armies

Following is a diagram of the typical organization and range of strength of a Civil War army:

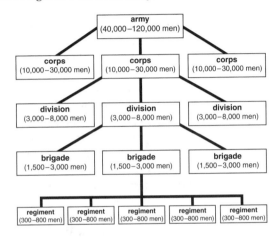

The Basic Battlefield Functions of Civil War Leaders

In combat environments the duties of Civil War leaders were divided into two main parts: decision making and moral suasion. Although the scope of the decisions varied according to rank and responsibilities, they generally dealt with the movement and deployment of troops, artillery, and logistical support (signal detachments, wagon trains, and so on). Most of the decisions were made by the leaders themselves. Their staffs helped with administrative paperwork but in combat functioned essentially as glorified clerks; they did almost no sifting of intelligence or planning of operations. Once made, the decisions were transmitted to subordinates either by direct exchange or by courier, with the courier either carrying a written order or conveying the order verbally. More rarely, signal flags were used to send instructions. Except in siege operations, when the battle lines were fairly static, the telegraph was almost never used in tactical situations.

Moral suasion was the art of persuading troops to perform their duties and dissuading them from failing to perform them. Civil War commanders often accomplished this by personal example, and conspicuous bravery was a vital attribute of any good leader. It is therefore not surprising that 8 percent of Union generals—and 18 percent of their Confederate counterparts—were killed or mortally wounded in action. (By contrast, only about 3 percent of Union enlisted men were killed or mortally wounded in action.)

Although any commander might be called upon to intervene directly on the firing line, army, corps, and division commanders tended to lead from behind the battle line, and their duties were mainly supervisory. In all three cases their main ability to influence the fighting, once it was underway, was by the husbanding and judicious commitment of troops held in reserve.

Army commanders principally decided the broad questions— whether to attack or defend, where the army's main effort(s) would be made, and when to retreat (or pursue). They made most of their key choices before and after an engagement rather than during it. Once battle was actually joined, their ability to influence the outcome diminished considerably. They might choose to wait it out or they might choose, temporarily and informally, to exercise the function of a lesser leader. In the battles of the Civil War, army commanders conducted themselves in a variety of ways: as detached observers, "super" corps commanders, division commanders, and so on, all the way down to de facto colonels trying to lead through personal example.

Corps commanders chiefly directed main attacks or supervised the defense of large, usually well-defined sectors. It was their function to carry out the broad (or occasionally quite specific) wishes of the army commander. They coordinated all the elements of their corps (typically infantry divisions and artillery battalions) in order to maximize its offensive or defensive strength. Once battle was actually joined, they influenced the outcome by "feeding" additional troops into the fight— sometimes by preserving a reserve force (usually a division) and committing it at the appropriate moment, sometimes by requesting additional support from adjacent corps or from the army commander.

Division commanders essentially had the same functions as corps commanders, though on a smaller scale. When attacking, however, their emphasis was less on "feeding" a fight than on keeping the striking power of their divisions as compact as possible. The idea was to strike one hard blow rather than a series of weaker ones.

The following commanders were expected to control the actual combat—to close with and destroy the enemy:

Brigade commanders principally conducted the actual business of attacking or defending. They accompanied the attacking force in person or stayed on the firing line with the defenders. Typically, they placed about three of their regiments abreast of one another, with about two in immediate support. Their job was basically to maximize the fighting power of their brigades by ensuring that these regiments had an unobstructed field of fire and did not overlap. During an attack it often became necessary to expand, contract, or otherwise modify the brigade frontage to adapt to the vagaries of terrain, the movements of adjacent friendly brigades, or the behavior of enemy forces. It was the brigade commander's responsibility to shift his regiments as needed while preserving, if possible, the unified striking power of the brigade.

Regiment commanders were chiefly responsible for making their men do as the brigade commanders wished, and their independent authority on the battlefield was limited. For example, if defending they might order a limited counterattack, but they usually could not order a retreat without approval from higher authority. Assisted by *company commanders*, they directly supervised the soldiers, giving specific, highly concrete commands: move this way or that, hold your ground, fire by volley, forward, and so on. Commanders at this level were expected to lead by personal example and to display as well as demand strict adherence to duty.

Civil War Tactics

Civil War armies basically had three kinds of combat troops: infantry, cavalry, and artillery. Infantrymen fought on foot, each with his own weapon. Cavalrymen were trained to fight on horseback or dismounted, also with their own individual weapons. Artillerymen fought with cannon.

INFANTRY

Infantry were by far the most numerous part of a Civil War army and were chiefly responsible for seizing and holding ground.

The basic Civil War tactic was to put a lot of men next to one another in a line and have them move and shoot together. By present-day standards the notion of placing troops shoulder to shoulder seems insane, but it still made good sense in the mid-nineteenth century. There were two reasons for this: first, it allowed soldiers to concentrate the fire of their rather limited weapons; second, it was almost the only way to move troops effectively under fire.

Most Civil War infantrymen used muzzle-loading muskets capable of being loaded and fired a maximum of about three times a minute. Individually, therefore, a soldier was nothing. He could affect the battlefield only by combining his fire with that of other infantrymen. Although spreading out made them less vulnerable, infantrymen very quickly lost the ability to combine their fire effectively if they did so. Even more critically, their officers rapidly lost the ability to control them.

For most purposes, the smallest tactical unit on a Civil War battlefield was the regiment. Theoretically composed of about 1,000 officers and men, in reality the average Civil War regiment went into battle with about 300 to 600 men. Whatever its size, however, all members of the regiment had to be able to understand and carry out the orders of their colonel and subordinate officers, who generally could communicate only through voice command. Since in the din and confusion of battle only a few soldiers could actually hear any given command, most got the message chiefly by conforming to the movements of the men immediately around them. Maintaining "touch of elbows"—the prescribed close interval—was indispensable for this crude but vital system to work. In addition, infantrymen were trained to "follow the flag"—the unit and national colors were always conspicuously placed in the front and center of each regiment. Thus, when in doubt as to what maneuver the regiment was trying to carry out, soldiers could look to see the direction in which the colors were moving. That is one major reason why the post of color-bearer was habitually given to the bravest men in the unit. It was not just an honor; it was insurance that the colors would always move in the direction desired by the colonel.

En route to a battle area, regiments typically moved in a column formation, four men abreast. There was a simple maneuver whereby regiments could very rapidly change from column to line once in the battle area, that is, from a formation designed for ease of movement to one designed to maximize firepower. Regiments normally moved and fought in line of battle—a close-order formation actually composed of two lines, front and rear. Attacking units rarely "charged" in the sense of running full tilt toward the enemy; such a maneuver would promptly destroy the formation as faster men outstripped slower ones and everyone spread out. Instead, a regiment using orthodox tactics would typically step off on an attack moving at a "quick time" rate of 110 steps per minute (at which it would cover about 85 yards per minute). Once the force came under serious fire, the rate of advance might be increased to a so-called double-quick time of 165 steps per minute (about 150 yards per minute). Only when the regiment was within a few dozen yards of the defending line would the regiment be ordered to advance at a "run" (a very rapid pace but still not a sprint). Thus, a regiment might easily take about ten minutes to "charge" 1,000 yards, even if it did not pause for realignment or execute any further maneuvers en route.

In theory, an attacking unit would not stop until it reached the enemy line, if then. The idea was to force back the defenders through the size, momentum, and shock effect of the attacking column. (Fixed bayonets were considered indispensable for maximizing the desired shock effect.) In reality, however, the firepower of the defense eventually led most Civil War regiments to stop and return the fire—often at ranges of less than 100 yards. And very often the "charge" would turn into a stand-up firefight at murderously short range until one side or the other gave way.

It is important to bear in mind that the preceding description represents a simplified idea of Civil War infantry combat. As you will see as you visit specific stops, the reality could vary significantly.

ARTILLERY

Second in importance to infantry on most Civil War battlefields was the artillery. Not yet the "killing arm" it would become during World War I, when 70 percent of all casualties would be inflicted by shellfire, artillery nevertheless played an important role, particularly on the defense. Cannon fire could break up an infantry attack or dissuade enemy infantry from attacking in the first place. Its mere presence could also reassure friendly infantry and so exert a moral effect that might be as important as its physical effect on the enemy.

The basic artillery unit was the *battery*, a group of between four and six fieldpieces commanded by a captain. Early in the war, batteries tended to be attached to infantry brigades. But over time it was found that they worked best when massed together, and both the Union and Confederate armies quickly reorganized their artillery to facilitate this. Eventually, both sides maintained extensive concentrations of artillery at corps level or higher. Coordinating the fire of 20 or 30 guns on a single target was not unusual, and occasionally (as in the bombardment that preceded Pickett's Charge at Gettysburg) concentrations of well over 100 guns might be achieved.

Practically all Civil War fieldpieces were muzzle-loaded and superficially appeared little changed from their counterparts of the seventeenth and eighteenth centuries. In fact, however, Civil War artillery was quite modern in two respects. First, advances in metallurgy had resulted in cannon barrels that were much lighter than their predecessors but strong enough to contain more powerful charges. Thus, whereas the typical fieldpiece of the Napoleonic era fired a 6-pound round, the typical Civil War—era fieldpiece fired a round double that size, with no loss in ease of handling. Second, recent improvements had resulted in the development of practical rifled fieldpieces that had significantly greater range and accuracy than their smoothbore counterparts.

Civil War fieldpieces could fire a variety of shell types, each with its own preferred usage. *Solid shot* was considered best for battering down structures and for use against massed troops (a single round could sometimes knock down several men like ten pins). *Shell*—hollow rounds that contained an explosive charge and burst into fragments when touched off by a time fuse—were used to set buildings afire or to attack troops behind earthworks or under cover. *Spherical case* was similar to shell except that each round contained musket balls (78 in a 12-pound shot, 38 in a 6-pound shot); it was used against bodies of troops moving in the open at ranges of from 500 to 1,500 yards. At ranges of below 500 yards, the round of choice was *canister*, essentially a metal can containing about 27 cast-iron balls, each 1.5 inches in diameter. As soon as a canister round was fired, the sides of the can would rip away and the cast-iron balls would fly directly into the attacking infantry or ricochet into them off the ground, making the cannon essentially a large-scale shotgun. In desperate situations, double and sometimes even triple charges of canister were used.

As recently as the Mexican War, artillery had been used effectively on the offensive, with fieldpieces rolling forward to advanced positions from which they could blast a hole in the enemy line. The advent of the rifled musket, however, made this tactic dangerous—defending infantry could now pick off artillerists who dared to come so close—and so the artillery had to remain farther back. In theory, the greater range and accuracy of rifled cannon might have offset this a bit, but rifled cannon fired comparatively small shells of limited effectiveness against infantry at a distance. The preferred use of artillery on the offensive was therefore not against infantry but against other artillery—what was termed "counterbattery work." The idea was to mass one's own cannon against a few of the enemy's cannon and systematically fire so as to kill the enemy's artillerists and dismount his fieldpieces.

CAVALRY

"Whoever saw a dead cavalryman?" was a byword among Civil War soldiers, a pointed allusion to the fact that the battlefield role played by the mounted arm was often negligible. For example, at the battle of Antietam—the single bloodiest day of the entire war—the Union cavalry suffered exactly 5 men killed and 23 wounded. This was in sharp contrast to the role played by horsemen during the Napoleonic era, when a well-timed cavalry charge could exploit an infantry breakthrough, overrun the enemy's retreating foot soldiers, and convert a temporary advantage into a complete battlefield triumph.

Why the failure to use cavalry to better tactical advantage? The best single explanation might be that for much of the war there was simply not enough of it to achieve significant results. Whereas cavalry had comprised 20 to 25 percent of Napoleonic armies, in Civil War armies it generally averaged 8 to 10 percent or less. The paucity of cavalry may be explained in turn by its much greater expense compared with infantry. A single horse might easily cost ten times the monthly pay of a Civil War private and necessitated the purchase of saddles, bridles, stirrups, and other gear as well as specialized clothing and equipment for the rider. Moreover, horses required about 26 pounds of feed and forage per day, many times the requirement of an infantryman. One might add to this the continual need for remounts to replace worn-out animals and that it took far more training to make an effective cavalryman than an effective infantryman. There was also the widespread belief that the heavily wooded terrain of North America would limit opportunities to use cavalry on the battlefield. All in all, it is perhaps no wonder that Civil War armies were late in creating really powerful mounted arms.

Instead, cavalry tended to be used mainly for scouting and raiding, duties that took place away from the main battlefields. During major engagements their mission was principally to screen the flanks or to control the rear areas. By 1863, however, the North was beginning to create cavalry forces sufficiently numerous and well armed to play a significant role on the battlefield. At Gettysburg, for example, Union cavalrymen armed with rapid-fire, breech-loading carbines were able to hold a Confederate infantry division at bay for several hours. At Cedar Creek in 1864, a massed cavalry charge late in the day completed the ruin of the Confederate army, and during the Appomattox campaign in 1865, Federal cavalry played a decisive role in bringing Lee's retreating army to bay and forcing its surrender.

Appreciation of the Terrain

The whole point of a battlefield tour is to see the ground over which men actually fought. Understanding the terrain is basic to understanding almost every aspect of a battle. Terrain helps to explain why commanders deployed their troops where they did, why attacks occurred in certain areas and not in others, and why some attacks succeeded and others did not.

When defending, Civil War leaders often looked for positions that had as many of the following characteristics as possible:

First, it obviously had to be ground from which they could protect whatever it was they were ordered to defend.

Second, it should be elevated enough so as to provide good observation and good fields of fire—they wanted to see as far as possible and sometimes (though not always) to shoot as far as possible. The highest ground was not necessarily the best, however, for it often afforded an attacker defilade—areas of lower ground that the defenders' weapons could not reach. For that reason, leaders seldom placed their troops at the very top of a ridge or hill (the "geographical crest"). Instead, they placed them a bit forward of the geographical crest at a point from which they had the best field of fire (the "military crest"). Alternatively, they might choose to place their troops behind the crest so as to conceal their size and exact deployment from the enemy and gain protection from long-range fire. It also meant that an attacker, upon reaching the crest, would be silhouetted against the sky and susceptible to a sudden, potentially destructive fire at close range.

Third, the ground adjacent to the chosen position should present a potential attacker with obstacles. Streams and ravines made good obstructions because they required an attacker to halt temporarily while trying to cross them. Fences and boulder fields could also slow an attacker. Dense woodlands could do the same but offered concealment for potential attackers and were therefore less desirable. In addition to its other virtues, elevated ground was also prized because attackers moving uphill had to exert themselves more and got tired faster. Obstacles were especially critical at the ends of a unit's position—the flanks—if there were no other units beyond to protect it. That is why commanders "anchored" their flanks, whenever possible, on hills or the banks of large streams.

Fourth, the terrain must offer ease of access for reinforcements to arrive and, if necessary, for the defenders to retreat.

Fifth, a source of drinkable water—the more the better—should be immediately behind the position if possible. This was especially important for cavalry and artillery units, which had horses to think about as well as men.

When attacking, Civil War commanders looked for different things:

First, they looked for weaknesses in the enemy's position, especially "unanchored" flanks. If there were no obvious weaknesses, they looked for a key point in the enemy's position—often a piece of elevated ground whose loss would undermine the rest of the enemy's defensive line.

Second, they searched for ways to get close to the enemy position without being observed. Using woodlands and ridge lines to screen their movements was a common tactic.

Third, they looked for open, elevated ground on which they could deploy artillery to "soften up" the point to be attacked.

Fourth, once the attack was underway they tried, when possible, to find areas of defilade in which their troops could gain relief from exposure to enemy fire. Obviously, it was almost never possible to find defilade that offered protection all the way to the enemy line, but leaders could often find some point en route where they could pause briefly to "dress" their lines.

Making the best use of terrain was an art that almost always involved trade-offs among these various factors—and also required consideration of the number of troops available. Even a very strong position was vulnerable if there were not enough men to defend it. A common error among Civil War generals, for example, was to stretch their line too thin in order to hold an otherwise desirable piece of ground.

Estimating Distance

When touring Civil War battlefields, it is often helpful to have a general sense of distance. For example, estimating distance can help you estimate how long it took troops to get from point A to point B or to visualize the points at which they would have become vulnerable to different kinds of artillery fire. There are several easy tricks to bear in mind:

Use reference points for which the exact distance is known. Many battlefield stops give you the exact distance to one or more key points in the area. Locate such a reference point, and then try to divide the intervening terrain into equal parts. For instance, say the reference point is 800 yards away. The ground about halfway in between will be 400 yards; the ground halfway between yourself and the midway point will be 200 yards, and so on.

Use the football field method. Visualize the length of a football field, which of course is about 100 yards. Then estimate the number of football fields you could put between yourself and the distant point of interest.

Use cars, houses, and other common objects that tend to be roughly the same size. Most cars are about the same size, and so are many houses. Become familiar with how large or small such objects appear at various distances—300 yards, 1,000 yards, 2,000 yards, and such. This is a less accurate way of estimating distance, but it can be helpful if the lay of the land makes it otherwise hard to tell whether a point is near or far. Look for such objects that seem a bit in front of the point of interest. Their relative size can provide a useful clue.

Maximum Effective Ranges of Common Civil War Weapons

Rifled musket	400 yds.
Smoothbore musket	150 yds.
Breech-loading carbine	300 yds.
Napoleon 12-pounder smoothbore cannon	
Solid shot	1,700 yds.
Shell	1,300 yds.
Spherical case	500–1,500 yds.
Canister	400 yds.
Parrott 10-pounder rifled cannon	
Solid shot	6,000 yds.
3-inch ordnance rifle (cannon)	
Solid shot	4,000 yds.

Further Reading

Coggins, Jack. *Arms and Equipment of the Civil War*. 1962; reprint, Wilmington NC: Broadfoot, 1990. The best introduction to the subject: engagingly written, profusely illustrated, and packed with information.

Griffith, Paddy. *Battle Tactics of the Civil War*. New Haven CT: Yale University Press, 1989. Argues that in a tactical sense, the Civil War was more nearly the last great Napoleonic war than the first modern war. In Griffith's view the influence of the rifled musket on Civil War battlefields has been exaggerated; the carnage and inconclusiveness of many Civil War battles owed less to the inadequacy of Napoleonic tactics than to a failure to properly understand and apply them.

Jamieson, Perry D. *Crossing the Deadly Ground: United States Army Tactics, 1865–1899*. Tuscaloosa: University of Alabama Press, 1994. The early chapters offer a good analysis of the tactical lessons learned by U.S. Army officers from their Civil War experiences.

Linderman, Gerald F. *Embattled Courage: The Experience of Combat in the American Civil War*. New York: Free Press, 1987. This thoughtful, well-written study examines how Civil War soldiers understood and coped with the challenges of the battlefield.

McWhiney, Grady, and Perry D. Jamieson. *Attack and Die: Civil War Military Tactics and the Southern Heritage*. Tuscaloosa: University of Alabama Press, 1982. Although unconvincing in its assertion that their Celtic heritage led Southerners to take the offensive to an inordinate degree, this is an excellent tactical study that emphasizes the revolutionary effect of the rifled musket. Best read in combination with Griffith's *Battle Tactics*.

Sources   In general the works cited in the "Further Reading" sections of each stop provide information, interpretation, and insight. The citations of those works in those sections should in every case be taken as an attribution of credit for the material presented there. The sources for specific quotes in each stop are provided here.

FIRST MANASSAS

The Road to First Manassas

"You are green it is true": U.S. Congress, *Report of the Joint Committee on the Conduct of the War*, 3 vols. (Washington DC: Government Printing Office, 1863), 2:37–38 (hereafter cited as JCCW).

Stop 1   "On the evening of July 21": Erasmus D. Keyes, *Fifty Years' Observation of Men and Events* (New York: Charles Scribner's Sons, 1884), 432; "We were leading the brave, lighthearted division": Martin A. Haynes, *A History of the Second Regiment, New Hampshire Volunteer Infantry, in the War of the Rebellion* (Lakeport NH: n.p., 1896), 23–24; "The enemy made his appearance": U.S. War Department, *The War of the Rebellion: A Compilation of the Official Records of the Union and Confederate Armies*, 70 vols. in 128 parts (Washington DC: Government Printing Office, 1880–1901), ser. 1, vol. 2: 558–59 (hereafter cited as OR; all references are from series 1).

Stop 2   "When we arrived at the ford": Thomas M. Aldrich, *The History of Battery A: First Regiment Rhode Island Light Artillery in the War to Preserve the Union* (Providence RI: Snow and Farnham, 1904), 19–20; "Here is the battlefield": John D. Imboden, "Incidents of the First Bull Run," in *Battles and Leaders of the Civil War*, edited by Robert U. Johnson and Clarence C. Buel, 4 vols. (New York: Century, 1885–87), 1:232; "They are running!": Henry N. Blake, *Three Years in the Army of the Potomac* (Boston: Lee and Shepard, 1865), 16; "Mounting the hill": William M. Robbins, "With Generals Bee and Jackson at First Manassas," in *Battles and Leaders of the Civil War*, vol. 5, edited by Peter Cozzens (Urbana: University of Illinois Press, 2002), 45–46.

Stop 3   "My little battery was": Imboden, "Incidents of the First Bull Run," 1:234.

Stop 4   "Will you follow me back": John J. Hennessy, "Jackson's 'Stone Wall': Fact or Fiction?," unpublished manuscript, Manassas National Battlefield Park, Manassas, Virginia; "turned my guns upon the house," "We started for the hill": JCCW, 1:243, 168–69; "General, the day is going": James I. Robertson, *Stone-*

wall Jackson: The Man, the Soldier, the Legend (New York: Macmillan, 1997), 266; "yell like furies": John J. Hennessy, *The First Battle of Manassas: An End to Innocence, July 18–21 1861* (Lynchburg VA: H. E. Howard, 1989), 97–98.

Stop 5   "Colonel Elzey . . . moved us first": McHenry Howard, *Recollections of a Maryland Confederate Soldier and Staff Officer under Johnston, Jackson, and Lee* (Baltimore: Williams & Wilkins, 1914), 37–42.

Stop 6   "There is no alternative": OR, 2:316; "army was more disorganized": Joseph E. Johnston, "Responsibilities of the First Bull Run," in Johnson and Buel, *Battles and Leaders*, 1:252; "In the final struggle": Haynes, *A History of the Second Regiment*, 35–36; "Our movements may be of a few days": Evan. C. Jones, "What Did They Do to Sullivan Ballou?," *America's Civil War* 26 (July 2013): 60–66.

SECOND MANASSAS

The Road to Second Manassas
"I hear constantly": OR, vol. 12, pt. 3: 474; "a miscreant" "to be suppressed": Clifford Dowdey and Louis H. Manarin, eds., *The Wartime Papers of Robert E. Lee* (1961; New York: Da Capo, 1987), 239, 240.

Overview of August 28, 1862
"we shall bag": OR, vol. 12, pt. 2: 72.

Stop 1   "The Pike passed": W. W. Blackford, *War Years with Jeb Stuart* (1945; Baton Rouge: Louisiana State University Press, 1993), 120–21; "along the turnpike": Rufus Dawes, *Service with the Sixth Wisconsin Volunteers* (Marietta OH: E. R. Alderman & Sons, 1890), 60–63.

Overview of August 29, 1862
"push forward into action": OR, vol. 12, pt. 2 (supplement): 826.

Stop 2   "to be cashiered": OR, vol. 12, pt. 2 (supplement): 1051; "a Division Commander's": Carl Schurz, *The Reminiscences of Carl Schurz*, vol. 2: *1852–1863* (New York: McClure, 1907), 362–68; "A Yankee sharpshooter": John J. Hennessy, *Return to Bull Run: The Campaign and Battle of Second Manassas* (New York: Simon & Schuster, 1993), 226, 278; "The moment was an important one": Douglas Southall Freeman, *R. E. Lee: A Biography*, 4 vols. (New York: Scribner, 1934–35), 2:325; "It may be necessary":

OR, vol. 12, pt. 2: 76; "too far out": Hennessy, *Return to Bull Run*, 234; "Here it comes": Henry Kyd Douglas, *I Rode with Stonewall* (Chapel Hill: University of North Carolina Press, 1940), 138; "push forward": OR, vol. 12, pt. 2 (supplement): 826; "Forward boys": Hennessy, *Return to Bull Run*, 278; "Tell him I knew": Douglas, *I Rode with Stonewall*, 138; "Ten hours of actual conflict": Edward McCrady Jr., "Gregg's Brigade of South Carolinians in the Second Battle of Manassas," in *Southern Historical Society Papers*, 52 vols. (1876–1959; Millwood NY: Kraus Reprints, 1980), 13:32–35 (hereafter cited as *SHSP*).

Stop 3   "Don't shoot here!," "hurried some two miles": A. P. Smith, *History of the Seventy-Sixth Regiment New York Volunteers* (Cortland NY: Truair, Smith, and Miles, 1867), 129–35.

Overview of August 30, 1862
"signal victory": Dowdey and Manarin, *Wartime Papers of Robert E. Lee*, 268.

Stop 4   "all contrary to my orders": OR, vol. 12, pt. 3: 723; "I am clear": OR, vol. 11, pt. 1: 98; "I regard him": Hennessy, *Return to Bull Run*, 324; "comparatively quiet for many hours": John Gibbon, *Personal Recollections of the Civil War* (New York: G. P. Putnam's Sons, 1928), 62–63.

Stop 5   "The enemy were": A. M. Judson, *History of the Eighty-Third Regiment Pennsylvania Volunteers* (Erie PA: B. F. H. Lynn, 1865), 51; "Boys, follow me!," "Go back": E. E. Stickley, "Stonewall Brigade at Second Manassas," *Confederate Veteran* 22 (1914): 231; "For half a mile or more": Theron W. Haight, "Gainesville, Groveton and Bull Run," in *War Papers Read before the Commandery of the State of Wisconsin, Military Order of the Loyal Legion of the United States* (Milwaukee: Burdick, Armitage & Allen, 1896), 2:367–71.

Stop 6   "The heavy fumes": James Longstreet, *From Manassas to Appomattox* (Philadelphia: J. B. Lippincott, 1896), 188; "The Zouaves": Joseph Benjamin Polley, *A Soldier's Letters to Charming Nellie* (New York: Neale, 1908), 75–76; "It was a singular coincidence": J. B. Polley, *Hood's Texas Brigade: Its Marches, Its Battles, Its Achievements* (New York: Neale, 1910), 93–94.

Stop 7   "Much to my surprise": OR, vol. 12, pt. 2: 286–87.

Stop 8   "he had not sent": Cecil D. Eby, ed., *A Virginia Yankee in the Civil War: The Diaries of David Hunter Strother* (Chapel Hill: University of North Carolina Press, 1961), 96–97; "We moved into position": Charles Folsom Walcott, *History of the Twenty-First Regiment Massachusetts Volunteers* (Boston: Houghton, Mifflin, 1882), 148–50; "Whose command is this?": Gibbon, *Personal Recollections*, 66.

First Manassas Campaign Excursion

"Fairfax Court House": Augustus Woodbury, *The Second Rhode Island Regiment: A Narrative of Military Operations* (Providence RI: Valpey, Angell, 1875), 28–29; "It appeared to me": Hennessy, *First Battle of Manassas*, 19; "With a sudden": Alexander Hunter, *Johnny Reb and Billy Yank* (New York: Neale, 1904), 55–62.

Jackson's Line Excursion

"We crossed the summit": Imboden, "Incidents of the First Bull Run," 1:234–36; "as if two thousand demons": Ethan S. Rafuse, *A Single Grand Victory: The First Campaign and Battle of Manassas* (Wilmington DE: Scholarly Resources, 2002), 153; "After taking our position": John O. Casler, *Four Years in the Stonewall Brigade* (Girard KS: Appeal, 1906), 41–46; "For God's sake boys": Hennessy, *First Battle of Manassas*, 81; "Colonel Stuart and myself": W. W. Blackford, *War Years with Jeb Stuart* (New York: Charles Scribner's Sons, 1945), 28–30.

Second Manassas Campaign Excursion

"Banks is in our front": Hunter McGuire and George L. Christian, *The Confederate Cause and Conduct in the War between the States* (Richmond VA: L. H. Jenkins, 1907), 197; "After what seemed": Charles M. Blackford, *Letters from Lee's Army* (New York: Scribner, 1947), 104–5; "make the Yankees pay," "You have my hat": Hennessy, *Return to Bull Run*, 48, 79; "The tidings of our mishap": Heros von Borcke, *Memoirs of the Confederate War for Independence* (Philadelphia: J. B. Lippincott, 1867), 72–74; "come to you": *OR*, vol.12, pt. 3: 474; "From the summit": Longstreet, *From Manassas to Appomattox*, 161–62; "Crossing at Waterloo": Blackford, *War Years with Jeb Stuart* (1993), 99–108; "Oh, it won't get up": Terry L. Jones, ed., *Campbell Brown's Civil War: With Ewell and the Army of Northern Virginia* (Baton Rouge: Louisiana State University Press, 2004), 145; "*Jackson's* Headquarters": Douglas, *I Rode with Stonewall*, 132–33; "everything was risky": William Allan, "Memoranda of Conversations with General Robert E. Lee: February 19, 1870," in *Lee the Soldier*, edited by Gary W. Gallagher (Lincoln: University of Nebraska Press, 1996), 17; "proven a surprisingly adept foe": Joseph L. Harsh, *Confederate Tide Rising: Robert E. Lee and the Making of Southern Strategy, 1861–1862* (Kent OH: Kent State University Press, 1998), 131; "I beg your pardon": Henry W. Thomas, *History of the Doles-Cook Brigade, Army of Northern Virginia, C.S.A.* (Atlanta GA: Franklin Printing and Publishing, 1902), 352; "After a march of twenty-five miles": R. L. Dabney, *Life and Campaigns of Lieut-Gen. Thomas J. Jackson (Stonewall Jackson)* (New York: Blelock, 1866), 517; "in very heavy force": *OR*, vol. 12, pt. 2: 451; "A scene around": John H. Worsham, *One of Jackson's Foot Cavalry: His Experience and What He Saw during the War 1861–1865* (New York: Neale, 1912), 119–22; "at the very earliest blush" "at day-dawn" "daylight to-morrow" "If you will march promptly": *OR*, vol. 12, pt. 2: 72; "if on arriving there": *OR*, vol. 12, pt. 2: 360; "up to the second story": Jim Burgess, "Violent Prologue: Thoroughfare Gap and the Road to Second Manassas," *Sentinel* 2 (Summer 2012): 7; "considering our position": *OR*, vol. 12, pt. 2: 384; "The enemy has retreated": *OR*, 12, pt. 3: 717.

Chantilly Excursion   "a signal victory": Dowdey and Manarin, *Wartime Papers of Robert E. Lee*, 268; "A few rounds": *OR*, vol. 12, pt. 2: 744; "The troops," "By God": Hazard Stevens, *The Life of Isaac Ingalls Stevens*, 2 vols. (New York: Houghton Mifflin, 1901), 2:484, 488; "Give my compliments": Hunter McGuire, "General T. J. ('Stonewall') Jackson, Confederate States Army," in *SHSP*, 25:99; "That's a Yankee officer!": David A. Welker, *Tempest at Ox Hill: The Battle of Chantilly* (New York: Da Capo, 2002), 186; "As we moved forward": Walcott, *History of the Twenty-First Regiment, Massachusetts Volunteers*, 162–67.

In the wake of battle. BLCW 2:686.

Camp gossip. From a photograph. BLCW 1:ix.

For Further Reading

This bibliography lists the works of most use in preparing this guide as well as suggestions for further reading.

Cooling, Benjamin F. *Counter-Thrust: From the Peninsula to the Antietam.* Lincoln: University of Nebraska Press, 2008. Examines the Second Manassas Campaign in the context of the series of Confederate offensives in 1862 that carried the war in the East from the outskirts of Richmond to the gates of Washington and into Maryland.

Cozzens, Peter. *John Pope: A Life for the Nation.* Urbana: University of Illinois Press, 2000. An admirably balanced, first-rate study of the central figure on the Union side in the Second Manassas Campaign.

Davis, William C. *Battle at Bull Run: A History of the First Major Campaign of the Civil War.* New York: Doubleday, 1977. An older but still useful account of the First Manassas Campaign.

Detzer, David. *Donnybrook: The Battle of Bull Run, 1861.* New York: Harcourt, 2004. The most recent significant study of the first major battle of the war in the Virginia.

Gaff, Alan D. *Brave Men's Tears: The Iron Brigade at Brawner Farm.* Dayton OH: Morningside House, 1985. An informative, well-executed study of the opening engagement of the Battle of Second Manassas and the units engaged.

Gottfried, Bradley M. *The Maps of First Bull Run: An Atlas of the First Bull Run (Manassas) Campaign, including the Battle of Ball's Bluff, June–October 1861.* New York: Savas-Beatie, 2009. Useful, handsomely crafted maps and a textual account of the First Manassas Campaign.

Harsh, Joseph L. *Confederate Tide Rising: Robert E. Lee and the Making of Southern Strategy, 1861–1862.* Kent OH: Kent State University Press, 1998. The best study of the first two years of the war in the East and the making of Confederate strategy during the period during which the two campaigns of Manassas were fought.

Hennessy, John J. *The First Battle of Manassas: An End to Innocence, July 18–21, 1861.* Lynchburg VA: H. E. Howard, 1989. A first-rate tactical study that offers a clear account of what happened on the battlefield in July 1861.

———. *Return to Bull Run: The Campaign and Battle of Second Manassas.* New York: Simon & Schuster, 1993. A study of the entire Second Manassas Campaign that is not only the standard work on the subject but is one of the best studies of a major Civil War campaign ever published.

———. *Second Manassas Battlefield Map Study.* Lynchburg VA: H. E. Howard, 1990. A detailed, unit-by-unit breakdown of the battle of August 28–30, 1862.

———. "Thunder at Chantilly." *North & South* 3 (March 2000): 47–60.

Johnson, Robert U., and Clarence C. Buel, eds. *Battles and Leaders of the Civil War.* 4 vols. New York: Century, 1885–87. A compilation of postwar writings by participants in the Civil War. Volumes 1 and 2 have over a half dozen first-person accounts of the First and Second Manassas Campaign, including contributions by *Joseph Johnston, Pierre G. T. Beauregard,* and John Pope.

Krick, Robert K. *Stonewall Jackson at Cedar Mountain.* Chapel Hill: University of North Carolina Press, 1990. A thorough account of the fighting at Cedar Mountain that opened the Second Manassas Campaign.

Patchan, Scott C. *Second Manassas: Longstreet's Attack and the Struggle for Chinn Ridge.* Dulles VA: Potomac Books, 2011. An excellent focused study of the fights for Chinn Ridge and Henry Hill that took place on the afternoon of August 30, 1862.

Rafuse, Ethan S. *A Single Grand Victory: The First Campaign and Battle of Manassas.* Wilmington DE: Scholarly Resources, 2002. A full study of the campaign that considers the larger political, military, and cultural context that shaped its course, conduct, and outcome.

Ropes, John Codman. *The Army under Pope.* New York: Charles Scribner's Sons, 1881. A very good early account of the Second Manassas Campaign.

U.S. War Department. *The War of the Rebellion: A Compilation of the Official Records of the Union and Confederate Armies.* 70 vols. in 128 parts. Washington DC: Government Printing Office, 1880–1901. Volume 2 contains official reports and correspondence that are essential for understanding the course and conduct of the First Manassas Campaign; volume 12 contains official reports and correspondence related to Second Manassas.

Welker, David A. *Tempest at Ox Hill: The Battle of Chantilly.* Cambridge MA: Da Capo, 2002. A readable, well-crafted account of the final action of the Second Manassas Campaign.

Zenzen, Joan M. *Battling for Manassas: The Fifty-Year Preservation Struggle at Manassas National Battlefield Park.* University Park: Pennsylvania State University Press, 1998. An intriguing study of efforts to preserve the Manassas battlefields in the face of unrelenting suburban sprawl.

In This Hallowed Ground: Guides to Civil War Battlefields series

Antietam, South Mountain, and Harpers Ferry:
A Battlefield Guide
Ethan S. Rafuse

Chickamauga: A Battlefield Guide with a Section on Chattanooga
Steven E. Woodworth

Gettysburg: A Battlefield Guide
Mark Grimsley and Brooks D. Simpson

Manassas: A Battlefield Guide
Ethan S. Rafuse

The Peninsula and Seven Days: A Battlefield Guide
Brian K. Burton

Shiloh: A Battlefield Guide
Mark Grimsley and Steven E. Woodworth

Wilson's Creek, Pea Ridge, and Prairie Grove:
A Battlefield Guide with a Section on the Wire Road
Earl J. Hess, Richard W. Hatcher III, William Garrett Piston, and William L. Shea

To order or obtain more information on these or other University of Nebraska Press titles, visit www.nebraskapress.unl.edu.

Counting the scars in
the colors. BLCW 3:284.